ALL WRITE ALREADY

YEAR OF YOUR BOOK

GENA SHOWALTER

JILL MONROE

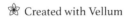 Created with Vellum

From Gena and Jill:

Thank you to the wonderful authors who donated quotes and inspired us with their words. Also, this book would not have been possible without the hard work of our editor, Lauren Floyd, and proofreader, Naomi Lane. THANK YOU!!!

Gena: I would also like to thank the wind beneath my wings, the person who always has my back and the best friend a girl could have - Jill Monroe.

Jill: I would like to thank my dog for putting up with my nonsense.

Gena: Oh sorry, my hand slipped. That should have read "I would like to thank...myself."

INTRODUCTION

Do you dream of being a published author, but don't know where to start? Maybe you have a packed schedule and can't find the time to write. Or you've tried to write a story but didn't know how to edit it—or even finish it. Good news! This book can help you tackle these problems and work on your goals.

Welcome to *All Write Already: Year of Your Book,* a handy how-to guide to help you write and edit an entire novel within a twelve month period.

Crafted by two bestselling authors with over 90 published books, *All Write Already* is a daily plan for anyone in need of help with their writing.

They take you through a step-by-step program, with short daily assignments meant to teach you how to 1) streamline your idea 2) create a solid foundation for your story and 3) draft and revise the entire novel, whether you're writing 50k or 100k words. No matter what genre of fiction you're drawn to, *All Write Already* has something to help you make your dream a reality.

If you've tried workbooks and writing challenges in the past but found them too vague, too dry, or just plain daunting, don't worry. We guide you through every stage, each assignment contributing to the overall arc of your story. We help you focus, magnify, accomplish and triumph!

Day one doesn't have to be the start of the month or the beginning of a new year. Our program includes exercises designed to encourage you to write a little bit each day. We begin with 16 days of pre-writing assignments to help you get to know your story and characters better. From day 17 on, we ask you to write or edit 6 days a week, leaving the seventh day for catch up and story reflection.

We tackle your book one thought, one page, one day at a time.

These short, daily assignments begin with fun activities meant to get you into the habit of writing. From there, we'll delve into the actual writing and editing of the book, and also share publishing information along the way. It helps to know where to take this story after you've written it, right? We even offer advice from other amazing authors who've been where you are now.

Following our method, you can have a completed, self-edited book ready for the next stage of the publishing process. Even better, you'll have the much-needed assurance that you did it once, so you can do it again. Here's to making this the Year of Your Book!

DAY 1

GETTING STARTED!

Dear Author,

Yep. That's you! If you bought this guide, there's a very good chance you've played with the idea of writing a book for years. Or maybe you dreamed of writing a novel, you just haven't sat down to put words to paper, but now you're ready to begin. We could not be prouder of you!

A lot of people who enjoy writing as a hobby only put pen to paper when inspiration hits. But here's the thing: You will get better at writing when you write *without* inspiration. That is when writing becomes a habit.

Sometimes you'll feel incredibly inspired, yes. Other times—let's face it, most times—you'll wish you were doing anything else. You might even reach a point in your writing that you want to give up because the words aren't flowing easily, or you've lost your passion for the story. *All Write Already* has ways to help!

Before anything else, let's take steps to ensure you're ready to begin writing.

First, we recommend reading the passages of *All Write Already*—in order—and completing each accompanying assignment. It might seem tempting to jump around, but there's a method to our sequence.

Next, we suggest you begin each project with a new notebook, even if you plan to type your story. You'll keep notes, ideas, lists and reminders in the notebook. You can even paste pictures of your characters inside it, or sketch a map of your world, or create a decision tree—more on that later.

Are you ready to get started? There's a task you can complete right now. Grab a piece of paper and a pen and jot down three reasons you want to write a book and what you hope to gain with its publication. Simply the joy of holding the finished work in your hands? Money? Career? There are no wrong answers.

GENA: My reasons are pretty consistent from book to book.

1. I have a story idea I must see come to life.

2. I'm ready to fall in love with new characters.

And 3. I want to be paid. As much as I love writing, it is my job, and like everyone else on the planet, I want to be paid for my work.

JILL: My reasons mirror Gena (see why we're friends?). I get obsessed with a story idea, working it out in my mind as I walk my dog, drive my car, cook dinner, etc..

1. I MUST get that story out of my head.

2. The thrill of seeing my book cover for the very first time.

3. I, too, love to get paid for my hard work.

Once you've finished your own list, keep it close and refer to it as often as possible throughout the year. We believe the more you focus on a specific goal, the more power it will gain in your life. When feeling discouraged, remind yourself of the reasons Future You would be disappointed if you quit. Let why you started be your inspiration for the day.

Your assignment: Take another look at your list. Then, in a brand new notebook or digital document, expand on each of your reasons for wanting to write a book. Get down to the nitty-gritty details.

Example: I want to make money

1. Buy a new house
2. Pay for daughter's college
3. Afford...life

Focus. Magnify. Accomplish. Triumph!

Happy writing!

Gena and Jill

DAY 2

THE ART OF MESHING IDEAS

A lot of new authors have an idea for a novel but no characters or plot points. Or, they have a couple vague ideas, but aren't sure how they can coexist within the same story. Whether your novel is a blank slate or a fully fleshed idea in your mind, our Combination Method could help you take it to the next level.

The formula looks like this:

Ordinary Idea + Ordinary Idea = Extraordinary Concept

Now, let's see the formula in action.

Vampires + Finishing School = *House of Night* series by PC and Kristin Cast

Pandora's Box + Demon Possessed Immortals = *Lords of the Underworld* by Gena Showalter

Russian Mafia Man Who Doesn't Like to be Touched + Woman on the Run in Desperate Need of Cash = *The Master* by Kresley Cole

You don't have to write about something the world has never seen before. Readers like relatability and good storytelling above out of the box surrealism. When you combine two familiar things, you can create one incredible idea!

Your assignment: Take out your notebook or open your digital document. Set a timer for five minutes and begin brainstorming a list of ideas that appeal to you. Don't censor yourself, just let the concepts and dreams flow.

Your list may look something like this:

Vampire
Small town
Archeology
Sandwich maker
Slow burn romance
Tattoo artist
Professional poker player
Nice clowns
Real paper dolls
Queen's soul
Alien father returns
Evil clowns
Balloons
Subway reunion
Cursed toy
Time stands still
Child prodigy grows up
Jury duty
Perfect guy has a tail

Now, begin pairing those ideas.

Slow burn romance + sandwich maker = Hallmark movie in the making?

Tattoo artist + real paper dolls = tattoos come to life?

Balloons + subway reunion = a party turns into a massacre?

Balloons + cursed toy = *Seed of Chucky* meets *It*?

Circle the ideas that excite you most. Think of ways you can expand the two ideas. Could your hero be a tattoo artist with a tail? Is your heroine a nice clown who can bring balloon animals to life? Did the villain just inherit a cursed toy that accidentally makes time stand still? Ask yourself what if, what if, what if? During this stage, "what if" is your best friend.

DAY 3

IDENTIFY YOUR VOICE

Every writer possesses a voice or style unique to them. This encompasses the words they use, sentence structures, choice of tense, character details, and plot, as well as the focus of narration, action and setting. Some writers are more descriptive than others. Some have a poetic slant. Others leave out any extraneous details.

Just remember: What you mention, readers will notice. Focus = magnify. Using precious page time to name, introduce and build a character who has one line and never shows up again can feel like a dropped thread.

It might help to think of your "author voice" as a fingerprint. Fingerprints do not develop on the surface, but from the very bottom layer of the skin. As that foundation tier grows, it tugs and bends the other layers. Your fingerprints represent the outcome of your conflicts, experiences, and growing pains. The same is true for your voice as a writer. No one else has lived your life, or has the same background, so there's not another voice like yours. But, like everyone else's, your writing style will come with strengths and weaknesses, and those can change as you do. The way you tell a story can even shift between projects. Your voice doesn't have to be the same throughout your writing career, but it does have to remain consistent throughout one project.

Today, let's focus on finding out your strengths and weaknesses in terms of "voice."

Your assignment: Think of a scene you'd like to have in your book. If you don't have a scene in mind, consider a childhood memory that might serve as backstory for one of your characters. Then, write it out, letting the words flow freely and unedited.

Note: Your internal editor might say: *Why can't you write more like X?*

Or: *People will think this is stupid.* Learn when to ignore your internal editor. Fear is not your friend; it can derail your goals.

When you're done writing your scene, give it a read and ask yourself some questions. What tense did you use—past or present? Are you lacking any details? Does your passage elicit or show any emotion? Did you describe the setting? If there is dialogue, does it move the scene forward? Where can you improve? What are your strengths?

DAY 4

You probably know a genre is a category of artistic composition characterized by similarities in form, style, or subject matter while a subgenre is a subcategory within a particular genre. But did you know readers of certain genres can have specific expectations for your story?

Examples of genre expectations:

- In romance novels, a happy ending or happily-for-now is key.

- In murder mysteries, multiple characters have distracting secrets that add an element of suspicion.

- Readers of sweet, closed-door romances do not want graphic love scenes in their books.

- Readers of erotica do not want a sexless romance.

- A sci-fi novel will offer some kind of advanced technology or futuristic concept.

Those expectations are the reason you need to know your book's genre and subgenre.

What genre and subgenre are you writing in? Ask yourself: What makes my book this genre? Do I know what aspect readers expect from this particular genre?

A few different genres:

Romance
Fantasy

Science Fiction
Western
Mystery
Young Adult
Historical
Thriller
Literary

A few sub-genres within romance:

- Contemporary (example: *Fun & Games* by Jill Monroe)
- Historical (example: *An Extraordinary Union* by Alyssa Cole)
- Category (example: *The Captain's Baby Bargain* by Merline Lovelace)
- Paranormal (example: *The Darkest King* by Gena Showalter)
- A fairy tale retelling (example: *The Glass Queen* by Gena Showalter)
- Dystopian (example: *Poison Princess* by Kresley Cole)
- Fantasy (example: *Moon Chosen* by PC Cast)

Side note: Throughout *All Write Already*, we will share more about the art of writing a romance novel than any other genre. This isn't only because we are romance writers. No matter the genre you choose to write, your characters will have relationships with other characters throughout the story. Romance is all about relationships.

Think about some of your favorite movies. Chances are good there's some kind of romance in it, whether that romance involves two lovers, two family members reconciling, or even a hero coming to understand an enemy.

GENA: My novel, *The Evil Queen*, is a young adult novel. As a retelling of *Little Snow White*—from the evil queen's point of view—it falls within the fantasy/fairy tale retelling subgenre. Going in, I knew readers would expect my story to follow the same general timeline as *Little Snow White*, and that I would have to bring the most iconic aspects of the fairytale into my story: The evil stepmother and her two different types of magic (scrying in mirrors and casting illusions of old ladies) as well as the poisonous apple, the seven dwarfs and a glass coffin.

JILL: As an example, my book *At the Heart of Christmas* is a sweet contemporary romance that falls into the holiday romance subgenre. The title lets the reader know the book centers around Christmastime—a very popular subgenre readers enjoy more and more as December approaches. Since this book was published by Hallmark Publishing, it matched the sensuality levels seen in their popular movies. Sweet romances have little to no heat between the main characters.

Your assignment: Identify and write down the genre(s) and subgenre(s) you'll be writing in. A book can be part of multiple genres and subgenres at the same time, and it helps to identify them. Each genre and subgenre could have certain expectations from your readers, and even if you're not married to a genre yet, this is a good way to brainstorm possible plot points.

DAY 5

T IS FOR TROPES

Tropes are common plot conventions, elements or themes that help drive your plot and/or characters forward throughout the book. Tropes are common and easy to spot, and that's a good thing! And yes, tropes can be cliches, but moreso, they are a way of expressing parts of life that can relate to the majority of others. Almost all stories have a trope of some kind, because tropes make characters seem more sympathetic and relatable, and can also be a foundation on which you can build your story.

You might recognize most, if not all of the tropes from this list.

- Enemies to lovers
- A race against the clock
- Redemption arc
- Girl/Boy next door
- The one–the savior of something
- Second chances
- Monsters among us: vampires/aliens/clones
- Monster hunting: werwolves/dragons/robots
- Family beating the odds
- A battle against technology
- Adventure awaits: space pirates/wormholes/time travel
- Deathbed confession
- Mysterious dead body
- Conspiracy to unravel
- Secret Society to infiltrate
- Mad Genius
- Mistaken identity

GENA: *The Glass Queen* is an enemies-to-lovers story at heart, as well as a second chance for my characters to right past wrongs. I made sure to craft character backstories around the "enemies" part—*why are they enemies? how does their past interactions shape their goals and desires?*—and used the "second chance" as fuel for the present, putting both characters in the midst of a savage gladiator-like tournament to keep them close, force them to work together, and showcase their individual skills.

JILL: *Lord of Rage* is a retelling of Goldilocks and the Three Bears with a redemption arc along with a ticking clock. I had so much fun crafting Osborn, the male lead. First, I got to make him a berserker and consumed by rage, but also, he must raise his two younger brothers. To support them all, he becomes a killer for hire, while also protecting and preventing his brothers from succumbing to the berserker rage as they approach adulthood. It was a blast crafting a complex character taking on seemingly opposing life roles. He battles this unique anger his entire life, but finds redemption when he learns to channel his fury as the tool it was always meant to be.

Your assignment: Write down the tropes you plan to use in your manuscript and explain why they are important to the story. Add this to your brainstormed ideas list. (If you are struggling to list your tropes, you might benefit from reading a more extensive list of examples online.)

Bonus assignment: Think about your favorite book. What tropes did the author use? How did those tropes work within the story? *Why* did those tropes work within the story?

DAY 6

The theme of your book is the underlying message you wish to convey to your readers. In other words, the theme is the big idea that is unveiled as your story progresses.

Theme examples:

- Love conquers all
- There's more than one type of strength
- Family and everything that comes with it (love, bloodlines, reconciliation, coming of age)
- God is good
- Self care is necessary
- What has a beginning has an end
- The difference between good and evil
- Hate isn't the answer
- Money doesn't buy happiness
- Power corrupts
- Survival matters most
- It's us versus them

If you know the theme of your book—the foundation upon which your scenes will stand—you can ensure one scene builds upon another, creating a seamless journey with a cohesive message and unifying vision.

JILL: In *At the Heart of Christmas*, I utilized a love triumphs over fear theme as well as reckoning with the past to have a future.

GENA: In *The Evil Queen,* I wanted to show the evil queen's descent into darkness, delving into what actually makes someone evil to others. So, as the theme of my book unfolded, it became "every hero is a villain, and every villain is a hero, it just depends on who you ask." To showcase this theme, I had to show my characters doing truly awful things for the best reasons and truly good things for the worst reasons.

Your assignment: Brainstorm a list of themes that might fit your book. What message are you trying to convey to your readers? What resonates with you?

Having trouble? Think of a favorite movie or book that draws you in over and over again. *Why* does it draw you in? Does the answer reveal a theme you're excited to explore?

DAY 7
PATCHWORK QUILT: PUTTING IT ALL TOGETHER

Now that we've gone through the first week of lessons, it's time to put it all together.

Let's say we have the grain of an idea for a suspense novel. A woman walking down an abandoned dirt road, alone, dirty with no memory. To expand the idea, we can list any ideas that come to mind and fit within the confines of this story:

- Forced amnesia—Magic? Medical? Foreign?
- Baking when stressed
- Suddenly heals from any injury in seconds
- Has needy sister
- Small town gossip
- Assassins on her trail
- Mystery savior

How can we combine those ideas? Let's start playing around.

She has amnesia + healing super fast = must find out what was done to her. That can act as a catalyst to spur her into motion and get the story flowing.

Small town gossip abounds + baking when stressed = a house full of pies so people are always coming over to eat and ask prying questions. Bonus: for a little comedic levity, she can daydream about a visit from her favorite fictional character Dean Winchester from *Supernatural*. He would know what to do!

Healing super fast + visits doctor = assassin shows up and attacks.

Mysterious savior enters the picture + he has questionable motives = who can she trust?

You can even twist your tropes!

Finds out she has been invaded by an alien + she's no longer fully human = a parasite is overtaking her slowly but surely, changing her personality.

Then, we take those ideas and find possible tropes hidden within them:

- Is evil born or made?
- Small town where they take justice into their own hands
- Good versus Evil
- Rebuilding a ruined life
- Dealing with change
- How far will you go to survive?
- A danger to others

From there, we craft our theme:

- Redemption is always possible (rebuilding a ruined life)
- Family doesn't have to be blood (who can she trust)
- Letting go of a tragic past to embrace a brighter future (rebuilding)
- Important to love yourself whatever you are going through (rebuilding)

It's looking like the most prominent theme is "rebuilding a ruined life," huh? So, now we know our direction: helping the heroine survive the assassins in order to craft a new life for herself, and get rid of her parasite...if she can.

For your second week of pre-writing lessons, we'll be expanding all of this, turning our attention to building your characters, the world, and the plot! Get ready, because we start tomorrow!

DAY 8
WORD VOMIT

Word vomit isn't as gross as it sounds. It's a simple exercise where you type or write down everything that comes to mind about your story—scene ideas, character traits, anything and everything you've considered adding to your tale—without allowing your internal editor a chance to slow your progress.

You might find yourself writing things like "he likes to fish" "hats" "car crash" "eats a corndog, spits it out." Don't worry about formatting or even logic. Spew nonsense if necessary. The brain works in mysterious ways, and you might be surprised by the ideas you derive from these word vomit sessions.

JILL: Because inspiration can be a jerk, the idea for *Fun & Games* came to me when I was on a strict deadline, writing another book. An editor and formatter had been scheduled, and both were waiting on me to finish, so I had to word vomit out my idea as quickly as possible and then return to my work in progress. (I do not trust my mind when it tells me I'll remember–I *always* write down my ideas.) The inkling of the concept was this: The heroine of a romance novel hears the back cover blurb. I also wrote down ideas for the kind of blurb she will hear, and moved on from there. Below is my word vomit. No judgement, please.

WORD VOMIT BLURB: On the outside, being a romance novel heroine looks like a lot of fun. Sure, you may get the sexy CEO billionaire or the hunky, shirtless single dad, but what if you wind up as a character being chased by a killer? What if you're paired with the undead? The zombie kind, not the hottie vampire.

What kind of person is the author? I mean really, who does this to someone? I'm not sure what I'm more irritated about. That my boyfriend, *ex*-boyfriend, is a complete tool who took all my money, but left me with years of student loan debt yet I was thoroughly oblivious. Or that I broke my arm and can't work, so my life's plans are on hold or that I'm back in Oklahoma LIVING WITH MY MOTHER (yes, I'm yelling). It's the oblivious part. In real life, I'm a lot smarter than this author wrote me.

RANDOM WV: Thanks to book time, we can fast forward to the interesting part where Josie and I are at the restaurant. And the coolest thing about book time – the appetizer is already here.

How negotiable do you think this whole romance thing is? Because check this out. I just think something... and there it is. So I have free will.

Coffee is revolting. <– See that? Written.

Gerblerhbuchlsj. I just thought all those letters and now I see them on the page in my mind. (For you I'm assuming they're on an actual page.)

JILL: Make sure you're as detailed as you can be when you word vomit, because there are also things I'd written down that I later had no idea what I'd meant. Like this one. *Match = rematch.* What did I mean, dang it?

Your assignment: Word vomit for 10 minutes. Don't censor yourself in any way, shape or form. If you think it, write it. Characters. Plot. Dialogue. Emotion. And as an added bonus, this could help get your mind in the writing groove.

DAY 9

Don't know anything about your main characters? Don't worry! Character Design 101 is in session!

It's important to know as much as you can about your characters, because their thoughts and actions depend on their previous life experiences, beliefs and current goals. If you do not know these things, you cannot know why the hero does what he does, so you might be unable to stay true to his character and the different aspects of his personality.

Note: While you might not utilize every detail in your book, this information will help you make decisions for your character, both small and large.

Also: You only need to make bullet points right now. You will elaborate tomorrow.

1. Appearance? Hair, eye and skin color? Height? Build? Any distinguishing marks? Gender? Age?
2. What is your character's name? (We sometimes search for names with a specific meaning to fit a character's personality.)
3. What are three major events that occurred in their past?
4. Past relationships? What kind of person draws and holds their gaze? Their attention?
5. Favorite food? Favorite drink?
6. Religious and political beliefs? Values?
7. Schooling? Hobbies?
8. Family and friends? Parents or parental figures alive? Siblings? Feeling about certain family members? Upbringing? Special bonds outside of family? Closest friends?

9. Socioeconomic status? What vehicles do they drive? What do they prefer to wear?
10. Special skill set, like sewing, knife throwing, navigating through space?
11. Job? Salary? Savings?
12. Level of happiness and ambition? Ultimate goal(s) for the future?
13. How do they treat other people? Are they a good communicator? Do they tell jokes? Are they confrontational? Peacemaker?
14. What is something others can see about this character that he/she cannot see for themselves?
15. How do they move through the world? Are they impulsive? Are they wise? Are they dumb? Do they hold onto regrets?

Your assignment: Give short and sweet answers to all of the above questions.

Pro-tip: Always save character questionnaires and interviews. Once you've published your novel, you can use these as teasers or as promotional materials later!

DAY 10

Yesterday, we focused (and magnified) the here and now. Today, we'll expand the backstory for each of your main characters.

Knowing and understanding the backstory of your characters is extremely important for you as the author. Their past, whether tragic, angst-ridden or joyous, will affect their thoughts and actions throughout the story. History, both recent and from childhood, explains their hopes and fears, and provides a solid foundation for their opinions and behavior.

As important as consistency is to your writing voice and genre, your readers will notice if a character is being inconsistent with their behavior or personality. Their past experiences shape the decisions they make today.

RANGE is a simple formula that can help you shape your characters.

Reasons
Ambitions
Needs
Growth
Emotion.

R - Reasons they do what they do. (If they wake up every morning sad, tell us why.)

A - Ambitions (What do they want more than anything else in the world?)

N - Needs (What do they need to be happy? What can't they live without?)

G - Growth (How will they grow throughout the book? If they start off sad, what must happen to make them happy by the end of the book —if happiness is your goal?)

E - Emotion and effect (What drives them wild? What makes them mad? What do they hate? Love?)

Your assignment: Answer the above questions to determine your character's RANGE and figure out why those events helped shape them into the person they are.

Bonus assignment: List other childhood memories your characters have, what school they attended, their best friends, jobs they've loved and lost or hated and shed, past lovers, and friends. You never know what detail will need to pop up later in the story.

DAY 11

Plotting Basics Through SEARCH!

Is your story driven by people and their goals and relationships (character driven), or by external forces in the story world (plot driven)?

For *All Write Already*, we have developed a 6 point plot structure. This structure can be a useful tool, whether the plot or characters drive the story. The system gives you the flexibility to expand each point as little or as much as you choose. We like to call it SEARCH.

Symmetry
Encounter
Adversity
Reflection
Climax
Harmony

S – Symmetry - The point where both your main characters begin the story. Their life is in balance, or at least they think it is. They may be working toward a goal, living large or feeling as though they're barely keeping their head above water. Balance isn't always necessarily good, but it's what your character is used to experiencing on a daily basis. This is their reality.

E – Encounter - The encounter that sparks the action and begins the story. In a romance, it's where your romantic leads meet. Hollywood gave us the phrase "meet cute". To writers of other genres, that definition might be too narrow, which is why we refer to it as the "memorable meet" instead. In the first released **Star Wars** movie, George Lucas placed the encounter in the spot where Luke Skywalker activates R2D2 to play the message from Princess Leia. They didn't meet in person, but he did get to learn about her, propelling him into action. The first encounter can be anything—awful, funny or scary. Just make sure it's memorable.

A – Adversity - The difficulties you put into the paths of your characters in the external or visible plot. Each new problem should raise the stakes a little bit more. So, give your characters a problem. Then make it worse.

R – Reflection - The emotional dilemmas you toss at your characters and their thoughts, feelings and gut level reactions. Think about the ways and reasons your characters will fight for what they want. As soon as they solve one problem, it's time to think up another. Events happen to us every day, some things we expect and others come as a surprise. The moment your characters feel comfortable with their plans and feelings, consider introducing an element to make them think/choose/fear/doubt, something to put a wrench in their plans. Here are some questions to ask yourself:

- What are their gut level reactions to these events?

- What happens when your character gets what they wanted, only to realize that nothing has changed. Or that everything has gotten worse!

C – Climax - This is the turning point for your plot, main characters and villain. Every scene you've written has been leading to this moment. For example, in *1984* by George Orwell, the climax occurs when Winston must choose between the love he has discovered and the Party he has devoted his life to serving. In romance novels, the climax is the point where the characters realize they're in love, or recognize that they have a major grovel—aka major apology—to present to their significant other.

H - Harmony - Your characters have faced down their foes in the climax. They've made their decisions and are now on the path that leads to a bright future. Show what your characters have learned and how they'll move on from here. Let the reader believe they've earned their happy ending.

We will explore all 6 elements of SEARCH in more detail later.

Your assignment: Come up with at least two ideas for each of the 6 points.

There are many great plotting books and tools to help you if you wish to delve more deeply into these areas of your writing. Here are just a few:

The Story Grid by Shawn Coyne
Romancing the Beat by Gwen Hayes
Story by Robert McKee
The Power of Myth by Joseph Campbell with Bill Moyers

DAY 12

SETTING

You've heard the phrase, right place at the right time? The setting of your novel boils down to two simple things, time and place, but those two things can make or break your character. These two elements will affect your character's vernacular, the sights and scents they encounter, the food they eat, and even financial status. Will you let your character be in their element, or a fish out of water?

When you imagine the setting in which your characters live, what do you see? Take note of all details, big and small. Do they inhabit a small town or a big city? Are they on Earth or another planet? Is there overcrowding? Are families fleeing? Is a main character part of a secret immortal society and only they can see the true world? Are they too afraid to leave their bedroom, so they watch the world from a screen?

Whatever the answers, your readers will see the world through your characters' eyes. You can use what they see to set the scene and breathe life into your world. But first, let's start with the basics: descriptive words.

GENA: My book, *The Glass Queen*, is set in the magical land of Enchantia. This world is imaginary, so I began with a list of words to describe the Enchantia I saw inside my head. My top ten:

Creepy

Mythical

Mysterious

Eerie

Elegant

Violent

Peaceful

Opulent

Elaborate

Dilapidated

A fictional world can be many things at once, it just depends on what part of the world you're focusing on, or through which character's eyes you're looking.

Your assignment: Make a list of all the places your main characters might visit in the course of your novel. Note if you will need to research those areas. Travel articles and online maps provide great resources. Now, write snippets to describe each place your characters will visit.

Side Note: Every genre has its challenges. When writing about a real location, there's a chance someone has visited or researched the place you are describing. What if you get something wrong? We recommend interviewing professionals, finding an expert in what you are writing about and having them proof the details. Or, you can make up the town/country, history, language—anything you want—just make sure you remain consistent, and that there's a logical reason for anything out of the ordinary.

DAY 13

YOUR CHARACTER'S MANY DIFFERENT WORLDS

Wait. Did we say "worlds," plural? We sure did! These mini-worlds differ from your setting–but they work *within* your setting. They are the individual compartments of your characters' lives. For clarity, we'll call them realms. Their work realm. Home realm. Family and friend realms. The possibilities are endless. Each of these realms comes with a different emotional undertone.

GENA: In my book, *The Evil Queen*, the heroine narrates the entire story. She has a home—a big city with a small-town feel that makes her feel unloved. A school—it's basically a battleground, so she's always on guard. A family—loving and necessary for her peace of mind. Her safe space. A fairy tale—magical, dark, eerie, fantastical. A mystery for her to solve. And a boyfriend—electric, consuming. Once I knew the vibe I wanted for each individual world, I had a much easier time building that world around her.

JILL: In 2016, the wonderful Roxanne St. Claire invited me to write for **Barefoot Bay**. The loyal fans of the series love the stories and the vibe, so I made sure to honor the already established rules in Roxanne's beloved series. Always respect the reader.

Creating a fictional place within an already established world gave me more flexibility as a writer, so I gave Molly her own special places. The orange grove world–decimated from the ravages of a hurricane, filled with broken trees and mangled limbs—roots Molly to her past and gives her a sense of purpose as she attempts to return the orchard to its former glory. The world of the ocean–with its predictable tides and soothing waves—gives Molly a refuge from her job and the responsibilities of supporting her grandmother.

Your assignment: Determine how many worlds your character will inhabit in your story and figure out how each one makes them feel.

DAY 14

For the story we're crafting in this book, let's refer back to our plot–A woman has no real memory of her abduction; she only knows she's lost a chunk of time. As assassins chase her, she tries to piece together her past.

Now let's focus on getting to know her better, using the assignments provided in the past week.

First, we build her up.

Appearance: dark hair, dark eyes. 5'7. A runner. Toned. Has a scar on her calf and a tattoo of some sort on her arm. Female. Twenty-eight years old.

Possible Name: Calypso means "she who conceals." Andy means brave. Rashana means a creation. Annabeth means curious. Emily means hard working.

Past relationships: Has always struggled to bond with others, so has never had a serious relationship. But she is attracted to strength.

Favorite food and drinks: Loves anything spicy. Hates sugary desserts.

Religious and political and values: Believes there is a higher power, wants justice for all. Values truth, knows it's rare.

Schooling and hobbies: Loves painting and reading. Loves people watching, trying to understand their motives, and collecting paintbrushes.

Family and friends: Never spends time or talks with father. Has a younger half-sister she adores and takes out on some kind of educational trip once a week. Loves spending time with friends, drinking wine and discussing books.

Financial: Middle class. Drives an older Mercedes. Prefers to dress casually and doesn't have much occasion to dress up.

Special skill set: Incredible artist, saving the money from her paintings to buy a better house with a better studio. Ultimate goal is to be a full-time painter. Has her ups and downs emotionally, but generally happy until her abduction.

Treats others: She's kind until someone crosses her boundaries. She's articulate and has a dry sense of humor that can sometimes be cutting. She doesn't like confrontation, but sometimes her temper gets the better of her and she explodes. She is not usually impulsive. She prefers to think and plan. She is street smart and tends to hold on to her regrets and grudges.

Her backstory:

Three major events in her life: 1. Losing her mother at a young age–afraid she'll die early, too. 2. Discovering a love of art, thanks to finding a collection of her mother's drawings. 3. Being publicly dumped by her high school boyfriend.

She never got along with dad and stepmom. Has always felt alone and has had no luck with relationships. Loves cats, drinks with friends, and her work at a museum restoring old paintings. Has always had a fear of sharks–will never step foot in an ocean for any reason!

Now let's discuss these as they relate to her RANGE as a character.

R - Reasons she does what she does—she fears what is growing inside her and of what happened to her. She's desperate to remember.

A - Ambitions—she wants answers more than anything else in the world, and she'll cross any line to get them.

N - Needs—she thinks she needs answers, but they won't satisfy her because she truly needs peace.

G - Growth—she will be afraid of people in the beginning but as the story progresses, she'll become a badass woman willing to do anything to protect herself and her loved ones.

E - Emotion and Effect—she can't tolerate lies, might climb the walls if she can't bake while she's stressed, hates cars–lost her mother in a crash–and loves cats. Except, her cats are now afraid of her, and she doesn't know why.

Now let's do SEARCH for the plot.

S - Symmetry - She is walking down a dirt road, barefoot, hungry, unsure how she got there. The seasons have changed, and now the weather is warm and humid, when she remembers it snowing just last week. There's a sudden flashback of torture that makes her flinch. This is her new reality.

E - Encounter - After she is found and taken to a hospital, tested and interviewed by police, someone sneaks in and tries to kill her but a mystery man swoops in and gets her out of there. After this first encounter, she doesn't know who to trust.

A - Adversity - They are now on the run, being hunted. Mystery man says he knows of someone else who was abducted with no memory of what happened, so they set out to find and question her. They'll need to figure out how assassins are always able to find them, as well as get new identities to travel without being detected. When they find the person who went through something similar...they are only plagued by more questions, raising the stakes.

R - Reflection - Emotionally, she's a mess but fighting to survive. Her thoughts revolve around her next steps. Should she stick around with her mystery man–she's attracted to him–or are his intentions sinister?

C - Climax - They find out the truth after being abducted again together, her memories restored. They'll seem trapped, like they are both going to die. Or maybe she finds out he is an alien, and they fell in love after her first abduction. He fought to save her. Now, they must face down their foe.

H - Harmony - They won the battle. They are free. They decide to forge a life together, keeping his secret.

Time for setting!

The story begins in a small town, but as she goes on the run, she visits other states. Road trip? Bigger cities to get lost in the crowds? A cabin in the woods.

Small town—stifling, too many prying eyes

Texas—familiar but not comforting, too close to home

New York—overly crowded, makes her paranoid
A cabin in the woods—safe place, ready for final showdown

Her different individual realms:
Solitary (frightening)
Doctor (hopeful turned frightening)
Mystery man(hopeful again but still frightening)
Traveling (always looking over shoulder)
Self-improvement (learning and preparing to fight back)
Alien (frightening with a chance at redemption)

DAY 15

PLANNING AHEAD

By now you have an idea for your book, a trope or two, and a theme. Our next goal is to fine tune some of the nitty gritty details that will help bring your big ideas to life. We will do this with a little pre-writing planning to organize your thoughts and prepare you for each new day of work.

This is not a time to think about anyone else's opinion. Only yours matters right now. Try not to censor yourself. You can always nix a scene later. Right now, let your imagination run wild!

GENA: For all of my earlier books, I was a "seat of the pants" type author. I had a grain of an idea, but little else, then sat down and just started writing, figuring things out as I went. And I still do that sometimes. But I mostly prefer to pre-plan now, figuring out my trope, theme and message before ever writing a word. I also figure out the kinds of necessary scenes I'll need to make my idea viable. The method I use works for those who have written random scenes, but don't know how to tie them together.

I use notecards, giving each pre-written idea (or already written scene) a title—the main thing that happens in it. Examples: "A kiss." "Hero fights the bad guy, revealing his strength." "The big secret is revealed."

Then I lay out or pin the cards in the order I think they'll occur, with a note about the purpose of the scene. *Always know the purpose of your scenes!* Then I make more cards with things that need to happen in order to reach those scenes.

Examples:

- Hero and heroine argue at a club (leads to the kiss)

- Hero is in a bad mood for some reason, and buys a bottle of whiskey in middle of night (which leads to the fight)

- Heroine suspects the hero is hiding something...heroine investigates...heroine confronts hero... the secret is revealed

I like using notecards or notebooks because I can leave added notes for myself.

When it comes to the actual writing, I never stop at the end of a scene. I always write the introduction to the next day's scene, so my mind ponders the direction I want to go for the rest of the day, unconsciously working out any kinks. By morning, I've figured out what mistakes I made and what needs to happen next.

Your assignment: Pick from one of two assignments today.

1. Make a list of every scene you already have in mind for your book and arrange them in the order you think they'll go. If possible, use bullet points to expand them.
2. Don't have any scene ideas? Think about your main characters, their goals and invent ways they can achieve each one. Follow this same procedure with problems they might encounter along the way.

DAY 16

The opening of your novel is important. It is a reader's introduction to your voice and sets the tone for your story. In fact, many readers often flip to the first page, scan the first line and paragraph and decide if they wish to read further.

There's a piece of advice often given to new writers: begin your chapter or story with a killer hook–a sentence or paragraph that leaves the reader wanting to read more. Many hooks pose a question to the reader, relay a bit of shocking information, or instill a sense of urgency. We think the first line simply needs to intrigue in some way, shape or form.

JILL: These opening sentences are from two two novels originally published by Harlequin in their Blaze line:

Maybe she could just fake it.

Sworn Enemies by Jill Monroe
Previously released as *Hitting the Mark*

What was she doing? Or had just done? Miriam Cole sucked in a breath and squeezed her eyes tight. It didn't change a thing. *He* was still there.

Sworn by Instinct by Jill Monroe
Previously released as *Primal Instincts*

GENA: Two of my favorite first lines are:

"Isn't it amazing how one seemingly innocent decision can change your entire life? For me, that decision came in the form of a grande mocha latte."

Playing With Fire by Gena Showalter

"Every night death came, slowly, painfully, and every morning Maddox awoke in bed, knowing he'd have to die again later. That was his greatest curse and his eternal punishment."

The Darkest Night by Gena Showalter

What are some of your favorite first lines, and what made them stand out?

Your assignment: Brainstorm possible first lines for your novel.

Tomorrow, you begin writing your first scene!

DAY 17

Today is the day you begin your novel! Where to begin? Maybe you've already drafted some scenes that you can use as a starting point. Maybe you'd like to begin with something new, at the beginning or even the end. That's up to you! You can start with any scene you prefer. If necessary, you can put everything together when you finish.

GENA: For my drafts, I always start at the beginning and work my way to the end, using single spaces and Times New Roman. When working on a rough draft, I tend to write an entire chapter in a day, and those chapters come in anywhere from 2000k - 4000k words. That word count has taken anywhere from an hour to 15 hours to write. My completed rough drafts have come in anywhere between 65k and 85k words. As I edit, adding things I missed and layering in other details I might have glossed over, that word count grows.

JILL: I prefer breaking my book into chunks and segments and then piecing them together at the end. I rarely write in order and often write the scenes I'm most excited about first. I've forgotten good ideas more times than I care to think about (sob). Notes scatter my desk and bullet points fill my manuscript. My preferred pace is to write 2,000 words a day or 10,000 words a week. I don't like working on the weekends, so if I can keep up with that 2k word pace Monday through Friday, I'm happy. Monday is my favorite day to write, and I avoid scheduling anything on that day at all. I'm most creative in the morning and leave marketing, emails and social media stuff for the afternoons.

Note: We're often asked about the number of words on a single page and the total length of our novels.

- A single page of a manuscript is usually around 250 words. So, you'll be writing one page a day, six days a week. Well, sometimes two pages a day. Keep this pace up until you have a completed rough draft, anywhere from 45k words to 75k words. Then we'll begin with editing assignments. If you're feeling inspired to write more, go for it! If you finish your rough draft before we reach those editing days, don't stop reading *All Write Already*. You'll pick up tips for revising and editing your story along the way.

- The length of a book is based on the word count, not the page number. This is because font, margins and chapter headers can contribute to the amount of pages, but not the actual words.

- A typical full-length novel can be anywhere from 45k and 100k. The genre you are writing in usually dictates the length. This is where your genre research comes into play. It's helpful to have a rough estimate of your end goal before you begin, because some storylines need more words due to the complexity of plots, subplots and characters.

Your assignment: Write roughly 250 words for your novel.

DAY 18

WHEN TO SELF-EDIT

Now that you've written the first part of your novel, your internal editor might be offering unsolicited advice, commentary or insults. Some authors like to edit as they write. Some prefer to write an entire draft, making notes about needed changes as they go. Then, after they've completed the draft, they go back and edit. Still others will send their manuscript directly to beta readers and only complete one edit at the end.

Sometimes authors who edit as they write get stuck and can't bring themselves to move on, because what they've written isn't "good enough." They focus on that one problem area for days, weeks or longer. Don't fall into this trap. You can't publish without a complete story. Forget perfect. If you lay the foundation today, you can build the house tomorrow.

Your assignment: Write roughly 250 words for your novel.

Bonus assignment: Find the best method of writing and editing for you. Pick a scene related to your story and start a timer for 10 minutes. Write as much of the scene as possible without letting yourself stop to think. When the timer goes off, stop writing. Do not edit what you wrote. In fact, set it aside.

Reset and start the timer again. This time, don't give yourself a time limit. Just time how long it takes you to write a second scene about the same topic. Carefully consider every sentence as you type it. When you finish, read it again to make sure it's right, then stop the timer.

Which method worked best for you? How different are the sentences? Is one better than the other? Is the time difference worth the extra effort?

DAY 19
HOOKS

Open up a favorite book and flip to the end of each chapter. Notice how the author ended scenes and take note of what kinds of "frosting" the author used to keep you reading.

JILL: As an experiment, I chose the book closest to me which was *Naked Thrill* and flipped to the last page of the first chapter. The context is this: Hayden Taylor just woke up naked beside an equally naked man. Their clothes have been burned, and there is a car painted like a ladybug parked outside. They find a pile of cash in the glove box. They're terrified they stole everything the night before.

He eyed the front seat. "I think I should drive."

"Why?" she asked.

His eyes softened, and a rueful smile touched his lips. "Because if we're caught I can make them believe you had no idea I'd stolen the car. Only one of us gets arrested."

It was strangely chivalrous. Hayden reached up, sank her finger into the hair at the nape of his neck so she could draw him nearer. The reality of his kiss was way better than the fantasy.

"Besides," he said, his gaze dropping from hers to study something far off in the distance. "I've been to jail before."

When I wrote this scene, I aimed for several different emotions to crash into the heroine one after another. At first I wanted her to question if she'd been stuck with the kind of dude who thinks only men should drive. Then she realizes Anthony is trying to protect her and it touches her. As she's feeling desire and tenderness toward him, he breaks focus, and the reader knows he's about to say something to Hayden that he can't say eye-to-eye. When he drops that he's been in jail and the chapter ends, the reader turns the page because they want to know why.

GENA: I borrowed Jill's grab-and-look method and picked up *The Evil Queen*. Here are 3 examples of chapter ends.

> "With his gaze still locked on mine, he bit into the poisonous apple." (I wanted the reader to wonder what happens after Prince Charming eats Snow White's apple. Does he die?)

> She appeared in a flash, her silver eyes wild, her cheeks pale. She shouted one word, "Run!" (Again, this points to something terrible about to happen.)

> "Refuse, and you won't like what happens next." (The hero says this to the heroine, and I like it because it shows him as an alpha while making readers wonder what he'll do and how the heroine will react.)

Your assignment: Double your word count today! Write roughly 500 words.

DAY 20

DIALOGUE

Have you ever read a bit of dialogue and wished you'd said something similar to a real person? We have! It made us love the character so much more. Dialogue is another tool a writer can use to connect a reader to their characters.

Realistically, not everything your characters say is going to impart some kind of knowledge, draw out a grin or a tear, or teach someone a lesson, but the words they speak should be in line with their personality or goals.

- Write down the first response that comes to mind. Then flip it toward a different angle or go the exact opposite direction. When you, the author, are shocked by a fictional person's words, your readers might be shocked, too.

Customer: What's your soup of the day?
Waitress: Whiskey with H2o croutons.

- When it feels as though you are transcribing a conversation in real time, you've hit a sweet spot! Run with it! You can always go back and weave in emotion, tone, thought/narrative, and physical reaction later.

- Find balance. Having too much dialogue can distance a reader from your story. They never get a glimpse at the character's innermost thoughts. But, having too little dialogue can reduce supporting characters to caricatures. It can also be an indication the story lacks a strong enough conflict.

- Most studies suggest that the majority of human

communication is nonverbal, and that our words don't always convey what we're really thinking or feeling. Your characters might spout things they don't mean.

- Dialogue should mirror conversation between real people. To make sure it rings true, you can read it out loud, then cut out the things that don't sound natural or that are just plain boring, like the little pleasantries we use in everyday greetings. (Nice day. How are you? The weather is nice.) And yes, people will catch you talking to yourself. They might even tease you. Been there, survived that.

JILL: Dialogue is my absolute favorite thing to write. (My least favorite is clothing descriptions, as I have zero sense of style.) I've been known to become so involved in writing a scene that I've called my own kid by a character's name.

"Just a second, Breena!" (From *Lord of Rage*.)

GENA: I've done the same as Jill and accidentally called my children Jorlan and Katie after the main characters in my first book, *The Stone Prince* (now re-titled as *Prince of Stone*). I've caught myself saying dialogue out loud as I'm writing, and I often leave notes for myself in my manuscripts. BE FUNNIER HERE, SHOWALTER!

Your assignment: Write roughly 250 words for your novel. Is today a good day to focus on dialogue?

DAY 21

REFLECT AND CATCH UP

Everyone needs a break.

We believe self-care is every bit as important as knowing how to construct a compelling scene. So, for the rest of the book, we'll suggest one day a week to reflect on your story or to catch up if needed. Maybe you've fallen behind in word count. Or perhaps this is a time to give the creative side of your brain a break.

We know it's possible to burnout from any task—even the ones you're most passionate about. Hopefully these reflect and catch up days will make you feel recharged and eager to return to your book, ready to see your word count fly. Some of these rest days will offer advice from other authors, and some will give a piece of advice or words of encouragement that you might be needing depending on where you are in your novel.

Today is a great day to rest. Your mind and body will thank you.

Where would Sherlock Holmes be without John Watson? Could Harry Potter have met his destiny without Ron and Hermione at his side? These iconic relationships are part of what make their stories so popular. They didn't have to meet at birth to share a special bond, and your character's don't either. Think about movies you've watched and other stories you've read, and the first encounter between two characters. Think about the heroes/heroines in your own favorite tales or movies. Does anything about their first encounter stand out?

While Hollywood has dubbed this first encounter a "meet cute," we find the term too limiting. The first encounter doesn't have to be sunshine and rainbows. It can be awful, wonderful, horrific, euphoric —anything! It just has to be important and interesting to help keep your readers turning the pages. That is why *we* call it "the memorable meet."

If you've already written a memorable meet, great. Take an extra look to make sure it stands out. If not, start thinking of ways to increase the memorability factor.

Let's look at some of our favorite fictional memorable meets.

JILL: One of my favorite tropes is mistaken identity. In my book *Fun & Games*, my heroine thinks the handsome man with a lanyard around his neck is the librarian. She asks him to help her find some rather embarrassing books.

GENA: One of my most memorable meets takes place in *The Darkest Whisper*. I like it because it's bloody and mysterious. The hero stumbles upon a group of immortals trapped in glass-like cages. In one of those cages, there is a lone woman. The door opens for a split second, and she's gone. A split second after that, she reappears with a bloody trachea in hand. It isn't cute, but it's definitely memorable and makes the reader ask questions.

Your assignment: Write roughly 250 words for your novel.

DAY 23

Characters have been introduced, scenes have been set, and your reader has an idea about where the story is going–but wait! Does your story need an element of adversity?

Adversity propels a story into action and brings your main characters together with a common goal. Good and bad. Will they hatch a plan? Will it go well? You don't have to know the answer yet. Just consider this as a jumpstart for your plot.

Many stories start by showing the main characters going about their normal lives. Then something shocking happens, dropping the hero/heroine into an unexpected situation.

In *Harry Potter and the Sorcerer's Stone* by J.K. Rowling, Harry lives under the stairs in his Aunt and Uncle's home. Things start getting strange when a letter arrives inviting him to attend Hogwarts.

Still other writers opt to begin the story with the adversity itself. In the opening scene of the TV Show *Lost*, Jake wakes up wearing a suit...while on the floor...of a jungle. Although the viewer doesn't know what is wrong, they understand something isn't right.

Whichever track you take, today's readers expect that adversity to be introduced fairly early on in the story. Too much "before" time can be boring. Ask yourself: *If everything changes for the character when <PLOT> happens, what do I need to show to make <PLOT> most impactful?* That might be where your story needs to begin.

JILL: In *At the Heart of Christmas*, Quinn learns that the legacy of her family's ornament shop has fallen to her. For Nolan, he loses his home and business in a fire on the same day, setting him on the path that would change his life.

GENA: In the book I'm working on as I type this—*The Glass Queen*—I have two points of adversity to kick off my story, and they feed off of each other. The first: when the heroine's mother gives birth to her, then bargains with an evil witch to help save her dying infant...and the evil witch possesses the child instead. That is my opening scene. The second—when the heroine is a little girl and the evil witch living inside her head demands her due...a complete takeover of the girl's body. The first is the ember, and it leads to the second, the wildfire— aka my plot.

Your assignment: Write roughly 250 words for your novel.

Bonus assignment: Think about what would really throw your character off kilter. What's the worst thing that could happen? What's the best? What emotions would these events trigger in your characters? What actions would they inspire?

Now that you have ideas for the encounter and how to torment your characters with adversity, it's time to consider what your characters will reflect on emotionally.

In real life, we must make hard choices. Take a chance on a new job, or stick with what you know? Buy a house or wait? Stand up for someone or sit aside?

Earlier, we talked a little about those hard choices your characters will have to face. Here, we delve deeper into how you can make those choices even more difficult by creating roadblocks to overcome, forcing the characters to reflect. One of our favorite things! It's not everyday you get to make someone's life miserable (or is it?).

One way to craft your roadblocks is to think about the major highs and lows your characters will experience. What will have to happen for them to *reach* those highs and lows, and how you can make the process more difficult for them.

Now it's time to play connect the dots!

GENA: Be careful that you do not make the roadblocks and therefore the decisions your characters make too easy. When I wrote *Firstlife*, I ran into a "too easy to pick" problem, and that was, well, a problem. In the book, there are two realms in the afterlife. The light and the dark. Both realms recruit people who are still among the living, who want to choose where they're going to live after they die. Originally, I made the light realm too appealing. Because it's the realm I would have chosen to live, I was biased against the other. I had to set my bias aside and figure out the appealing aspects of the other realm.

As for creating roadblocks and connecting the dots, I usually start with the grain of an idea. An immortal warrior is killed every night, knowing he'll awaken the next morning...and die again in *The Darkest Night*.

Roadblock: He has a limited amount of time to try to save himself.

After that, I asked a trillion questions, many of them steeped in "what if." Why is he killed? Who kills him? How is he killed? How does he awaken afterward? What if he is immortal? What if he is being punished? What if he's cursed? But why is he cursed? Did he commit a crime? What if he killed someone important and his punishment has to fit the crime? How can I make this worse for him? How can I make it better? I kept asking myself questions until I had answers that blew my mind.

Your assignment: Double your daily word count today! Write roughly 500 words for your novel.

DAY 25

SEARCH: THE HOPELESS DESCENT, AKA THE CLIMAX

The hopeless descent is the ultimate climax of your book. All the roadblocks, conflicts and adversity have led to this point. Everything your character has been fighting for is coming to a head. At this point, all hope seems lost. Evil appears to have won. Everything your story has been building toward has finally occurred, and your main character doesn't know what to do. So what comes next?

Every part of your character's RANGE hangs on this point in your story.

When it comes to the end of your novel, what will be the climax? What needs to happen to reach that point? How will your characters fix everything when they get there? Challenge yourself to think beyond the obvious and easy. If it's too easy for your characters, it might be too easy for your readers.

Your assignment: Write roughly 250 words for your novel.

Bonus assignment: Consider the climax of one of your favorite novels or movies. Work backwards to determine how the author or director reached that climax. What clues did they drop along the way? What actions did their characters have to take? What emotions had to be pricked?

DAY 26

By now, your characters have triumphed against their adversities and roadblocks. They've defeated their foe and have earned their happily ever after. But what did they learn along the way, and did it come at a cost? Have their goals changed along the journey? Has their belief system or worldview changed?

GENA: I love when a character gets what they wanted so badly...and they realize it doesn't make them happy, because it's not what they needed.

Your assignment: Write roughly 250 words for your novel.

Bonus assignment: What do you want your character to learn on their journey? Do their roadblocks and problems fit their growth? Now that you've planned your plot, work backwards to add additional details, events, or flaws that will make their journey more powerful.

DAY 27

CONSTANTLY RAISE THE STAKES

Throughout your novel, circumstances will force your characters to make choices. Sometimes these choices will be a clear moral dilemma between right and wrong, but other times those choices will be murkier, like choosing between right and right or wrong and wrong. But what makes those choices matter to the reader? Well, in the past when you have been reading someone else's work, what compelled you to care about *their* characters?

- The consequences the characters would face, both good and bad?

- A similar situation in your life?

- A pure heart? A broken heart?

- Their emotional state?

- Their hopes and dreams?

- How other characters treat them?

Use the answer to craft your own compelling characters! Just remember, readers need to know what your characters want most and what they are willing to do to get it. This will help establish what the characters have to lose and the potential for sacrifice, helping to raise the stakes of your story.

And don't forget to advance your character's RANGE at least once in every scene they appear. (Need a reminder about RANGE? Go back to Day 10)

JILL: I like to do something called "problem stacking." I think of my plot in terms of moving one step forward, two steps back. When my main characters think they've fixed something, I like to give them another problem so that it's harder for them to reach their ultimate goal..

Your assignment: Write roughly 250 words for your novel.

DAY 28

REFLECT AND CATCH UP

Don't Stop At the Finish Line

There's something I do every single day I write, and it helps me in ways I didn't realize at first. I never stop writing when I finish a scene. Before I end my workday, I write the introduction to the next scene and leave bullet points about what I hope to accomplish in it. That way, I always have a head start the next day, and I can easily slip back into my story.

–Gena Showalter

DAY 29

No one can relate to perfect people because perfect people do not exist. Since real people aren't flawless or without quirks, your characters shouldn't be perfect either. When it comes to fictional works, perfect characters can cause something known as "Mary Sue syndrome." The only cure? More cowbell. We kid, we kid. But trust us, you want to avoid the dreaded MSS.

That means you'll need to give your characters physical, mental and/or emotional imperfections. You can even give them a combination of the three.

Need help thinking of *your* character's flaws? Go back and reread your character interviews. Sometimes their strengths can go hand in hand with their flaws. Is she smart, but has no filter? Does he care a lot but has trouble expressing his feelings? Are they funny, but can't stay organized? Are they generous, yet needy? Do they have a great memory that prevents them from letting things go?

When it comes to imperfections, context is key. What works for a fun, quirky character might not work for a savage warrior bent on conquering the galaxies. Example: Clumsiness can be an endearing, humanizing trait in a school teacher, but not a surgeon or ballerina.

Flaws can also be the thing that brings two characters together. Do their flaws create a special bond? Like two klutzes comparing scars. Are their flaws and quirks similar or complementary? Like, say, two best friends who both love sending their friends things they hate, because it's hilarious. (Cough Gena and Jill Cough.)

GENA: The day I heard Jill hated garden gnomes, I went and bought every garden gnome I could find, snuck over to Jill's house in the middle of the night and peppered her front porch with an endless sea of gnomes. I soon discovered Jill possessed the same quirk, because she bought me a singing lobster—I despise toys that sing—then snuck over and took it back so she could send me ransom demands. It was such a joy to find someone with a similar sense of humor, with the same adorable quirk. Adorable. Yes. I said what I said.

Just like with beauty, flaws are in the eye of the beholder, and insecurities can be a plot device.

Flaws can also be understood and accepted. In our romance novels, we aim for the love interests to understand or relate to each other's flaws in ways other characters do not. It helps create that special bond we mentioned.

Your assignment: Write roughly 250 words for your novel.

Bonus assignment: Create a list of flaws for each of your main characters. Think of how those flaws will affect their relationships and ways they'll react.

DAY 30

CHARACTER FEARS

Fear is a primal emotion, and it sparks a survival instinct like nothing else. As an author, you can harness your own anxiety, dread and doubt to add layers of emotion to your writing, and thereby your characters. This is true of any emotion you've experienced, but today we'll focus on fear.

You can give your characters your phobias or something unique. But either way, they should have at least one fear. Fear is relatable; it helps connect them to the reader. After all, who *hasn't* experienced anxiety, dread and doubt at some point in their life? If your readers see a part of themselves in your character, they are more likely to root for a victory.

And when we talk fears and phobias, we don't just mean external creep factors like serial killers, ghosts living in the walls of your home, or your car breaking down in the middle of the night. We're talking about the deep-seated fears that strike an emotional cord. The fear of losing the one you love. The fear of being alone. The fear of having to talk to people in a social situation. You can use your own experiences to add realism to what your character is feeling.

Writing this type of deep emotional fear can work for your book, even in a comedy. At its core, the *Wedding Crashers* movie tackles themes of acceptance, loneliness, and aging.

Your assignment: Write roughly 250 words for your novel.

Bonus assignment: Write down the physical reactions you've experienced when facing your own fears and ways you were able to calm. How can you apply these to your characters? Maybe they want to avoid a person or place or event. How will it affect other aspects of their life? Will it challenge your character throughout the story, making them deal with what they hate most and hope to avoid?

DAY 31

VILLAINS, ANTAGONISTS AND MONSTERS, OH MY!

For the purpose of simplicity and clarity, we will refer to your fictional bad guy/beast as "villain" or "he/she/they" from here on out.

Villains can be a perfect foil for your main characters. Any bad guy, beast or antagonist can be a villain, and it's important that your bad guys are just as fleshed out and defined as their "good" counterparts, because their beliefs, experiences and expectations will determine every decision they make. You can even build your villain the same way you build your hero and heroine, using the same character building questions found on Day 9, as well as RANGE found on Day 10.

We suggest asking additional questions of your villain.

1. What will it take to defeat this villain?
2. What's something really likable about the villain?
3. What kind of bad are we talking about here? Criminal? Straight up evil? Or does circumstance force him to do bad things?
4. Is this villain redeemable?

If your villain is a monster, we have even more questions.

1. What type of creature? Animal? Otherworldly? Experiment gone wrong?
2. What is the creature's physiology?
3. What are the creature's physical, mental and emotional strengths and weaknesses?

Your assignment: Double your daily word count today. Write roughly 500 words of your novel.

DAY 32

MULTIDIMENSIONAL SIDE CHARACTERS

You'll find side characters in most fictional books. These characters can help breathe life into the story as they interact with the main characters. Often, readers may gravitate to a certain side character, and even start a cult following that turns into spinoff opportunities, like Saul Goodman from *Breaking Bad*.

Here are our best tips to crafting vivid side characters, who might even end up being the star of your next book.

1. Does the character have a shared memory with the main character? Let him/her think about it.
2. How does the side character react emotionally to different situations?
3. Mystery. Does the character do something the hero can't understand?

JILL: To make my side characters as realistic as possible, I try to give them as rich a life and backstory as I can without going over my word count or overshadowing my main characters. The hero in the book *Lord of Rage* has two younger brothers. They are heartbroken boys who'd lost their parents and were being raised by their distant and cold older sibling. As Osborn learns to love and forgive, his relationship with his brothers changes and grows. The brother also provided some comic relief, and I have readers ask me to write their stories.

GENA: Nowadays, I prefer to leave my side characters a bit of mystery, feeding out just enough details to intrigue. I hope! 1. It gives readers something to think about once they finish the book and 2. It gives me room to play with the character's backstory if I decide to give them a book of their own. Too many times I've spilled too many details about side characters and trapped myself on a specific path, giving me no room to play. I've even hurt and offended longtime, dedicated readers by changing a character's path without fully fleshing out why or easing into the change—don't make that mistake!

Your assignment: Write roughly 250 words for your novel.

Bonus assignment: Make a list of secondary characters who will appear in your story. Also note their relationship to the main characters, physical descriptions and what they'll add to the story.

DAY 33

Think about the closest relationships you've experienced over the years. Chances are good that you two have visited important places together and your plans have gone awry. You've shared laughter and arguments. Witnessed accidents, mistakes and victories. Depending on how long your characters have known each other and the type of relationship they have, they'll have shared experiences. You can use those shared experiences to highlight or fracture a bond, show new aspects of their personality, or explain why these characters are like they are.

Think about some of your favorite characters in beloved books or movies. How did the author or director create these types of shared experiences? Flashbacks? Action scenes? Dialogue? Did it work? Did it fail? What kind of overall impact did it have on the character and/or story arc?

GENA: I remember a time Jill and I were inside a fancy museum. She was fascinated by the art and telling me the history of some of the pieces, and I was responding. *Really. Hmm. Yes.* When she turned around to ask me a question, she spotted me powdering my nose and checking my teeth in a compact mirror, and we both burst out laughing. The experience showcased one of our differences—I like pretty art, she likes boring art, and that will forever be my takeaway—but also brought us closer together. We still tease each other about it. Professor Facts and Miss Mirror.

Your assignment: Write roughly 250 words for your novel.

Bonus assignment: Create a shared experience between two of your characters.

DAY 34

EVERYONE ARGUES

If real people argue, and they do...a lot...chances are good that your characters will argue about something sooner rather than later. How will your story people handle the argument?

Arguments can spring forth for different reasons. Falling in love, finding a dead body, exploring a new planet—these types of things engage deep, primal emotions which can lead to quick tempers and an even quicker spout of thoughtless words. Maybe your main character is in some kind of physical discomfort. We all know someone who becomes a real beast when they are hangry. (Cough Gena cough). Work and family stresses can also needle your characters. Past mistakes can come back to haunt them. Anything can sour their mood!

Whatever the reason for the emotional upheaval, you need to know how your characters will deal. Are they quick-tempered and ready to rumble, or easy-going peace seekers? What pushes their hot buttons? Do they forgive and move on or hold a grudge?

And what happens after the fight? Do they hold a grudge? Can they go back to the way things were?

Developing a connection between characters means more than a simple "I'm sorry." For the relationship to heal, should there be true regret and forgiveness? What about a commitment to working together, taking a step toward rebuilding trust?

Pro-tip: Sometimes short, choppy sentences can help convey action and sharp emotion. And don't forget the multiple ways to signal irritation, anger, or upset. 1. physical action, like teeth grinding, 2. physical reaction, like a racing heart 3. facial expression, 4. word choice and 5. tone of their thoughts.

Your assignment: Write roughly 250 words for your novel.

Bonus assignment: Write a full scene with your main characters arguing. Think of it like a mini-story within your story; there should be a beginning, middle and end. Identify any key emotions the characters experience during and after the argument. Hurt? Injured pride? Loss? Euphoria? Glee? Wicked delight? Do your characters understand their own feelings? How do they recover from the fight? Is it physical or with words? Do your characters name call, curse or yell?

DAY 35

REFLECT AND CATCH UP

JILL: I prefer two methods of organizing. Notecards and to-do lists. I keep a stack of index cards nearby at all times, and post them on a bulletin board in my office that is within eyesight of my computer. These index cards are usually about characters: name, hair color, style, personality traits, etc. RANGE and SEARCH go on the bulletin board, too.

For my to-do lists, I love using the "Notes" application with the bubble and check mark. I relish checking those bubbles off–I feel so accomplished every time I complete something! I also enjoy being able to access that list from every one of my digital devices. I try to keep my to-do list as "tasky" as possible—things I can do to improve my story. Like doing a word search for an overused phrase or step-by-step instructions to fix a plot hole.

The best way to make your lists work for you is to personalize them. I've tried filling character sheets, keeping lists on the fridge and specialized apps on my phone, but in the end it was the simple bubble and index card method that worked best for me. Gena logs everything into a notebook and will add tabs to help her find the information she's looking for. Maybe a three-ring binder or specialized organizational tool will be good for you. Now go discover what works best for you.

Side note: The next handful of assignments will focus on list creation.

DAY 36

MAP YOUR WORLD!

As you write and develop your story world, keep a map or rough outline of the town/kingdom/realm you are building. Depending on your story, this can save you a frantic search through your manuscript or notes just to reminder yourself whether the library is located on Main Street or if the Province of Fleur is mountainous or flat.

If drawing isn't your thing, consider creating note cards with facts in bullet points for each location. As you flesh out your world, be sure to add the new details to your map or cards. That way, you'll never forget that the town library is in a red brick building within walking distance of your hero's childhood home, or that the school's parking lot is full of potholes.

Your assignment: Write roughly 250 words for your novel.

Bonus assignment: Using the list of places your characters will visit throughout your novel, draw a map of your world/city/town. Keep this list and map handy because you'll refer back to them the deeper you get into your story.

DAY 37

You've already started your novel and named your characters. And, though we've talked a little about character names, we want to delve deeper today. Sometimes, after you get to see your character in action, their original name no longer fits. Thankfully, there are many ways to find a new and perfect name. You can use baby books, websites, or even watch the credits of different movies and TV shows to pick out the names you admire.

JILL: I prefer to use names I picked out when I was pregnant, but didn't ultimately give to my children. I also like to find an underlying meaning for a character's name that might not be obvious to the reader, but helps my writing on a subconscious level. *Lord of Rage* is a retelling of *Goldilocks and the Three Bears*. The hero Osborn is a berserker and bear, and his name, along with his brothers', were various plays of the word *bear* in other languages.

GENA: Like Jill, I sometimes choose names with meaning. Torin = watchtower. In my **Lords of the Underworld** series, he guards his friends by sourcing info through computer hacking. Maddox—mad —deals with rage issues. Strider takes great strides to win any battle. In my **Forest of Good and Evil** series, Farrah is Snow White, the "fairest...fair...Farrah" of them all.

On a practicality standpoint, try to avoid giving too many characters names that are similar, begin with the same letter or rhyme. This can confuse or downright annoy some readers. (As always, there are exceptions to the "rules.")

Your assignment: Write roughly 250 words for your novel.

Bonus assignment: Make a list of other possible names for your characters. Research the meaning of those names to see if anything sparks your imagination or helps you flesh out the character's personality traits.

DAY 38

UNIQUE TO YOUR CHARACTERS

By now, you know when and where your characters live. You've realized the story realms they'll venture. Tomorrow, you'll get to create unique words they can use in their everyday life. For today, let's talk about what makes the book's setting special to your characters specifically.

The places we visit can evoke different emotions in us, depending on our past experiences. Even if something is new, it can remind us of something we loved and lost/want and need. In other words, your setting can be a catalyst for anything! A memory flashback. A spot, a clue or dead body is found. An ambush. A breakdown. A rejuvenation.

Does your main character have a favorite spot they like to visit? Is there something they'll notice thanks to a past experience that others might overlook? Do they have a routine jogging route a kidnapper could utilize? Do certain locations rouse different emotions?

JILL: In *Naked Pursuit* (also known as *The Wrong Bed: Naked Pursuit*, now a movie from Lifetime) the hero wakes up with no memory of what happened in the days before. Before that, he totally avoided visiting his hometown, and his boyhood home, for reasons revealed later in the book. To anyone else, that house has no real meaning. To him, it's everything. But now he's in trouble and feels responsible for the woman handcuffed to him, so returning home for help is his first instinct.

Your assignment: Double your daily word count today! Write roughly 500 words of your novel.

Bonus assignment: Think about the places your main characters will visit within your story world. Create a list of 5 unique descriptions those characters might notice or memories they'll encounter while standing in that location.

DAY 39

GENA: In my book, *Playing With Fire*, the heroine (Belle) drinks a spiked mocha latte and develops superpowers over the four elements. Now a (sexy) government agent is hot on her trail and she's on the run, trying to survive. (I just gave you my elevator pitch. You'll learn about those later in *All Write Already*.) Soon Belle learns there's a whole other realm out there, one filled with all the superheroes of myth and legend.

This "realm" exists alongside modern society, so it needed words to distinguish it from the natural world. I'm not talking descriptive words, but actual words used by my characters in their everyday lives.

I created "PSI." Paranormal Studies and Investigations.

PSI had a motto: *To the rest of the world, we are ghosts. Nonexistent.*

PSI needed opposition, so I created "OASS." Observation and Application of Supernatural Studies.

People with superpowers are referred to as "paras" and they had terms for those without a supernatural ability.

Even if your book is set in the contemporary world, your narrator will use specific and unique words associated with their job, family, or some other aspect of their life.

- A lawyer might use trial language in everyday life. "I object!"
- A doctor might say "STAT" to non-medical family members.
- Someone who watches reality TV will understand more pop culture references than someone who never watches TV.

Your assignment: Write roughly 250 words for your novel.

Bonus assignment: Create a list of unique words your characters will use throughout your book.

DAY 40

MORE THAN JUST SIGHT

When writing, you can utilize the five senses to elevate a scene to the next level, adding realism and grounding the reader in the familiar. Think SHTTS. Sight, hear, touch, taste, scent.

JILL: Think what now?

GENA: This is MEMORABLE, Jill. Go with it.

JILL: And that's why mnemonics work. When you want to add realism to a scene, think NOW IS THE TIME FOR A SHTTS. (Sigh)

What textures do your characters feel/encounter? Silk? Rough calluses? What do they taste when they eat? Or when they kiss? How does their personality affect what they see? Do they focus on the positives or the negatives? What sounds do they hear? Are locusts buzzing? Cars honking? Dogs barking?

Make sure the verbs associated with the fives senses aren't used repeatedly. Something that is easier to do than you think. These words include *look, see, hear, taste* and *smell*. Be aware, and when you can use a more dynamic word—go for it.

Examples:

He looked around the room for his prey.
He searched the room for his prey.

She felt his body heat against her skin.
His body heat seeped past the thin cotton of her T-shirt.

Your assignment: Write roughly 250 words for your novel.

DAY 41

THIS WAY OR THAT WAY?

There are many different ways to write a novel. Some authors write their first draft in longhand, then type everything in a document, giving them their first chance to edit. Others prefer to type everything from the start, using Word, Pages, Google Docs, or writing software like Scrivener. Another favorite is using dictation.

There's no right way or wrong way; there's only your way and what works best for you. Do not listen to anyone who tells you otherwise. But wait! Be aware: What works for you one day may not work the next time. Be open to change and try experimenting with different methods when needed. If one approach stifles your creativity, try something else.

JILL: Your writing space can also change from day to day and book to book. *Tall, Dark and Filthy Rich* I wrote in a notebook while waiting in the car at the school pickup line. *Lord of Rage* found its way onto the page while camping and *At the Heart of Christmas* was written almost exclusively on my laptop. Rules don't dictate where and how we write. Just because one book was written at a noisy coffee shop doesn't mean you must mirror that same environment for the next book. As you change, your methods can change.

Your assignment: Write roughly 250 words for your novel.

Bonus assignment: Write one paragraph longhand, and type another paragraph into a digital document. Get a feel for both methods. Do you feel more creative one way? Did you want to keep going when typing, but struggled to form ideas when writing longhand, or vice versa?

DAY 42

REFLECT AND CATCH UP

Anyone who wants to write professionally needs to figure out her process. Each author works in her own unique way. For example, I write by the seat of my pants – meaning I have a scene in my head that inspires me, I sit down and start writing, and I let my muse guide me along the way. I never know for sure what my characters will do or say and they surprise me all the time. For me, the process is almost like reading a book, because each page unfolds with new surprises.

Other authors want/need to plot in advance. I have an author friend who creates scenes and then ties them together, and yet another friend who writes the ending first and then backtracks.

If I tried any of those methods, I'd never complete another book because I'd be so frustrated, and if they tried my method, they say they'd ramble all over the place without any coherency.

I also write "complete," meaning I don't do first or second drafts. I edit as I go, often rereading the previous 10 pages before diving into the next part of the story. That way, when I'm done I'm done! I have friends who write a first draft, and some who write three.

I get bored very easily and rereading my own work would be painful for me, but the point is that there's no wrong way as long as it works for you. Whatever helps you take a story from start to finish is what you need to do, because a book isn't finished until... it is.

One thing I've always felt passionate about is the avoidance of critique groups. I know they work for some authors (see paragraph 1!) but in this flooded market, the most unique thing any author has to offer is her voice. If multiple voices have gone through your book, you've diluted that filet mignon to beef stew... and everyone sells beef stew, right?

Lastly, write for YOU. If you don't enjoy the process, if you don't love your characters and aren't involved in each scene, the reader won't be either. Worse, the entire process will become a heinous chore, and seriously, there are less stressful jobs than making yourself write a book you don't love. If you laugh with your characters, if you cry and curse alongside them, if you finish your book to complete satisfaction, the reader will too. Happy writing to all!

–*New York Times* bestselling author Lori Foster

DAY 43

POV: POINT OF VIEW

The point of view you use determines how your reader will see the world and the characters within it. Some authors prefer a single point of view throughout their books. Others like to use a double point of view. In romance, we often use a double point of view to showcase both love interests. You can even write scenes from a secondary character's viewpoint...or a dog...or a door—whatever or whomever you'd prefer!

Think about your narrator's personality and flaws. How do they see the world differently than the people around them? Are they aware of those differences? Are they reliable, only speaking the truth, or do they lie to themselves? Do their feelings and opinions cloud their judgement? How do you want your narrator to come across to your reader?

Can't decide on a narrator for a particular scene? Ask yourself which character has the most to gain or lose by what is about to occur.

Some authors keep a running tally of screen time for each character. Just remember, it's your world and your rules. Don't create artificial scenes in an attempt to maintain some kind of balance.

To build suspense about a certain character's thoughts, you can stay out of their head.

Your assignment: Write roughly 250 words for your novel.

Bonus assignment: Write a short scene involving two main characters witnessing a fight, having an argument, or going to an event, but use only one point of view. Then, write the same scene from another character's point of view. Which works better for that scene and why?

DAY 44

When writing your novel, you have several tenses to choose from.

> Present: I am eating a cookie.
> Past: I ate a cookie.
> Future: I will eat a cookie.

But there's also:

> Present perfect: I have eaten a cookie.
> Past perfect: I had eaten the cookie.
> Future perfect: I will have eaten a cookie.

In terms of your narrator, you get to choose between:

> First person: I ate a cookie.
> Third person: She ate a cookie.

We know authors who like to write their first draft in first person to help them delve deeper into character emotion and thought. When the book is complete, they write a second draft with everything in third person.

GENA: I've written books in third person past, first person past, and first person present. The tense I chose always depends on my target audience, storyline and characters. In *Playing With Fire*, I decided to stay inside the heroine's head exclusively, leaving the hero shrouded in mystery. (He's a sexy government agent sent to neutralize her after she develops superpowers over the 4 elements.) As the two seem to fall in love, I wanted the reader to wonder if he truly had her best interests at heart.

Your assignment: Write roughly 250 words for your novel.

Bonus assignment: Yesterday, you wrote a scene from two different points of view. Today, we'd like you to take one of those scenes and flip the tense. If you wrote it in past tense, change it to present, and vice versa. If you wrote in third, change it to first, and vice versa. Do you notice any differences in terms of emotion, feeling, or mood?

INSIDE JOKE

In real life, people who are close often have inside jokes. It's fun to give our main characters inside jokes as well. This adds a new layer of authenticity.

JILL: I know Gena has mentioned this, but you need to know my side of the story. When Gena dropped by my house and STOLE a garden gnome right off my porch, I only discovered the theft when she sent me a picture of the poor statue with a knife to its throat. The nerve! I loved that gnome I also hated. Of course, I had to retaliate by stealing the stuffed singing lobster I'd given her, putting it in a pot, as if I planned to boil it...while filming it all. And that's how the battle of Lobby and Gnomie began—Gena's fault. Now, we tease each other about this and most people have no idea what we're talking about.

GENA: Gnomie had it coming! Sorry, I just had to get that out of the way. Anyway. In *The Darkest King*, the heroine is a killer unicorn-shifter. Yes. I said unicorn-shifter. In her society, they repay every wrong with a diabolical punishment à la *The Good Place*, like forcing the commitment-phobic hero to pretend to be her boyfriend in order to gain something he wants more than breath. Throughout the book, the two tease each other about this fake relationship in ways others find confusing.

"The wedding's off! We're broken up."

"Hate to break it to you, baby, but we just got back together."

Your assignment: Write roughly 250 words for your novel.

Bonus assignment: Create an inside joke for two of your characters.

DAY 46

A vision or dream board is a collection of images and quotes meant to inspire you. People do this to focus on and magnify their dreams and goals.

You can also make a vision board for your story!

By using images that remind you of your characters and the locations they visit within your story, you can remind yourself of the most important visual details at a glance.

- The physical appearance of your characters
- Their home
- Their office
- Outfit ideas

A storyboard is a little different. Rather than photos, you keep plot points arranged in the order they need to be written. This creates a visual blueprint to follow as you write.

Some authors find storyboards and vision boards to be a helpful part of their brainstorming process, as well as aiding in their need for organization. You might be one of them!

Your assignment: Double your daily word count today! Write roughly 500 words for your novel.

DAY 47

The weather can play a large part in your story, affecting the scene's setting, the character's clothing choices, whether or not someone's plans need to change, and any number of other things.

We have tips to navigating these weather situations!

- Referring to the seasons of the year can act as shorthand. As soon as you read the word "summer," you automatically think sunshine, heat, swimwear.
- Seasons can affect your characters' moods. Too hot in summer, too cold in winter, too rainy in spring, and too dreary in fall, and someone might complain.
- Tornadoes and hurricanes can create danger and chaos. Lightning can illuminate and electrify. Storms can be frightening or cleansing.
- Location changes everything! Rain may be falling in town while it's clear in the mountains above. Traveling south will bring warmer weather. Don't forget that the northern and southern hemispheres experience the seasons at opposite times of year

Your assignment: Write roughly 250 words for your novel.

Bonus assignment: Determine what season(s) take place during your story. How does the time of year affect your characters? Does weather play a significant role? Does the weather play a role in character behavior. Did it trigger a memory?

DAY 48

INTERVIEW YOUR MAIN CHARACTERS

You know your characters better now. But do you know them well enough? Today, you're going to interview your main characters, asking silly questions to get to know them on a deeper level.

Bonus: You might want to find ways to pepper their answers throughout your story!

We'll help you start!

- Would you rather fight a zombie and get bit, or be a zombie and do the biting?
- You're in trouble. Do you involve others or handle it on your own?
- If you were a movie, what would be your title?
- What pizza toppings are you?
- Would you rather be invisible for the rest of your life or never have another moment of privacy?
- If you were a car, what kind would you be?

Believe it or not, there is meaning to the madness. Knowing if someone views themselves as a sports car or a junker held together by duct tape and a prayer can give true insight into a character.

Your assignment: Write roughly 250 words for your novel.

Side Note: You can save your character interviews to use as promo later!

DAY 49

REFLECT AND CATCH UP

The words in the first line of a book are some of the most important lines you'll write. Yet when that thought puts me into a panic, I tend to think of what my character would say about first lines. It often comes off dramatic, sarcastic, or in some cases, a bit murderous. If I leave that first line to what my character needs, even if it's only a small shadow of who they are as a person, I can let those words flow.

–*New York Times* bestselling author Carrie Ann Ryan

DAY 50

ACTION THEN REACTION

When good or bad things happen in someone's life, they react physically, mentally, and emotionally. Don't gloss over those details in your story! What physical changes come over your characters? Do their thoughts fragment? What emotions unfurl inside them?

In most scenes, you might notice the action comes first, followed by a reaction. (For reference, a flashback is a way to show reaction before action.) As in real life, we react to something first—we flinch/smile/gasp—*and then* we think about it. This don't have to be a long, drawn out rumination, especially when you're in the midst of an action scene. You can make a brief mention and expound later. Allow your characters to react emotionally, then process what they are feeling and figure out a plan of action.

Your assignment: Write roughly 250 words for your novel.

DAY 51

TOO MUCH? TOO LITTLE?

How much should I be writing a day?

Honestly, every author is different. One person's pace might not work for another. And really, your pace can even vary from day to day. Your health, energy, motivation and spare time can change, often depending on outside factors.

Every book is different, too. Sometimes the words just flow, your fingers flying over the keyboard. Other times, you may struggle to craft a single paragraph.

Some writers are adamant about writing every single day. Others prefer to deliberate for weeks, even months, then word vomit a draft as quickly as possible. Don't be afraid to give different methods a try; it might take a little trial and error to find the pace that works for you. Monitor how much you are writing in any given hour, where your writing flows, and the environment that best stimulates your creativity.

Be careful not to make comparisons with other authors. It can take as little as three days for a lettuce seed to germinate, but up to two weeks for a parsnip. Even though they have different timelines, they're both still vegetables.

Your Assignment: Double your daily word count! Write roughly 500 words for your novel.

DAY 52

BLATANT FORESHADOWING

Foreshadowing is a warning or hint of a future event. It creates a sense of foreboding that can keep your reader flipping pages to find out what happens next.

Think of it this way: If the author takes the time to give a detail, it could be important later on. If someone in a TV show notices a strange noise coming from their car, chances are good the car will break down later and cause some trouble.

Your characters can notice or feel a prickle of unease. The fine hairs can rise on the back of their neck. Their blood can flash-freeze. Someone can say something that raises suspicions. *"Did you see that?"* You can use a prophecy: *As the moon swallows the sun, a dark warrior will rise to rule the land, but will he be good or evil?*

You can even use flashbacks. Like showing a murder that occurred in a haunted house a century ago in order to showcase what could happen to your main characters when they move in.

Foreshadowing doesn't have to be long and drawn out. It can be as simple as one sentence. *Game of Thrones* is practically branded on foreshadowing. Who hears the phrase *"Winter is coming"* and doesn't start thinking about *direwolves* and dragons?

Is it necessary to foreshadow? No, not always. But foreshadowing can do two things for your story. First, it can build apprehension or excitement and keep the reader reading. That's obviously good for you and your story. Second, it can prepare the reader for what's coming next. Some readers/viewers like to guess what will happen next.

Another bonus? It can be tons of fun for the writer!

At this stage of your manuscript, you might not know how your book will end and what to foreshadow. Use our old standby suggestion of keep writing and figure it out later. You can go back and weave in foreshadowing at any time.

Your assignment: Write roughly 250 words for your novel.

Bonus assignment: Think about whether there is some kind of omen in your book. A prophecy? A sign? Could you enrich your story by adding a hint at what's to come?

DAY 53

A subplot is a secondary story that runs parallel to the main story. Meaning, you are incorporating an *additional* story in your novel. This side-story can be written from the point of view of your main characters at a younger or older age than the time of your main tale, or side-characters known or unknown to your main characters. This side-story might seem to deviate from your main one, but it will always support your theme.

This side-story can intersect with the main story at any time in your tale. It can add tension, excitement, or a sliding door effect—moments in life where a decision somehow alters the character's entire life. The moments he/she could have chosen A but went with B instead, so they wonder what their lives would have been like if they'd made the opposite decision.

Examples of plot versus subplot:

Plot—Main protagonists move into a haunted house.

Subplot—A couple who moved into the house a century before the main protagonists.

∽

Plot—A woman discovers she's a long lost daughter of Zeus and must complete seven tasks to enter Mount Olympus.

Subplot—Told from the point of view of another daughter of Zeus, who sabotages the woman's efforts.

∽

Plot—Hero and heroine fall in love, fighting it the whole way.

Subplot—Hero's brother falls in love with the heroine's sister, but this couple does not fight it.

With this example, the author can use that secondary love story to show where the hero and heroine went wrong and vice versa.

Famous subplots:

- Inigo Montoya's quest for revenge in *The Princess Bride*.

- The other people affected by the war between the Montagues and Capulets in *Romeo and Juliet*.

- The adventures of Legolas and Aragon in *Lord of the Rings*.

GENA: In *The Evil Queen*, I made the heroine's sister the subplot. I hoped to show what happened when the two girls were faced with the same dilemma but made opposite choices. Who made the right choice, and who made the wrong one?

Do you have a subplot in your story? What is its purpose? What is your goal?

Your assignment: Write roughly 250 words for your novel.

Bonus Assignment: Develop a goal for another character that comes in contact with a main character. Do the two goals meet/clash?

DAY 54

OVER-EXPLAINING

GENA: I wrote 4 different rough drafts of *The Evil Queen*. You read that correctly. Four. From scratch. It took forever, but I kept making the same mistake. Whatever plot I placed my characters in, I kept over-explaining the world, the rules of the world, every mythological species and magical power, never allowing the information to roll out organically. For my fourth and final draft, I decided to write a heroine who was brand new to the story world I was crafting. As she learned about the world, the reader learned about the world. This mindset kept me from expounding on topics irrelevant to her current circumstances.

Although, you don't want to under-explain, either, which leads to confusion. Your goal is balance. Figure out what is needed, what is icing, and what is overkill. Just because you research something and it's smart or informative, the entirety of the details might not belong in your tale. Your goal is to hold the reader's interest in the story and stave off any confusion.

Your assignment: Write roughly 250 words for your novel.

DAY 55

PACING DAY BY DAY

Let's say you want to write a 60,000 word book in three months. To figure out how much you need to write each day, you'll divide 90 days into 60,000. The answer—670—is your daily word count goal.

Now let's say you want to write it in three months, but you don't want to write on the weekends. You'll subtract the weekends, leaving you with 66 days to finish your story. That means you need to write 910 words a day.

But (there's always a but, isn't there?) you want to give yourself a week to read through and edit, which means you'll subtract seven more days...which means you now need to write 985 words a day.

Oh, but now you realize Thanksgiving falls during those three months, so you need to take out 3 days for cooking, driving, visiting with friends or family and watching football.

Keep an eye on your calendar, there's always things like doctor appointments, work parties and family obligations that will eat into your writing time.

Your assignment: Write roughly 250 words for your novel.

DAY 56

Write the story on your heart, regardless of trends. Readers will feel your passion in it.

And please know that first drafts are ugly. They are like warped skeletons - bare bones that will make you cringe. The true beauty comes during the drafting process. Revise, rewrite, delete what you don't need, add details and layers - each draft you'll see the story progressing into what you've envisioned. It takes time. We as writers tend to be super hard on ourselves and incredibly impatient with the process, but every step is important when crafting a story. It's too easy to give up during the ugly stage. Keep going! You are the advocate for the characters and world you've created. If you love it, fight for it, even if it means fighting your own self. Insecurity can be crippling to a creative mind. You've got to believe and be gentle with yourself.

–*New York Times* bestselling author, Wendy Higgins

DAY 57

WHAT'S YOUR NUMBER?

Let's delve deeper into word count. So many new authors ask established authors how long their books are, because they are unsure how long their own book should be. The easy answer is: *As long as it needs to be.*

A full length novel can be anywhere from 40k to 100k (or more!) words. A novella is usually around 20k - 40k thousand words. Shorter stories are usually around or under 15,000.

Traditional publishers often have a specific word count they'd prefer you to follow. This information can be found on their website (usually under guidelines.) There might be some leeway, though, and you or your agent can negotiate the word count so that it's spelled out in your contract.

For those authors interested in self-publishing, you have the flexibility to make the book as long or as short as you want. Keep an eye on the genre, though; straying too far out of the norm can frustrate readers. For instance, paranormals are often over 80,000 words or more while cozy mysteries can clock in at 40,000. Reverse those numbers and you can see why readers might be disappointed or shocked if you deviate.

GENA: Most of my books are around 100k–120k words. My longest book, *The Darkest Warrior*, is 140k words. I tend to write longer novellas, as well, that come in anywhere from 30k - 60k. (A typical short story is usually under 45k words, which some consider the minimum count for a full length novel.) One time, I did write a short novella with an extremely complex plot–*Ever Night*. Looking back, I realize the story required 100k words. It was a mistake on my part, but a great learning experience.

JILL: My goal is always two thousand words a day or 10,000 words a week, so sometimes I must work on the weekend to catch up (and one of the reasons we gave you every seventh day off in this book). I aim for 50k words for my stories, but after editing and revising, they'll land closer to 65k.

There are factors you can consider to help you decide on your story's length. Is your plot simple or complex? The more complex the plot is, the more pages you'll need to let it unfold.

Are you building a whole new otherworld? If so, you'll probably need to write a longer book to paint the stage and explain the dynamics. How many characters populate your story world? The more there are, the more page room you need for descriptions and personalities. Do you have a subplot? If so, you might need to write a longer book.

If you're aiming for a specific publisher and your expected word count is too small, consider layering in additional descriptions or a subplot that runs parallel to your story.

Your assignment: Double your daily word count! Write roughly 500 words for your novel.

DAY 58

As a new author, you might not have a lot of practice writing different types of scenes or showcasing different kinds of emotions through thought/action/character. Look through the list below and see if you've written about these topics at some point. If not, consider writing one as practice. No time spent writing is wasted. You might even strike a well of inspiration!

- A kiss
- Being chased by bad guys
- Discovering a dead body
- A fight between two people
- Groveling/an apology for a terrible wrong
- Grief/sorrow
- Uncovering shocking news
- Embarrassment
- A first time to do something
- Being startled in the night

Your assignment: Write roughly 250 words for your novel.

DAY 59

Maybe you carved out a chunk of writing time, only to realize that you need to research something first. Anything from the fall of Rome to the average cost of a wool coat in New Zealand around 1859. So, you stop writing and fire up a search engine, and wind up passing minutes... then hours browsing your news feeds, reading articles, or looking at pictures, all or none of which is related to your query. By the time you get ready to write again, you've lost your flow.

When you choose to write on a computer, the danger of distraction is very real. Whenever you stop, it can be difficult to start up again! Unless the details are vital to your plot, we recommend not stopping to research. Instead, it helps to write yourself a note about what you need to study, then move on. Once you've left the inspiration-zone or completed your daily goal, you can go back and do some research.

If you feel you need to research now because the information could determine the direction of your story, go for it. Just be sure you are pressing forward in your draft, not standing still.

Your assignment: Write roughly 250 words for your novel.

Bonus assignment: Set a timer for 20 minutes and write straight through, expanding on what you wrote yesterday.

DAY 60

GENA: One of my most asked questions by new writers is "How long are your chapters?" While different authors will have different answers, I'm happy to give you a point of reference. I usually write 2000–3000 words per chapter. I've written less, and I've written more. Some chapters require more information/action/dialogue than others. But I never start writing thinking I need a specific number of words in any given chapter. I let the scene flow the way it needs to flow, stopping when it reaches a natural end or an excellent hook.

Your assignment: Write roughly 250 words for your novel.

DAY 61

HOW TO END A CHAPTER

As you are writing, you can look for spots that shout "This is the perfect scene ender!" Here are some organic ways to end a scene or chapter.

- A shocking bit of dialogue
- A big discovery
- A cliffhanger
- Foreshadowing
- The arrival of another character
- The need to move to a new location
- Spooky imagery
- A witty one-liner
- A point is made
- Someone walks away

How do your favorite authors end their chapters?

Your assignment: Write roughly 250 words for your novel.

DAY 62

YOU KNOW WHAT YOU KNOW

There's an old adage: *Write what you know*. But we say: *Write what you can imagine!*

We've never fought a vampire or flown through the clouds with an angel, but we were able to visualize it, so we were able to write it.

Whatever action you're writing, try to imagine experiencing it for yourself. How would you feel? Frightened? Excited? What would you see, smell, touch and taste? How would your body react?

Sometimes, writing about something you've never done can be difficult. You might need help to get yourself in the right frame of mind. Consider watching a movie or TV show with a similar mood and tone that you are going for. Listen to music that evokes the emotion you need. Remember, you magnify what you focus on, and not just in your writing. External factors can affect your imagination just as surely as your imagination can affect your characters.

Your assignment: Write roughly 250 words for your novel.

DAY 63
REFLECT AND CATCH UP

The First Fear For a Writer is the Fear of Getting Started

On the surface it sounds ridiculous. How hard can it be to get started? But it's easy to say you're going to be a writer. You tell people at work you're going to get going on that book. You tell your significant other that you need the spare bedroom for an office. And you start googling vacation homes you're going to buy when the money starts rolling in.

It's easy to talk about writing. It's a lot more difficult when you're sitting in front of the blank computer screen with that little cursor blinking at you.

Suddenly you're thinking that a hundred thousand words is a lot. Really, really a lot. And the idea that hit you in the middle of the night that seemed so fabulous is completely lame. And the characters who are constantly chattering in the back of your mind when you're trying to concentrate on something else, suddenly don't have a thing to say. The next thing that happens is that you're completely over-whelmed.

When that happens, I try to remember that it's just about doing something. Anything. It can be little. A description of the town where you're setting the book. Or a scene with the main character drinking coffee and reading the newspaper.

Big goals come from small steps. And if you want to do a lot, it sometimes means aiming only for a little.

We're told by those who've succeeded that you have to push toward your goal, that only hard work and sweat will allow you to reach the finish line. And that's great when your mind isn't blank and that stupid curser isn't blinking at you. Sometimes you have to give yourself a break. Don't sit down to write War and Peace. The key is creating goals that you can achieve. It's too easy to quit if you've set the bar too high.

Be kind to yourself, and know that as long as you're moving forward you're going to reach the finish line.

—*New York Times* bestselling author Alexandra Ivy

DAY 64

BREAK A LEG!

Not every character needs a fun motto or saying associated with their character, but a good catchphrase can provide added insight into their life and (hopefully) stick with a reader long after they finish reading the book.

A catchphrase can be something a character says as encouragement for themselves, like a rallying cry, a mantra, or a bit of advice they live by. This slogan should be important to them for one reason or another. It can point to a specific person, place, time, event or thought. It can be a joke, come from a traumatic past event, or spring from a fond memory. It can even be a hope or a dream they hold onto with all of their might, or as simple as, "Balls!" But, it is almost always short and sweet.

One of our favorites comes from the **Immortals After Dark** series by Kresley Cole. "Nucking Futs Nïx" is the nickname of Nïx the Ever-Knowing, and it tells you so much about her personality right off the bat.

GENA: I'd never really thought about character catchphrases until writing *Alice in Zombieland*. Kat, a reader favorite, likes to say "True story." Many readers loved her and used her catchphrase when speaking to me. I think it made Kat more relatable. Nowadays, I like to give one of my main characters a mantra they use to encourage or chastise themselves, and there's always a reason for it.

Do any of your favorite fictional heroes and heroines have a catchphrase? Should one of your characters have one?

Your assignment: Write roughly 250 words for your novel.

Bonus assignment: Brainstorm a catchphrase or mantra for one of your characters. For fun, maybe a friend, love interest or sidekick can have an opposite one.

DAY 65

FINDING INSPIRATION FOR DESCRIPTIONS

As you write, you might need to draw inspiration from the real world. Photos of a mansion, perhaps, to help you describe where your villain resides. For the sake of accuracy, you'll probably need to do some research. Maybe you can't immediately recall what houses in the Tudor style look like, or the kind of safety signage in front of a factory. Just as we write "RESEARCH" in a spot requiring further study, we often add "PUT DESCRIPTION HERE" when we're on a roll and don't want to stop to set the scene. This is helpful when the description just isn't coming to mind or you want to check the visuals against your memory.

Years ago, authors turned to fashion magazines and architectural guide books to help flesh out their descriptions. Nowadays, we're just a click away from stunning scenes, warm interiors, and the latest trends. You can even read reviews about real-world locations that might make an appearance in your book.

Don't forget to save inspiring photos for future reference or, if applicable, promo shareables!

Your assignment: Write roughly 250 words for your novel.

Bonus assignment: Take a couple of minutes to look up places that your character might visit. Will they inhabit a gothic castle? Work in a sterile high-rise in the middle of the city? Look for photos that inspire you, or fill in any of the missing details for yourself. Now, write it out! Take at least 250 extra words to set a scene, and be sure to sprinkle in the five senses.

DAY 66

How's it going?

If you're following the schedule, you've been writing for more than six weeks now.

- Do you have an idea for today's scene?
- How are you progressing on SEARCH?
- How are your characters showing off their RANGE?
- Do any of your scenes need fleshing out?

Consider keeping a checklist with everything you hope to accomplish in each individual chapter.

Focus. Magnify. Accomplish. Triumph!

Your assignment: Double your word count today! Write roughly 500 words for your novel.

DAY 67

THE BUSINESS OF FORMATTING

Will you be typing or writing longhand today? If you choose to type, you're probably wondering about spacing and fonts. We use our own personal preferences for our rough drafts and format once we're done. But, you might prefer to format for a publisher or publishing as you go, to see your work in its proper form right from the start.

Here's a handy informational tip sheet to help find the method that works best for you.

- Manuscripts sent to traditional publishing houses are double spaced, with fonts like Times New Roman and Courier New. Some authors like to use fun fonts as they write to reflect their creativity or the mood of the scene, then reformat when they finish.

- If you are self-publishing, your book will need to be formatted in book form, single spaced. (We use Vellum for this after we've completed the entire novel and finished all of our editing.)

Your Assignment: Write roughly 250 words for your novel.

DAY 68

CRAFTING YOUR MONSTER

Whatever genre you're writing, your plot might call for some kind of beast. Movies like *The Shape of Water*, *A Quiet Place* and TV shows like *V Wars* based on the graphic novels by Jonathan Maberry are wonderful examples of different types of beasts.

Things you need to know: How does your creature interact with your characters? How does the creature change over the course of the book?

How does its body differ from a human's? What is the texture of its skin? How do its physical needs differ from ours? What are its eating habits?

Does it have special powers? Can it see auras or hear a pitch only dogs usually hear?

How does it communicate? What language does it speak?

How does its homeland—if it has one—differ from ours?

Maybe your characters have only noticed the bigger picture items about your beast so far. Is it time to begin noticing smaller details? A glint in its eyes? A curl of steam from its nostrils? A scar on his claw? Just make sure there is a logical reason for every detail you provide!

Your assignment: Write roughly 250 words for your novel.

DAY 69

GETTING BUSY!

Whether you're writing a romance, mystery or epic fantasy, there may be a point where you must write an intimate scene between your characters. Affection, touching and sex are just another tool a writer can use to move the plot forward and show character growth.

A kiss or an accidental brushing of a hand can be as devastating emotionally as a full on sex scene, it just depends on your characters, story and how the act is performed. Whatever the sensuality level— slow burn, fast burn, steamy or sweet—the scene should flow from your characters and story organically. It should evolve naturally and make sense, just like every other element of your tale. We recommend sticking to whatever level makes you the most comfortable. Readers can sense awkwardness, and it can rip them right out of the story.

You can build up to a love scene by establishing awareness between your characters. To establish awareness, you can use all five senses and sexual tension. Also, character firsts help: first sight, first touch, first kiss and the first time their gazes met.

Consider what the characters noticed about each other during their first meeting. Play up those attributes.

Have you utilized the five senses? In other words, have you taken time for a SSHTS?

Sight: Consider letting the characters notice the big picture about each other to start, then begin to notice smaller details as the scene progresses.

Touch: What textures and temperatures do they feel? How does their partner react to their touch?

Scent and taste: Does their partner have a scent and/or taste?

Sound: What do they hear? The quickness of their breaths?

What is the tempo? Hard and fast, or slow and sweet?

When their gazes meet, what physical and emotional reaction do they experience?

Keep the scene in tune with the character's current predicament. Are they afraid they will die the next day? Have they declared a temporary truce? Do they think this relationship will only be a temporary arrangement? Perhaps they think they'll never see this person again, but what happens when they do?

How the characters act and respond to intimacy will be tied to their past. Have they been in love before? Hurt before? Abused?

A love scene is more than just sex and body parts. Attraction involves the mind, and in real life, people are drawn to voice, kindness, intensity, power and humor. Among other things. Don't be afraid to show the funnier side of human interaction, either. Touching another can be fumbling and awkward at times.

Reading your dialogue aloud can be an important step for this type of scene. If spoken words are awkward, too sweet or would make you laugh in real life, consider reworking it until the conversation sounds natural.

The beauty of a love scene is that they often serve more than one purpose. Think about the scene's objective—beyond sexual gratification, or whatever your characters are into. Does it draw the characters closer? Maybe it pushes them further apart. Will they regret this experience afterward? Do you hope to show a character's vulnerable side or create more problems?

While there are no hard and fast rules to writing a love scene, there are several aspects to consider.

- Using metaphors to describe body parts and sounds can be awkward or cringe-worthy
- Flowery dialogue can seem disingenuous
- In today's society, a discussion about consent and safe sex practices can be vital. Some fear having two characters (or more!) discuss consent and safe sex takes away from the romanticism. That is absolutely not true. In the hands of a skilled writer, nothing is sexier!

- Always research genre expectations

JILL: I write both sweet books and very steamy ones under my name. Thanks to the brilliant suggestion of Mandy M. Roth, readers who visit my website are now met with two choices: Sweet or Spicy. That way, the ones who like sweet romances don't have to sort through my spicier titles (and vice versa) to find what they want.

Something of note: If you are self publishing, make sure to thoroughly read the Terms of Service (ToS) for every store where you upload your book. Authors can and will lose access to markets by violating these terms.

For a deeper understanding of intimacy, consider reading *Intimate Behavior: A Zoologist's Classic Study of Human Intimacy* by Desmond Morris.

Your assignment: Write roughly 250 words for your novel.

DAY 70

REFLECT AND CATCH UP

Don't let someone else's success make you feel less. They're on their journey – you're on yours.

–Bestselling author Beverly Jenkins

DAY 71

INTERNAL EDITOR

Now that you've made a habit of writing, we're going to talk about your internal editor again. Remember the voice in the back of your head telling you a sentence isn't quite right or that you should go back and fix something? Yeah, that's your internal editor or "IE". This IE can be an amazing friend, a bitter enemy, or even both at the same time.

If your IE is criticizing every word you write, ensuring you cannot move on from a chapter, a scene, or a sentence, your story isn't progressing. That means your internal editor is doing more harm than good, wanting perfection at a time it isn't needed.

Consider turning off your IE and writing through the problems. This could help you figure out a solution. And, if you keep writing and realize later you must start from scratch, at least you learned something. No writing is wasted.

Sometimes it's important to write even when you have no idea how to end the book. The answer could come to you as you motor on. If not, you'll at least know what route not to take with your story, and you'll develop a better understanding of characters and plot. And don't worry that what you're writing sucks. As Gena likes to say, "You can fix suck."

Sometimes, just seeing the words on a piece of paper or screen is the magic answer, opening your eyes to a new solution.

During the first frenzy of getting ideas out of your head and onto paper, we recommend locking your internal editor away. Here are some tips that might help you ignore your biggest critic...at least for a little while.

1. Turn off spell check when you're writing your first draft or warming up. Those red squiggles can be distracting.

2. Word vomit! Let loose and get the words out, then clean them up during the editing process.
3. Remember that you have a built-in time to fix everything: editing! There's no way to edit a page with no words on them, so don't jump the gun and complete step two before you're done with step one.
4. Accept that the first draft doesn't have to be perfect. Any mistakes you write, you can correct later.
5. Remind your Internal Editor you'll be setting him/her/it free when it's time to edit. Just not to the detriment of your self-confidence.

The IE can challenge us to take risks and think outside the box, but we selective about when we pay attention to it.

JILL: I used to get up at 5:30 in the morning to write. Although it was tough (I am *not* a morning person), I did find a bonus in that my IE wasn't fully awake yet.

Your assignment: Write roughly 250 words for your novel.

Bonus assignment: Set a timer and write on your project for 20 minutes. Whatever it takes – ignore the internal editor!

DAY 72

THE SPICE: VARIETY

You are an author. You must try to write more varied sentences. You will learn that readers notice if you don't.

Read the above paragraph again. Do you notice how each of the three sentences has the same construction? All together, they're dry, right? So let's try it again, only this time, we'll vary the sentence structure.

You are an author. Try writing more varied sentences. Right? At some point, readers will notice if you don't.

The second one has more punch, yes?

Your assignment: Double your daily word count! Write roughly 500 words for your novel.

DAY 73
BEST ADVICE

What was the best writing advice you ever received?

JILL: Without a doubt, it was "Butt in Chair–Hands on Keyboard" (BIC-HOK). I'm not sure who came up with that phrase, but like how some use the *Godfather* as the answer to all of life's questions, BIC-HOK is usually the ticket to all writing quandaries.

How did you finish your book?

Butt in chair, hands on keyboard.

What was the secret to making the bestseller list?

Butt in chair, hands on keyboard.

Of course, writing is an art, wrapped up in myths and legends about inspirations and muses, and I respect the creative process. But there are also realities to consider, especially if your goal is to have writing be your main source of income. Mortgages, other bills and your kid's looming tuition come around like clockwork, so time management is the name of the game.

I've heard and yes, even used, phrases like, "I'm waiting for my muse" or "I'm just not feeling inspired to write". But I've found I use those as excuses to give myself permission to forgo my work. Because although "butt in chair, hands on keyboard" is simple advice, it's not easy to do. It requires incredible discipline.

No more waiting around for your muse today. Be your own muse and build up that writing stamina!

Your assignment: Write roughly 250 words for your novel.

DAY 74

ACCOUNTABILITY PARTNER

While you can be your own muse, you might find it's much harder to be your own drill sergeant. That's when a buddy comes in handy.

GENA: When I first began writing, I had a burning desire to get the jumble of ideas out of my head and onto paper. After an initial rush of excitement, however, I realized that writing a book can be hard. I was sixteen at the time, and I gave up.

Why did my excitement dwindle? Just the thought of doing hard work, or did the reason go deeper? Fear of failure? Fear of success? Maybe I didn't know how to fix issues with my plot and characters, or how to write myself out of a metaphorical corner? Yes! All of those things and more. But, once I graduated high school and dropped out of college three times, I had to face facts. Writing was the only thing I could see myself doing for the rest of my life. So, I had to buckle down and do it. The more I forced myself to write despite those fears and struggles, the more I learned about the process of crafting a book. I think the same will be true for you!

Know that declining enthusiasm is perfectly natural. Published authors have an advantage in this regard, because they have official deadlines and the contractual obligation to return their advance money if those deadlines are missed. When no one is waiting on you and the threat of your professional reputation or cold hard cash isn't on the line, it's much easier to stop when the passion fades.

So, how can you pre-plan for those times when you need to write, but don't want to? Find an accountability partner! Someone to encourage you when you're down.

This person doesn't have to be a fellow writer, just someone who cares about you and isn't afraid to approach you with a raised eyebrow or fierce emoji when necessary. Share with them your goal of writing a book in a year. Ask them to hold you accountable. Put reminders in your phone. Do whatever you have to do to push through to the end!

JILL: I've had a dream of beginning a podcast for a couple of years now. In 2019, I decided to make that happen and set a goal of a year. In November, I joined a 28 Day Challenge that put everything in place, so I could officially launch my podcast in 2020. Part of that challenge was to find an accountability partner, and I chose my daughter. Like any child who finally gets to turn the tables on a parent, my daughter took her duties seriously! She texted and called for my updates. Let me tell you, there was NO WAY I would tell her I hadn't met my deadline. By the end of those 28 days, I had a podcast title, domain name, social media handles, artwork necessary to make a trailer and a preview episode ready to go. That's what an accountability partner does for you.

Your assignment: Write roughly 250 words for your novel.

Bonus assignment: Start your search for an accountability partner. It could be a friend, a family member, a forum, or anyone else in your life that can give you that personal nudge in the right direction. You don't have to show them your work if you don't want to yet.

In the meantime, we're in stamina build-up mode! Can you set a lofty goal for yourself? Maybe things are starting to click into place with your narrative. Try to double or triple your usual word count.

DAY 75

If you watch a TV show or movie that evokes strong emotions, consider listening to the soundtrack as you write.

Next level: Keep a list handy, detailing what emotion each soundtrack evokes. Then, when you need to write a scene filled with a specific emotion, you can have the right music playing in the background, helping you delve into the right mental state.

When thinking about characters and music, consider the:

- Instrumentals
- Lyrics
- Mood of the song
- Emotion of the singer
- Reason for the song

Readers often love to know what songs inspired you as you created your book or what might be playing on your character's car stereo. Share those in a "Note From The Author" section or on your social media pages.

Your assignment: Write roughly 250 words for your novel.

Bonus assignment: Choose a song that means something to you, and could maybe mean something to your characters. Listen to it, and then spend some time mentally interviewing your characters about it. Write 300 words using the song as inspiration.

DAY 76

FINDING TIME TO WRITE

"I don't have time to write."

Have you ever spoken those words? Are you sure they are true?

While we have other posts about finding time to write, today is all about avoiding pitfalls of procrastination: after all, why do today what you could do tomorrow?

Schedule your work time!

You can prove to yourself that you do have the time. Over the next three days, write down every mandatory task you perform on a daily basis and when. This includes your job, travel time, childcare, housework, cooking, etc. Then, take a look at any open spots. That is your writing time!

No open spots? Consider getting up earlier in the morning or staying up a little later at night. What about recording your favorite show instead of watching it live? Or, what about setting a timer and writing 15 minutes every time you complete another task. Those sessions can add up until you've completed your word count for the day.

Today's sacrifice could lead to tomorrow's blessing. Focus. Magnify. Accomplish. Triumph!

Your assignment: Write roughly 250 words for your novel.

The most important advice I can give to a new writer is this: Develop friends within the writing community. Writing is a lonely, solitary business. As a writer, you'll spend long hours at the keyboard. You'll struggle to find the right plot/turning point/phrase. There'll be days when five or six rejections land in your inbox all at once. When you have to cancel a dinner date in order to meet a deadline.

People outside the writing community won't understand. They'll tell you, "Sitting so long is bad for your health. You should take a break every hour and walk around the block." As if. Or your brother-in-law's uncle will call you up one day to offer you his "perfect solution" to that thorny plot point you discussed with your sister *in total confidence*. Someone who hasn't experienced it will never understand the despair that darkens your soul when an editor or an agent responds with a cavalier, "Not for me," after you've entrusted them with a year's worth of your work. Family members might suggest a time management class when you're struggling to meet a deadline.

But another writer? They get it. They'll tell you about the neck wrap that eases cramped muscles. Or better yet, they'll lend you theirs. They'll talk through that turning point with you, and they won't stop until you say, "Aha!" They know rejections require more than sympathy and kind words; they understand that massive amounts of chocolate are necessary if you're going to face the keyboard again, and they don't judge. They'll drop off a casserole or have Uber Eats deliver a meal the week before your book is due. And when you sign that agent, when you sell your book, when you hit a list, when you win an award, your writer friends will be the first to show up with a bottle of champagne, a box of chocolate or a bouquet of flowers and tell you they knew you could do it all along.

–Award-winning author Leigh Duncan

DAY 78

The next several days we'll discuss writer's block.

For every problem, there *is* a solution. Always. Without fail. You simply have to figure out what it is.

Every author gets stuck at some point. Maybe a change of scenery will help. Maybe you need to close your eyes and imagine the scene over and over again, playing "what if" until you find the solution. Or, maybe you need to start with word vomit.

Methods that have worked for us:

- Going for a drive
- Taking a shower
- Watching a movie that evokes the same emotion you need for the scene
- Reading a book that evokes the same emotion you need for the scene
- Looking at artwork or stock photos online
- Walking around the house, talking out loud

Tip: If you're spending long periods of time staring off into space to think and struggling to finish the scene, write a note in the margin for Future You, explaining everything you have problems with, what you're hoping to accomplish with the scene, and any possible solutions you've already brainstormed, even if those solutions won't ultimately work. Then? Move on. Later, when you go back, you might discover your incredible mind was working out the solution from the shadows all along.

Your assignment: Write roughly 250 words for your novel.

Bonus assignment: Find the place where you're stuck right now (you know the one) and read through it. Is there anything you can add? Anything that isn't working, and is choking you up? Play doctor on this passage and see if you can get it running a little better.

DAY 79

STILL STUCK?

When you get stuck, it doesn't mean you've gone in the wrong direction. It *can* mean that, yes, but not always. There are many different causes for that "stuck" feeling. Here are just a few.

- The story setup is complicated and requires a complex solution you haven't figured out yet.

- You have too many choices laid out, and the direction has become illogical or muddied.

- The situation is too simple, or relies on problems that are easily solved with a conversation or other obvious fixes, and you're struggling to sustain conflict.

Think about your story, your characters and your plot. There might be a place where the wires are crossed, and figuring out where it happened will help you get back on track. Use the process of elimination until you hit on the block that's preventing your words from flowing.

If your characters are stuck and you don't know how to get them unstuck, chances are good your readers won't know, either. This is an opportunity to blow their minds with a shocking twist. Think beyond the expected. Shock yourself with the solution and you just might shock the reader, too.

Your assignment: Write roughly 250 words for your novel.

Bonus assignment: Spend more time with your project. Is it working better? Do you need to use a hacksaw on parts of it? Take stock, and remember to use your character's personality traits and flaws to your advantage.

DAY 80

Are you writing the first book in a series? We have tips!

Remember that you will be locked into any backstory you give your secondary characters, even if you later decide to give one or more a book of their own. What if the old backstory doesn't work with your new idea?

- Be certain about everyone's backstory before you publish the novel, even the villain, antagonist or monster.

- Be vague when and where you can, without compromising your main story or character development.

Consider keeping notes for each individual character, and write down any pertinent information. Be sure to note physical appearance, their backstory, major events that affected them in each story, and any personality changes that have occurred and why.

If you want to redeem your villain, antagonist or monster in a later book, it might be best not to let him do irredeemable things in other tales.

Do not solve all the overarching plot questions in book one. Save something for the next book!

Your assignment: Double your daily word count! Write roughly 500 words for your novel.

DAY 81

TO PROLOGUE OR NOT TO PROLOGUE

A prologue is an introduction to your story that takes place at a different time than your main story or with different characters. It can show an event from the past that changed your main characters in some way, or even show a moment that occurs later in your book. A prologue has to matter and set up something major in your book.

Sometimes prologues work, sometimes they don't. Everything depends on your story and your characters. Some editors, readers and authors have strong opinions on them, but we are firm believers in an author doing what they think is right for their story.

Ask yourself: What is the goal of this prologue? What purpose does it serve? If it's simply to give information, how can those details be parsed out later in the book without the prologue? Would the book be better served if the Prologue became Chapter One?

Your assignment: Write roughly 250 words for your novel.

DAY 82

TEMPER

If you claim a character has a temper problem, you'll need to show them losing their temper at least once during the course of the story. You can design scenes to highlight this particular type of temper, whatever it is. Violent? Eerie silence and stillness? Cursing? Cruel?

What sets them off? What calms them down?

Does their temper change throughout the story? Maybe it becomes necessary for them to learn how to control their fury, or they find a new outlet. This character's calm moments can help magnify their rages in other parts of the book.

Be sure to use words, actions and thoughts that convey anger. Like shorter, punchier sentences. Jerky motions. Quicker breathing. Flushed skin. A visible, bulging vein. Clenched fists. There are many ways to convey anger.

As with any scene, the character's emotion will cause a step-by-step evolution, affecting future thoughts and actions.

Example: The temper fuse is lit.

- First physical reaction and tone of thoughts change.
- Anger grows stronger the more they think about it. (Remember, what you focus on, you magnify.)
- Stronger physical reaction propels them into action.
- Punch a wall. Curse.

GENA: In my **Lords of the Underworld** series, the character Maddox is possessed by the demon of Violence. He has a dark, savage temper, and he gets physical. He fights dirty and thrills when he causes pain. Nothing calms him down...until he meets his heroine. Her gentle spirit calms his stormy one in ways he's never before experienced. As the story progresses, he learns to focus on his memories of her to calm himself.

Your assignment: Write roughly 250 words for your novel.

Bonus assignment: Write a scene showing a conflict between characters. What are their arguing styles? Make sure it's not simply yelling for yelling's sake. Arguments are a wonderful place to layer in conflict and reinforce the theme.

DAY 83

SUSPENSION OF DISBELIEF

Readers want to get lost in our stories. To do so, they willingly suspend their disbelief to accept the surreal events/creatures/situations we throw at them. But, to maintain the reader's willingness to believe, your story cannot break its own rules. Readers will not accept impossible things unless you have a concrete reason why it's possible within your story world.

For this reason, it is vital that your characters stay in character, one plot point leads to another, there are no unlikely coincidences, nothing is too convenient for your characters, your heroes and heroines aren't all powerful, and your narrative is sound. That doesn't mean they have to be fair or unsurprising. Logic makes the impossible possible!

Your assignment: Write roughly 250 words for your novel.

DAY 84

REFLECT AND CATCH UP

The thing about writing a series is that you have to 'hook' your reader. You want them to be invested in the characters. ALL of them, not just the hero and heroine in the book they're currently reading. They should feel a deep-seated need to read the next book. In book 1, you should tease about the couple coming out in book 2. In book 2, you should tease about the couple coming out in book 3, etc.

This doesn't have to be a long-drawn out obvious thing either. Maybe have the Hero talk about his greatest regret (example, not having kids), and in his book, he suddenly becomes an instant dad to a child he didn't know about, or to three orphans he came upon in the course of his job). You should foreshadow, make your readers curious about the characters they don't know a lot about yet.

And this is the most important part, at the end of the current book, you should always include a teaser to the next book. Maybe you show your hero being knocked out and dragged off by a womanly figure in black. Maybe he's reading a letter from his long lost love and vowing to go get her. Maybe you show the heroine in a blacked out cave wishing someone would come rescue her. This gives the reader a clear sense of what's coming next and hopefully will make them immediately go and one-click that book. Give your readers a reason to one-click.

–*New York Times* bestselling author Susan Stoker

DAY 85

Everyone likes to be rewarded for a job well done. That's human. Have you considered setting up a daily reward system for yourself? You have a daily word count goal to meet, after all, and a little extra incentive to finish it could give you the boost you need to power through.

What do you love? Naps? A favorite wine? Dinner with a friend? Pick something that motivates you. Once you hit your goal, celebrate! Growing your novel's word count is a great accomplishment!

JILL: Once I took my children on a playdate with six total children under the age of five. Afterward, the play area was a DISASTER, and I groaned as I spotted the mess. The other (and much wiser) mom grabbed a package of marshmallows and gave a child one for every fifth toy they picked up and put away. You have never seen such action and so quickly. At first I worried that this may give children the wrong message—rewarding children with treats for doing something that they should be doing anyway, but she actually taught those children (and me) a life lesson:

1. Tasks still must be completed.
2. By making it every 5th toy, they learned not everything is rewarded.
3. Look forward to the treat when the job is done well.

Your assignment: Write roughly 250 words for your novel.

DAY 86

PEOPLE WATCH!

Consider going to a public place, sitting and listening to other people's conversations. This can be a great way to harvest ideas for your story.

Always wanted to be a secret agent? Now's your chance to eavesdrop.

JILL: One time I was waiting in line at a fast-food restaurant when suddenly, the woman next to me looked at her partner and yelled, "Are you calling me a liar?" You better believe it drew my attention, and a half dozen plot bunnies.

Your assignment: Write roughly 250 words for your novel.

DAY 87

A critique partner is a fellow writer or bookworm who reads over your work to find the flaws, plot holes and inconsistencies you might have missed. This critique partner can also serve as your accountability partner, but be aware that the two jobs are quite different. An accountability partner is charged with helping you remain on track with your goals. Basically, the whip wielder.

Additionally, there are different types of software and websites that you can plug in your word totals to help you stay on track. One fun challenge is to participate in National Novel Writing Month (NaNoWriMo), which always takes place in November. Often, local groups complete this challenge together, offering support and encouragement along the way.

Critique partners can be wonderful, and they can be terrible, so choose wisely. Not every opinion is right. Not every suggestion is helpful, and not everyone is trustworthy.

JILL: I found my first critique group on the internet, and even though we no longer work together, I am still friends with many of those ladies today. Gena and I met at a local writing chapter, so you can find a group anywhere, local or an ocean away.

A word or two of caution. Learn to identify when a suggested change improves the story or merely fits someone else's personal preference. When in doubt, go with your gut. It will be YOUR name on the front of the cover; you are the one who must be happy with the end result.

Is it possible for critique relationships to grow toxic? Yes. Jealousy can come into play. Differences of opinions can cause rifts, and members can take sides. If you leave a critique session feeling unmotivated and like a hack, reconsider whether or not the group is right for you. There is nothing wrong with walking away.

You can join our exclusive group, secret word: **Triumph**
https://www.facebook.com/groups/AllWriteAlready/

Your assignment: Write roughly 250 words for your novel.

Bonus assignment: Consider sharing your work with someone you trust.

DAY 88

RULE OF THREE

The Rule of Three is a writing principle that suggests anything that comes in threes is more effective and believable than the things that do not.

The thought behind it is simple. If something happens once, it can be hailed as a mistake. If something happens twice, it can be called a coincidence. But three times? There's the proof.

Writer's often use this technique to build a case for whatever point they wish to prove. Here are a few examples:

She wanted him. He looked hot (1), smelled good (2), and when he smiled, her world felt right (3).

Wind whistled (1), and branches slapped together (2). Shadows writhed (3). Had a night ever creeped me out more?

Her house had become a menagerie, filled with dogs (1), cats (2), and the insects they brought in (3).

Other examples:
    Blood, sweat and tears
    Stop, drop and roll
    Past, present, future

Your assignment: Write roughly 250 words for your novel.

Bonus assignment: Locate a place in your project that you can utilize the rule of three. Does it enhance the realness of the scene?

DAY 89
YOU'RE NOT A JOURNALIST

Have you ever skipped over big blocks of information as you read a fictional book? Perhaps that information was something that excited the author...and only the author. Remember, as you write, you add more than a journalist detailing facts of a story, or a professor giving a lecture. You are an artist who breathes life into people, places and things.

To avoid crafting blocks of narrative that might bore the reader, consider scrolling through your story and rereading every wall of text you come across—possible information dumps. Can one or more of the facts in your exposition be placed elsewhere? Would the information be more exciting if separated from other information? Would it be better delivered through word of mouth instead of narrative? Is the information relevant to the story where it is? Are there places to weave in emotional responses and sensory details?

Focus. Magnify. Accomplish. Triumph!

Your assignment: Write roughly 250 words for your novel.

DAY 90

A decision tree is a thought tool that (might) resembles a tree by the time you finish. Or, if you are like Gena, it will resemble a jumbled ball of yarn. You start with a single question (trunk), add the different answers (branches), then add the possible consequences to each decision (leaves).

We like to use this method for our characters any time they must make a major decision. The goal is to avoid making your characters appear all-knowing, as though they have the right answer for every problem, and no thought is needed.

Here's an example of a simple decision tree. (Yours will be much more complex, with lines pointing to different answers.)

(Trunk)

Character comes to a crossroads. Should they choose:

(Branches)

Left: paved road
Middle: road straight ahead
Right: gravel road

(More branches)

Left: The paved road leads to Enchantia
Middle: The road straight ahead leads to nowhere
Right: The gravel road leads to Zombieland

(Leaves)
Left: Battle the evil sorcerer

Middle: Learn to fight
Right: Be crowned queen

Each choice leads to new choices that must be made, as well as fresh implications and complications, every decision causing the "tree" to branch out.

Your assignment: Write roughly 250 words for your novel.

Bonus assignment: Consider a choice your character must make and the possible outcomes of their decisions. Craft a decision tree to help.

DAY 91

REFLECT AND CATCH UP

Understand that there will be days you make a lot of progress toward your goal and days you don't. How you handle the setbacks can make or break you. Understand there will be certain things that are out of your control. Don't allow yourself to be discouraged. Keep going. You'll get to the finish line.

–*New York Times* bestselling author Mandy M. Roth

DAY 92

YOUR IDEAL WORK SPACE

Carving out time to write can be difficult. Finding a place to write can be just as challenging. When you *do* find the time and place, you may need to enact "on the job" rules for your loved ones. This rules can include:

- No texts or phone calls unless you're seriously hurt
- No blood, no vomit = no interruption
- Ask yourself if your query is worth awakening the beast lurking inside the author

Let's backtrack a moment, though. Today we'll focus on finding the best space for you to write. Tomorrow we'll cover the necessary boundaries.

So. What do we know about writing space? Every author needs one. Someplace comfortable to you, where you are at ease and able to focus for extended periods of time. Some authors work well with a messy desk (both Jill and Gena), some require organization. Whatever your preference, you may want to avoid leaving reminders of incomplete tasks. Every time you work, your mind will wander to those tasks, distracting you.

Often you'll hear of writers going to a favorite coffee shop, ordering a drink and then writing uninterrupted until their drink is gone.

As we mentioned on Day 41—This Way or That Way?—what works with one book might not work with another. If the words aren't flowing as smoothly as usual, allow yourself some flexibility. A change in scenery might just do the trick!

JILL: Even though Gena and I have collaborated on a book before —*Dating the Undead*—the process we used to complete this manuscript was different. For *All Write Already*, we divvied up assignments. Then, we did some brainstorming on two different seven-hour long car trips. We also spoke on the phone multiple times, typing in our shared document in real time.

Your assignment: Write roughly 250 words for your novel.

Bonus assignment: What can you do to set the tone for your workspace? Can you tidy your desk, hang up a sign, or light a candle? Try some things out and write an extra 350 words.

DAY 93

You might need to set work time boundaries with your family and friends. Occasionally, non-authors do not understand that writing is a job, even if you aren't getting paid—yet.

GENA: If you want to make money as an author, you must treat your writing like a job and do your required work even when you don't feel like it. This will help train you to meet your deadlines.

There are multiple tricks you can utilize to help set boundaries for yourself and others. If necessary, hang a sign on your door: *No Interruptions Unless There's Blood or Fire.* Silence your cell phone. Turn on your auto-reply email telling people you'll reply as soon as you're able. Lock yourself out of social media for a set time.

JILL: Honestly, this can be your biggest challenge. I still have family members who don't think I have a "real" job because I don't leave the house every day and work in an office. As a new writer, you may struggle with finding the balance between family obligations with children, appointments for aging parents/grandparents as well as the 9 to 5. The cold, harsh reality is that there is no perfect balance. Instead, I work for situational balance. Clearly, kids need attention, but eventually they'll learn to fold clothes, work the kitchen and entertain themselves, and these are good things. Designate one appointment day for your elderly relatives, so you're only chauffeuring one day a week instead of several.

There's a saying that goes something like this: *Real writers write every day.* But, that kind of schedule can be brutal if you've got a full time job, a family, or any number of other responsibilities. It's okay to write when you can. Once I gave myself permission to take a day off from writing due to other obligations, a weight was lifted. That thinking allowed me to enjoy those days with my grandparents instead of wondering if I'd have time to get my word count in before I had to pick up the kids from school.

This may mean your books will be published further apart. That rapid release schedule might not work for you. Harsh truths, I know, but one thing I can promise you is that change happens. You won't always have to divide your time. I recently became an empty nester, and as I always suspected, my productivity soared through the roof. (Sorry kids.)

You've had time now to evaluate your writing space. Is it meeting your requirements? Do you need to reassess? Create a plan of action so your current writing space/budget meets your needs. Look at your calendar and craft a plan of action to ensure your boundaries are respected.

Your assignment: Write roughly 250 words for your novel.

DAY 94

VILLAIN'S BACKSTORY

Like your main characters, your villain needs a backstory. This information can help explain why he's like he is, what he wants—aka his endgame—and any strengths and weaknesses he'll display as the story progresses.

What are three major life events that helped shape your villain? A traumatic incident or the loss of a loved one? The first stirring of a predatory instinct? A betrayal?

Are any of these events tied to the main character(s)?

Is your villain a created being or a born one? If created, what is the science/logic behind her creation? How does she react to certain stimuli?

Whatever type of villain you are writing, make sure to give them at least one redeeming quality. Most people—even monsters—are not all bad, just as heroes are not usually all good. By giving a villain a positive trait, you help flesh out the character to make them real, no matter the species.

Your assignment: Write roughly 250 words for your novel.

DAY 95

DROP A BOMB

Get stuck again? Consider dropping some kind of bomb on your characters to really shake up their world!

In the TV Show *Lost*, the writers always kept the viewers engaged by dropping a new revelation. These included discovering there were other survivors, when Walt was taken, finding the hatch or when Charlie warns Desmond the boat they thought was there to save them was not Penny's boat. The characters literally discovered a bomb in one season.

Adding a surprising twist will definitely keep your readers on their toes. They might even stay up extra late, despite having to work the next day, because they must, must, must know what happens next.

Keep your bombs logical so that they don't strain a reader's suspension of disbelief.

You can add unexpected suspense to your story to keep your readers turning the page.

- Give a character a secret they must keep from another.
- Add an eerie feeling to a certain room or character.
- If your characters have broken a bad habit, tempt them to do it again.
- One character catches another in a lie.
- Add a deadline or ticking clock. Think about the story of *Cinderella* and how you worried as midnight approached.

Unpredictability can ratchet up suspense. Think—*What would I, as a first time reader of this story, expect to happen next?* Then, consider writing the exact opposite.

Go with your gut. If it feels right for your story, run with it.

Your assignment: Double your daily word count! Write roughly 500 words for your novel.

DAY 96

LAYER, LAYER, LAYER

We've said it before, but we'll say it again. Your rough draft doesn't have to be perfect. You can fix any mistakes you find when you edit. The rough draft doesn't even have to be the full story.

The rough draft can act as the bones of the story. The main events and developments. Then you can go back and add the muscle—the emotion, transitions and connections. The flesh and frosting—the descriptions, one-liners, using more dynamic words.

Is your story missing any layers? Action? Reaction? Emotion? Thought/consideration? Hooks? Foreshadowing? Transitions between scenes? Sometimes it's easier to read the book once, adding the missing action, then reading it again to add the missing emotion, and so on. Sometimes it's easier to add everything at once. What method will work best for you?

Your assignment: Write roughly 250 words for your novel.

DAY 97

WORKS OUTSIDE BUT NOT IN

Just because something works outside of your story—a line you love, a situation you're excited about, a joke or stunt—doesn't always mean it will work *in* your story. Forcing something into your story just because it's awesome will not have an awesome result. It can tear readers out of a story faster than you can kick your own butt.

Your assignment: Write roughly 250 words for your novel.

DAY 98

Ideas Can Come From Anywhere

Have you ever woken up in the middle of the night with an idea burning to be told? Or how about when you're in the shower? Or at a restaurant? For me, the best ideas rarely strike when I'm sitting at the computer willing them to come. Often when I'm not thinking about it and I'm relaxed is when they tend to pop into my brain, and not always at the most convenient times.

In fact, I came up with this, my best beginning worldbuilding advice and the reasoning behind it, at 6 AM, sitting in a parking lot while waiting to go to a film shoot with my husband. I used voice to text on my phone because I wanted to remember what to tell you.

I don't know how many times I've thought I would surely remember an idea because it was so amazing. But in the end, I'd wake up the next morning only to find that the awesome idea had slipped through my fingers. Though, I do occasionally wake up to a very cryptic note I can't decipher. I'm still not sure where I was going with "bird men and potato chips".

I keep notebooks everywhere–my nightstand, the car, my purse. Some of them even have notes I scribbled on restaurant napkins. I know other authors also do this, and I highly recommend it to anyone working in this field. Whenever an idea strikes, write it down. Whenever you observe something interesting, write it down. Whenever you hear a snippet of inspiring conversation or unique dialog, write it down. Your ideas notebook is a wealth of inspiration.

How you organize it is up to you. Random observations I'll write in the back and turn the pages forward to separate them from the ideas relating to my current projects at the beginning of the notebook. Others I mark with symbols in the upper corner so I can quickly see what kind of idea it is, like a star for something I think is great and an empty box for something that needs checked off my list.

Whether you decide to type notes on your phone or keep a notepad by your nightstand, I find it a good idea to have something to write with at all times so that you can capture those brilliant thoughts and inspirations as they come to you. These will be the little snippets of ideas that you flesh out later when it comes to writing your book.

—*New York Times & USA Today* Bestselling Author Michelle M. Pillow

DAY 99

NOT BASED ON REAL PEOPLE

Have you ever noticed the paragraph in books and movies that claim "these fictional characters bear no resemblance to real people alive or dead"? There's a reason for that—liability. As enticing as it is, do *not* name and describe your characters based on real people or call a haggard otherworld species after your ex. Save yourself from a potential lawsuit later on.

Your assignment: Double your daily word count! Write roughly 500 words for your novel.

DAY 100

Anytime we begin a new scene, we try to ground our readers in the "reality" of the moment with a description of the world/scenery around the characters. This doesn't have to be an information dump —too much information offered in one place. You can sprinkle in the details throughout the opening, adding more as the scene progresses.

The five senses can help you paint this scene. Temperature? Smells? Sounds? Is the location crowded with multiple people having different conversations? Or is the place empty and silent? What landmarks do your characters encounter? Is anything unique about this location? What is the tone/mood/vibe? Help the reader read the room.

Tip: You can write your scene as usual. Then, go back and read that scene and highlight any descriptions. Then, go through your highlighted sections and add details as necessary. This is a more concentrated form of layering.

Your assignment: Write roughly 250 words for your novel.

DAY 101

Let's return our attention to our main characters. As we write, certain descriptive words can get lodged in our heads. Handsome. Fierce. Brave. Beautiful. Smart. Flighty. Bumbling. Brooding.

We have a tip to help prevent you from overusing the same descriptive words. And how to recognize if you might be *over-*describing your character.

1. Every time you write a descriptive word, highlight it in the same color.
2. When you finish your rough draft, scroll through your document or flip through your notebook to find the highlighted portions. Are there too many? Too few? Are they too close together, relaying the same information?
3. Make a list of at least 25 alternates and replace where necessary.

As an example, here are alternatives to the word *handsome*:
Arresting.
Stunning
Hot
Sexy
Delicious
Eye candy
Gorgeous
Glorious
Attractive
Exquisite
Flawless

Your assignment: Write roughly 250 words for your novel.

DAY 102

HALF-BAKED OR FULL-BAKED?

At the beginning of *All Write Already*, we talked about "problem stacking." One step forward, two steps back. But where do the ideas for those problems come from? What about the emotions, actions and characters?

Easy! Those ideas can come from anywhere. The key is looking for them.

Have you ever been around a child who is fixated on the question "why?"

Child: Why does the dog bark?
Mom: Because they can't talk, and they need to get our attention.
Child: Why?
Mom: Well, because they want to play. Or poop.
Child: Why?
Mom: Because everyone needs to poop.
Child: Why?
Mom: Someone save me. Please.

That child is searching for answers.

- Do you need inspiration for your murder mystery? Maybe you can't decide where to leave a clue. Why not pay attention to current events? *Law & Order* sometimes uses the tagline "Ripped From Today's Headlines."
- Need a universal experience for your characters? Pay attention to the discussions and complaints of your friends and coworkers.
- Want to craft the worst date ever? Search the web for real life experiences.

Ideas are out there, just waiting to be discovered. Sift through the dirt and you'll find the gold.

Your assignment: Write roughly 250 words for your novel.

DAY 103

Excited to write but wish you weren't? Here are our tried and true tips to snuffing out that excitement as quickly as possible!

- Chase "meh" ideas that feel commercial or fit trend but don't excite you
- Focus on every word being "perfect"
- Dwell on criticism
- Embrace fear
- Constantly second-guess yourself
- Magnifying the negatives

Your assignment: Write roughly 250 words for your novel.

DAY 104

A "word sprint" means setting a timer and writing until the clock zeros out. You can do this multiple times a day, once a week/month, or whenever the mood strikes. You can even increase your time by five minutes each instance that you reset the clock. The goal? Complete your required word count for the day and then some!

If you are on a roll but you've already reached your word goal and the timer has gone off, don't stop your momentum. Keep going. Think like an arrow—always moving forward!

Your assignment: With a word count goal of 250, set a timer for 20 minutes and word vomit. Did you meet your goal or did you go over? If you didn't meet your goal, set the timer for 25 minutes and go again.

DAY 105

REFLECT AND CATCH UP

Write. Handwriting in a notebook, typing on a computer, dictation into your phone, how you do it doesn't matter - just get the words down. That comes first, before covers or promotion or social media pages. Each time you write, you learn and strengthen your writing muscles. So write. Produce the work.

–*New York Times* bestselling author Nalini Singh

DAY 106

It can be difficult to polish your work when you don't have another person to help with edits. Writing software might come in handy.

Please note: Gena and Jill are not affiliated with any software or programs mentioned in this book. They do not sponsor the sites or receive any type of compensation. Also, this is not an in depth review of these programs. It is simply a quick overview of two types of software they use. While neither of the below is free, other programs are. Or, they are sold on a sliding scale. Think about what kinds of tools you need.

ProWritingAid: Checks grammar, spelling and delivers reports on style and overused words. This program is for both download and online use.

Scrivener: A word processing program that is specifically designed for writers. It organizes notes, research, outlines and more.

If you opt not to use a software and only rely on spell check, you could be missing grammatical errors—words that are spelled correctly but misused. Consider having a text to voice program read your writing aloud. Some free programs can even analyze your passages for clarity and overused words.

Your assignment: Write roughly 250 words for your novel.

DAY 107

HOP PLOT BUNNIES, HOP

Often you'll see a picture or read an article and inspiration will hit, your ideas multiplying like rabbits. While plot bunnies are fun, they can lead to never-ending rabbit holes that draw you away from your current project. That's why we recommend you write down any new ideas that excite you but don't quite fit into your current project, then get back to work on your manuscript in progress. Writing warmups can help get the mental juices flowing!

Focus. Magnify. Accomplish. Triumph!

Your assignment: Write roughly 250 words for your novel.

DAY 108

UNSYMPATHETIC CHARACTERS ARE JUST SUPERFICIAL

If your main characters are completely unlikable, the reader might not root for them to succeed. The characters might even reach the dreaded status of "irredeemable." The kiss of death when you do, in fact, hope to redeem them, because the reader doesn't care if they live or die. Heck, the reader might even want them to suffer a little.

That doesn't mean your characters can't make mistakes. No one gets everything right every time. The character doesn't even have to do the "good" thing most of the time. They don't need to be kind or sweet, either. But, for the reader to root for them, they need to be relatable in some way.

Did you kind of like Hannibal Lecter?

Did you have a soft spot for Darth Vader?

Did you want to give Gollum a hug?

Want to snuggle with Loki?

Think about your favorite unlikable-but-likable characters from books or movies. What made you root for/like them? What did you dislike about them? Did the other characters dislike this trait too? How did they win you over? Was there a moment that this character could have been redeemed, but they chose another path instead? What was the ultimate fate of this character, and was it satisfying or unsatisfying?

Now think about your own characters. Are your main characters sympathetic in some way? Do they have flaws or other balancing characteristics? If not, what can you do to make them relatable to readers? What is one relatable characteristic you can add?

Your assignment: Write roughly 250 words for your novel.

DAY 109

Today's exercise will help you to notice the little details that ground a scene in reality, and make your story more relatable to readers.

Let's practice with a night scene. When the sun goes down, consider standing outside or turning off the lights in your room to experience the sights, sounds, scents and sensations that are present in the dark. Light a candle to feel the heat and watch the shadows.

How does this change your environment? What insects do you hear? How does the wind feel against your skin?

Do the same thing with sunrise. What do you notice? What changes? What details can fit within your story?

Where else can you do this experiment? A crowded sidewalk? A shop? A park? Take note of anything that stands out, anything that changes or keeps you in the moment, or even disrupts your concentration. Those details can be used in your story to help make it real to the reader.

Your assignment: Double your daily word count! Write roughly 500 words for your novel.

DAY 110

IT'S NOT JUST A MEAL!

We talked about ways to set a scene. Did you know food can help with that?

Going out to eat? Take a photo of any food you might want to reference in your book. Keep track of the flavors and how you react to them. Perhaps you have a character who will react similarly. Any fancy decorations that fit with your story?

How do you feel when you haven't eaten all day? How does it feel to cook for someone, or to eat the food that someone has prepared just for you? Is cooking a hobby or a chore for your character? How does food taste when you haven't eaten all day? When you're sad? Is mealtime the heartbeat of your day, or a task that gets put off?

What kinds of conversations do people have over food? What kinds of nibbles are served at a party? At a community picnic? At a wedding?

Your assignment: Write roughly 250 words for your novel.

DAY 111

As you lay in bed, think about some aspect of your book. Any aspect! Try to let the scene play inside your head like a mini-movie. You might be amazed by the number of plot holes you discover, or the brilliance of your solutions.

When this happens, when you realize a problem or solution, your mind might tell you, "Don't worry. I'll remember."

LIES! There's an excellent chance you'll forget by morning. Write down or email yourself any problems and/or solutions when they come to you. Your story—and your readers—will thank you!

Will your tired brain convince you some of your ideas are amazing and you need to email them...but they're just crap? Probably. We've woken up to emails like:

- Twins are triplets
- Buy an invisible friend
- dow.p[/goe

Even if your ideas aren't workable, you'll never be able to judge their true worth if you forget them.

Your assignment: Write roughly 250 words for your novel.

Bonus assignment: Email yourself your nighttime ideas.

DAY 112

If it gets you writing, it's good. It's your process. Claim it, own it. Absorb only those tips and guidelines that get your fingers moving. Avoid the ones that freeze them over the keyboard. Avoid "rules". There aren't any. "Rules" will start a waltz with your fears and together they'll conspire to knock you off the side of the dance floor. The greatest education you can get as a writer is revising scenes you've already written and constantly reading books you're passionate about.

–Bestselling author Christopher Rice

DAY 113

As you progress in your writing journey, you may be keeping a second notebook with any new ideas you've had. Be sure to keep a running table of contents. There's nothing more frustrating than sifting through half a dozen pieces of paper looking for a list you began weeks ago but had to put aside.

We recommend attaching a list with a couple words about each idea on the cover.

Example of Gena's list:

Aliens among us
Pandora's box
Zombieland
Atlantis
Evil fairy tale
War gods

Your assignment: Write roughly 250 words for your novel.

DAY 114

DON'T GIVE UP!

Writing can be difficult. It can tax your mind and make you feel fried by the end of the day. But don't give up. Some days are difficult, yes, but some days are magic. Endure any tough times now in order to reap a reward later. Just think. If you keep going, you'll soon have a finished book. The blood, sweat and tears will be worth it!

And look at the progress you've made. You should have more than a hundred pages of your book written. Congrats!

Keep going and keep making progress! You've got this!

Your assignment: Double your daily word count! Write roughly 500 words for your novel.

DAY 115

Brainstorming is a great way to develop your ideas. If you can, find a creative person you trust and tell them your idea. They might see something you missed or offer a complementary idea to inspire you.

GENA: I love to brainstorm with my trusted writer friends! In fact, Jill and I brainstormed one of my books on a road trip (*Catch A Mate.*) The conversation started with the old stereotypical saying "Men are pigs." We jokingly stated, "And women are the slaughterhouse." We knew there was a story idea there, so we began to toss ideas around. Ultimately we came up with an idea about a woman who is paid by suspicious wives to smile and flirt with their men to prove that no man can be trusted...but what happens when the cynic for love begins to fall for a coworker?

Years later, I attended a book conference and ended up brainstorming in a hotel room with Jill and Kresley Cole. I presented my initial idea for *Can't Let Go,* and we played the "what if" game. What if this happens? What if that happens? They got me thinking about things I hadn't considered before, and I loved it!

Your assignment: Write roughly 250 words for your novel.

DAY 116

TOTAL IMMERSION

Do everything you can to immerse yourself in your story. Noise-canceling headphones or music that fits the mood and tone of your novel. Clean your desk before you start a new tale or cover it with objects of inspiration. Whatever works for you! Think about your story even when you aren't writing. In the shower. On a run. While cleaning. Play different sceneries through your mind. What if my character did that? What if my character did this?

Live and breathe it, and the words should come easier and faster!

Your assignment: Write roughly 250 words for your novel.

DAY 117

CONTRADICTIONS

You've probably come across a contradiction or two in your lifetime. The person who hates people but loves going to parties. Someone who is both humble and proud or smart and naive. Bottom line, real people can be complicated. Why not bring those same paradoxical traits to your characters?

No one we know fits into a convenient box. No one is sweet 100% of the time, and even dirtbags have good days. The smartest person in the world can mess something up, and an ignorant person can get something right. Someone can smile on the outside while crying on the inside. Along the same vein, someone can cry on the outside while laughing on the inside.

Challenge yourself to write characters with contradictions and complexities.

GENA: In *The Glass Queen*, the heroine abhors violence and yet she wants to make weapons and armor as a means to protect herself. In the original version of *Oh My Goth*, the heroine hates people who judge others...but she's always judging others. In *The Darkest Seduction,* the hero is possessed by the demon of Promiscuity. He needs to bed a new person every day or he weakens and dies. He jokes that he has the best life, but inside he is miserable and craves companionship with one person.

What is a contradiction you can give your characters?

Your assignment: Write roughly 250 words for your novel.

Bonus assignment: Come up with at least one personality contradiction for your main character and/or villain.

DAY 118

Are you stuck again?

- Have you written yourself into a corner? If there's a way in, there's a way out. Don't forget to play "what if" to brainstorm possible solutions.

- Are you bored with the story? Maybe your characters are bland and you need to spice up their personalities. Maybe your plot lacks urgency. Do you need to up the stakes? Have you layered in emotion? When you figure out *why* you are bored, you can figure out how to fix the problem.

- Did you realize you started in the wrong place or took a wrong turn? Can the scenes be retooled to fit your new direction? Yes or no, consider marking the spot with what you need to happen in the beginning of the book to support your new direction and move on to fix it later. Sometimes, though, a change can't wait, because you need to see it so you can figure out what comes next. If you go back and fix it now, consider meeting your daily word count goal as well.

- Need to start over completely, because nothing is salvageable? Consider using your catch up days to write the new opening scenes.

Whatever you do, don't give up. You've got this as long as you keep moving forward!

Your assignment: Write roughly 250 words for your novel.

DAY 119

If I had any advice to give new writers, it would be to persist. Keep writing, keep practicing your craft. No one plays a perfect Beethoven the first time they sit down at a piano; the same is true for writing a book. Practice, persist, and remember, nearly all authors started exactly where you are right now: unpublished and unknown. The difference between a published author and a non-published author is that the published author never gave up.

–*New York Times* bestselling author Julie Kagawa

DAY 120

TIME LEAP

Time leaps can be helpful, keeping the pace of your story moving along. Readers might not need to know what happened every day while a character was in hypersleep. On the other hand, too many "A week later" "Two days passed" "Months ticked by" "Eight minutes later" "Five seconds ago" "Two years ago" "Last week" can be distracting. You may want to consider restructuring your story. What needs to be shown? What needs to be told? What needs to be skipped?

Often, a simple scene break is all that is necessary. We denote a scene break with an ** and double return.

Chapter breaks can also convey a passage of time, without the need to add extraneous detail about what happens between the two scenes.

You can show the passage of time through description such as the change of weather:

The leaves outside his prison window turned from green to gold, and soon fell to the ground.

Dialogue can also be utilized:

"Stop your pacing, Hannah. It's only been a day."

Finally, character emotion and action can impart the passage of time.

He glared at the heart monitor, willing the solid white line to jump, only to squeeze his eyes in anguish. Five minutes was too long for the brain to go without oxygen.

Your assignment: Write roughly 250 words for your novel.

DAY 121

REGRET

Years ago, we used to blog. Those online journals were all the rage back then, and we set a goal to post new material at least once a week and interact with our readers.

JILL: A while back, I scanned some of my old blog posts, looking for a recipe I'd posted when I came upon this:

I almost didn't write today's post. Today is parent/teacher conferences, I had a ton of family obligations this week, so I'm not where I want to be in my work in progress... you know, the normal excuses. But I'd made a goal for myself at the beginning of the year. I'd blog once a week about writing. I also knew that I'd kick myself if I didn't meet my goal in March—not meeting goals should be something left for December.

Of course, I was joking. But the sentiment stuck with me. Not meeting goals = regret.

Many times, our friends and readers have mentioned that they'd like to write a book, too, and they'll ask us for advice. We'll give it. But, when we ask for an update about their progress, the most common response is that they haven't started yet, or they wrote a few pages and stopped. Time passed, and they had no real progress to show for it. The regret is strong.

Writing isn't easy. There's always something easier to do. For starters, reading or binge-watching some great TV show everyone is talking about. Why not put in the work now to see the fruition of your goal in the future?

Your assignment: Write roughly 250 words for your novel.

DAY 122

Sometimes you've got to skip ahead, even if you prefer to write your story from beginning to end, in order, don't be afraid to jot down a scene you feel inspired to write. While we've cautioned you not to wait for a muse, we also believe inspiration is precious and shouldn't be wasted.

GENA: Once I wrote the first 100 pages of a novel (*The Darkest Seduction*), got stuck and couldn't go on. I realized I'd paired the hero with the woman I wanted, not the one *he* wanted. But, stubborn as I was, I decided to rewrite those 100 pages using my choice with different circumstances. I got stuck again. Finally, I wrote a scene that would fall in the middle or end of the book to give the hero the woman he wanted. By seeing what could be between them, I was then able to sit down and write the book with the woman he wanted. The words flowed fast and sure.

Your assignment: Double your daily word count! Write roughly 500 words for your novel.

DAY 123

EMOTIONAL CONNECTION

Some authors feel emotionally connected to their characters as they write. They might cry as they craft a sad scene and laugh during a funny one. Other writers do not feel emotionally connected to their characters and do not react as they write. Whatever your reaction—or non-reaction—you aren't wrong. Your process is your process. Do what works best for you.

Your assignment: Write roughly 250 words for your novel.

DAY 124

Borrowing Another Author's Characters
Versus
Being Inspired by Them

Here's the thing. You cannot sell a book if it's based on someone else's characters or set in their story world. Not without the author's permission, anyway. Whoever created the characters and the story world owns both. But, other stories can inspire you.

How many books were inspired by fairy tales? How many books were inspired by the first vampire novel ever written? Inspiration is wonderful. Theft is illegal. Make sure you story can stand on its own!

Your assignment: Write roughly 250 words for your novel.

DAY 125

YOU WON'T PLEASE EVERY READER

You cannot and will not make every reader happy. That's why we prefer to write for an audience of one. Write the book your way, so that the final product is something that you love. That's where you'll find your literary magic.

Have you ever read an amazing novel, visited a site to review it and found a bunch of negative reviews left by readers who hated it? What one person loves another will hate and vice versa.

GENA: When I first started writing, paranormal romances were not selling. But, I really, really wanted to write paranormal romance. It was the genre of my heart. So, I thought I'd write a paranormal romance about an alien cursed to spend the centuries trapped in stone, freed only by a kiss. I downplayed his alien-ness, hoping I'd have an easier time getting people to read it. When I queried agents, however, the one I wanted most contacted me to say she loved my writing, but was troubled by the story itself. She told me she kept getting excited, thinking the hero was indeed an alien, but she couldn't be sure, because I'd skimped on all those details. At that moment, I realized there were more people like me, hungry for alien romance. Now I write what I love and don't worry about the rest.

Your assignment: Write roughly 250 words for your novel.

DAY 126

REFLECT AND CATCH UP

My advice is two-fold...and slightly contradictory. First, the revision process is your friend! Embrace and welcome the changes. Don't be afraid of completely rewriting anything – the story, the characters, the subplots, the pace, the turning points. Once you've finished writing a draft, revisions are when the magic happens and can be the most fun you've ever had at a keyboard. A good revision breathes life into every scene and character, and can take your book from a sleeper to a keeper. But...my other advice is know when to quit. Many new novelists cling to their manuscript, unable to stop making even the smallest changes. There comes a time when you have let that puppy out into the wild, no matter how much you want "one more read through" to get it right or solicit the opinion of one more beta reader. (All you're really looking for is validation, believe me.) As a writer, you should find the balance between the need to revise and the importance of letting go and, on both fronts, trust your instincts. If you've spent a lifetime reading (and what author isn't a reader first?) then you have absorbed the storytelling process, so trust your instincts!

–*New York Times* bestselling author Roxanne St. Claire

DAY 127

Remember our list for killing creativity? Today we have a list to help you fail at this novel-writing thing. Pick one or all. Your choice.

- Give up now. Why wait till later?
- Let one day of not writing turn into two...three...four...and so on
- Keep stopping your work in progress to focus on a new idea or change just one more thing in the beginning
- Be unwilling to listen to a smart critique by a professional editor
- Magnifying and giving in to your fears

Your assignment: Write roughly 250 words for your novel.

DAY 128

If you have trouble kicking off your writing for today or any day, go back and read the previous day's work to ground yourself in the world. If that doesn't work, set a timer for 10 minutes and word vomit. Still struggling? You might have written yourself into a corner.

Steps to get out of the corner:

1. Read your work in progress from start to finish until you figure out where you might have gone wrong. Won't hurt to make notes for yourself along the way.
2. Brainstorm ways to fix the problem. Adding new scenes? Going in a different direction? Deleting something? Starting over? Sometimes a work in progress *is* unsalvageable.
3. Implement your solution!

Your assignment: Write roughly 250 words for your novel.

DAY 129

GENA: I know we say your book should be as long or as short as it needs to be, and that's true...on the creative side. But on the technical side, size does matter. (Yes, pun intended.) Some publishing houses require a certain word count. Also, you wouldn't want to call a novella a novel, confusing or misleading readers.

When I'm learning something new, I love examples. So, I'm going to use my own novels as a gauge, rounding up or down, so you can have an idea of what a certain word count looks like.

- The Darkest Warrior: 140k words
- The Darkest King: 120k words
- The Darkest Night: 100k words
- Lord of Vampires: 75k words
- Oh My Goth: 60k words
- Dark Swan: 50k words
- Temptation in Shadow: 35k words (novella)

Your assignment: Double your daily word count! Write roughly 500 words for your novel.

DAY 130

RECIPE FOR SUCCESS

When you are baking, you mix different ingredients to create one incredible taste. Your book is the same. *Mix a dash of this, a sprinkle of that, and a heaping helping of goodness, then bake in your mind and enjoy!*

Every aspect of your story must work together. One sentence should transition into the next...one scene should flow into the next...and there should always be a logical reason for something to happen.

Your assignment: Write roughly 250 words for your novel.

DAY 131
DECISION FATIGUE

Decision fatigue is a real thing. After making a million decisions for our characters, we can find ourselves unable to make a decision for about *anything*. Thankfully, there are ways you can combat decision fatigue before it starts.

- A nice rest to help reset your mind.
- Pre-plan your clothes, meals and other daily tasks before a long day of writing.
- Go for a walk and be sure to take a break to eat a meal

Your assignment: Write roughly 250 words for your novel.

DAY 132

MOVE AROUND

In the past, we have finished our rough drafts and said, "Ow! My back!" rather than "Sweet! I'm done!" We recommend stretching as you write.

Sitting for prolonged periods of time can strain your muscles. If you set a timer to go off once every hour, you'll know when to stand and stretch to get your blood pumping for a few minutes, even when you are in the writing zone. Your back will thank you!

Your assignment: Write roughly 250 words for your novel.

DAY 133

REFLECT AND CATCH UP

A day without a book is a dark day indeed.
Don't endure a dark day.

Is today a good day to research items you've marked for further study
in your book? Focus. Magnify. Accomplish. Triumph!

DAY 134

GIVE THE STRANGER ON THE STREET A STORY

There is a mental exercise you can do to help train your brain to create organic backstory for your characters, and it's fun to boot. You start by giving people you see a made-up backstory.

Someone who drives past your car—where are they going? Why are they going there? What skeletons do they have in their closet?

See a couple at a restaurant—how long have they been together? How did they meet?

You can even do this for characters on TV. Make up events that might have shaped them into the people they became.

Your assignment: Write roughly 250 words for your novel.

What the heck is "high concept?" Well, high concept is a unique and easily communicable idea, with obvious and immediate mass appeal. When developing your own story, ask yourself what makes it original, unique and memorable? What makes it stand out? What makes it relatable to people today? Does it take the "what if" to a whole new level?

Sometimes it's just the title alone that intrigues.

The Devil Wears Prada by Lauren Weisberger
Pride, Prejudice and Zombies by Jane Austen and Seth Grahame-Smith
Any Duchess Will Do by Tessa Dare
Beautiful Bastard by Christina Lauren
Forget Tomorrow by Pintip Dunn
My So-Called Bollywood Life by Nisha Sharma
Nine Rules to Break When Romancing a Rake by Sarah MacLean
The Girl With the Dragon Tattoo by Stieg Larsson
Deathmaker by Lindsay A. Buroker
The Romanov Prophesy by Steve Berry
The Worst Best Man by Mia Sosa

You can even link your series titles to something specific, like Alexa Martin has done with the Playbook series centering around football romances: *Blitzed, Fumbled and Intercepted.*

You can use catchy word-play to name the series. An excellent example is **The Dogfather** series by Roxanne St. Claire, with the first book *Sit...Stay...Beg.*

In high concept, the idea sells the story.

- Vampire finishing school (**House of Night** series by PC and Kristin Cast – *Marked* Book 1)

- Contemporary *Twilight* for adults (*Fifty Shades of Gray* by EL James)

Can you boil down your plot, characters and unique premise in a sentence or two?

Your assignment: Write roughly 250 words for your novel.

DAY 136

As you write the scenes for your book, it might help to think beyond your own perspective, opinion and experience. Get out of your comfort zone and consider the other side of the coin.

We have an exercise to get you started. Have you written a scene where your hero makes a decision and it's the right one? Or, will your hero have to make a decision in an upcoming scene? Perfect! You've probably already built a case for why he's made/making the right decision. Now it's time to make a case for the "wrong" decision. What are the downsides to that "right" decision? Why would the "wrong" decision be better?

You can do the same thing for your villain. You know why he's bad...so remind us why he's good.

Your assignment: Write roughly 250 words for your novel.

DAY 137

MORE ON LAYERS

We've talked about layering. Now let's look at a specific example.

To "write in layers" you'll start with a simple scene snippet. Today we'll focus on a simple interaction between two characters.

> Their gazes met.
> "I love you."
> "I love you, too."

We have an action, then a line of dialogue from two different people. Now we'll layer in a physical reaction.

> Their gazes met, and her entire body jolted.
> "I love you."
> He smiled slowly, sending her pulse into overdrive. "I love you, too."

Let's layer in some emotion and tone!

> Their gazes met, and her entire body jolted. How long had she waited for this moment? Forever?
> "I love you," she rasped.
> Heat swirled in his irises. He smiled slowly, sending her pulse into overdrive. "I love you, too."

Do any of your scenes need new layers?

Your assignment: Write roughly 250 words for your novel.

DAY 138

TAG, WHO'S IT?

If a scene is dialogue heavy without enough tags, tones, actions and reactions a reader can lose track of who's talking. But, you don't want to go overboard with your tags, either.

"Why haven't you answered my text?" he asked.

"Because I didn't want to?" she replied dryly.

"That's not a good enough reason," he said.

"Well, it's the only reason you're going to get, bud," she told him.

Versus.

"Why haven't you answered my text?" he asked.

With a dry tone, she told him, "Because I didn't want to?"

"That's not a good enough reason."

"Well, it's the only reason you're going to get, bud."

Your assignment: Write roughly 250 words for your novel.

DAY 139

DOING THE UNEXPECTED IS FUN

How many times have you heard someone complain about a predictable book or film? If you're like us, the answer is *countless*. Doing something unexpected with your plot and/or characters can shock your readers, enhancing their reading enjoyment.

One example of this is *Lord of the Abyss* by Nalini Singh. The heroine is the beast, and the hero is the beauty. A wonderful twist!

What unexpected thing can happen in *your* story?

Your assignment: Write roughly 250 words for your novel.

Bonus Assignment: Take a look at your decision tree and a decision your character had to make. Did they make the expected choice? What would happen if they made the opposite choice, doing the unexpected? Does one of your characters bear the expectations of parents, mentor or supervisor? What would happen if they opted not to follow through?

DAY 140

REFLECT AND CATCH UP

So, the length of your rough draft is growing every day. You've gotten a more personalized feel for your main characters, your plot and your own writing habits. Here are some other things to consider:

- Check on your goals. Are you meeting your word or page count goal—the stepping stones to your main goal?
- Have you learned something new about your characters? Do you need to tweak their interviews?
- Are you continuing to use the same words over and over? Do you need to brainstorm a quick list?
- Have you learned to write when you really don't want to?
- Have you learned to manage your time better? Could you work on that?
- Are you taking care of you?

DAY 141

MUAHAHAHAHAHA

No matter how dark our story is, we like to insert moments of humor to break up the tension. And there are many different types of humor to choose from. Slapstick. Comparison. Truth/reality versus expectations. Unexpected answers. Irony. Pun. Brilliant wit. And more!

Slapstick: A type of physical humor.

Comparison: Comparing two unlikely things. In Gena's book *The Darkest Assassin*, the heroine thinks:

Men were like toilet paper. Necessary for a moment but happily discarded after use.

Truth versus expectation: The description on a personal ad compared to the person who arrived.

Unexpected answer to a question:

"What is Area 51?"
She smiled. "What else? It's a salt flat."

Irony: Language that usually signifies the opposite of what is being said.

Pun: A joke that focuses on the different meanings of a single word or words that sound similar but mean different things.

Wit: Keen intelligence.

What kind of humor do you prefer when you read someone else's book or watch a movie/TV series? How can you incorporate that type of humor into your own novel?

Your assignment: Write roughly 250 words for your novel.

DAY 142

You can take the tried-and-true from the public domain and add a twist to make it your own. That's how we get books like *Pride, Prejudice and Zombies* by Jane Austen and Seth Grahame-Smith.

GENA: I've taken multiple myths or stories from the public domain to create my own unique story.

Lords of the Underworld series—Pandora's Box. I didn't want to blame all the world's misery on one curious woman, as the traditional myth suggested. So, I decided to twist the legend my way and blame men.

The Evil Queen—*Little Snow White*. I used the story written by the Brothers Grimm as a blueprint for my own tale.

The Glass Queen—*Cinderella*. Again, I used the story written by the Brother's Grimm as a blueprint.

Alice in Zombieland—*Alice's Adventures in Wonderland*. I didn't use the story by Lewis Carroll as a blueprint for this one, but I did twist his title and use the idea of a girl stumbling her way into a whole new world.

Do you have a favorite story that is part of the public domain? If so, how could you twist it to write your own story?

Your assignment: Write roughly 250 words for your novel.

DAY 143

SUCKS TO BE THEM

What is the absolute worst thing that could happen to your character right now? Is it emotional? Physical?

In Nora Ephron's delightful movie *You've Got Mail*, the main character has been working toward saving her beloved bookstore she'd inherited from her mother. Losing her store would appear to be the climax. Not only has she failed, let her mother's memory down and very possibly her livelihood, this event actually happens earlier in the story. She thought losing the store would be the worst thing to happen, and yes, it was very sad, but Kathleen Kelly not only realized she'd been living another's dream but found depth and resilience she never realized she had.

Your assignment: Write roughly 250 words for your novel.

Bonus assignment: Think about what would hurt your main character(s) most at this moment. Write a scene where they think they're losing it all. What lessons do they learn about life and about themselves? How will this tie into Harmony in their SEARCH journey?

DAY 144

SCENE STEALER

As you write, keep in mind that each scene should contribute to the overall arc of your story. Every snippet should do one or more of the points below. If not, consider revising or cutting. (We have suggestions for what to do with your deleted scenes, so don't toss them).

- Did your reader learn something new about the character's RANGE? Did something change? Was something reaffirmed?

- How did this scene move the plot forward through SEARCH?

- Did the scene dive into the emotions of the main character(s), engaging the emotions of the readers?

- Did you clear up what the character(s) have to win or lose? Start or finish an argument?

- Would this scene interest you as a reader?

A lot of time we write scenes simply because they're fun and we enjoy them. Maybe you've conducted a ton of research and really want to show that off. But if they're not contributing to the story arc, then they might be considered fluff scenes. Too much fluff, and your readers may skip or skim—or worse, put down the book and never return.

Your assignment: Write roughly 250 words for your novel.

DAY 145

A PICTURE IS NOT WORTH A THOUSAND WORDS

We like to peruse stock photo sites and use the models as inspiration. But be warned! The Wild West Days of the internet are over. You cannot copy any photo or image off the internet to use on your site, social media or book covers. That is a violation of a photographer's intellectual property rights, and it is every bit as repugnant as book piracy.

There are free sites for pictures. Or, you can purchase an image for personal use. Just make sure you are on a reputable site, that you read the Terms of Service and understand the license that you are purchasing. Is it for commercial use? Is attribution required? Is the Standard license enough? Do you need the Extended license? Always always always check for a model release.

Your assignment: Write roughly 250 words for your novel.

DAY 146

Ever had an amazing dream in the middle of the night? If it happens again, remember to email the highlights to yourself, just like your other ideas, or you will probably forget it. That is why it's smart to keep your phone right next to the bed. Keep a notebook nearby, as well. (Actually, keep a notebook nearby ALWAYS. You never know when inspiration will strike.)

The mind works in mysterious ways. You might just wake up to find you've sent yourself the answer to a plot or character problem!

GENA: One night, I wrote myself an email. "Make paper dolls, and pretend they are real." With "night brain," I decided this was the best idea anyone had ever had, so of course I had to send it to myself. While the idea itself isn't workable—or is it?—I was able to use the idea of taking something that is made up, like a fairy tale, and making it real.

Your assignment: Double your daily word count! Write roughly 500 words for your novel.

DAY 147

REFLECT AND CATCH UP

Emotion. Every one of my brainstorming ideas had to elicit emotion. Emotion is what readers want to feel when they read your story. For some, they come to a book seeking adventure, a thrill, or suspense. For others, it's love, sense of family, or joy. Maybe all of the above. Know your target audience, what they're looking for when they pick up your book, and incorporate as much of those emotions into what you're giving them as you can. Pluck at your reader's emotions to the point you pull from deep within them. I try to write stories that run a gamut of emotions. I want my books to make readers laugh out loud, to make them shed a tear or two, to make them cheer the characters onward during their lows and to celebrate their successes. On occasion, I achieve that goal and get to share something beautiful with a reader.

–Bestselling Author Janice Lynn

DAY 148

Introducing a large group of characters at the same time can prove confusing. Readers may find themselves wondering, "Now who was *that* person?" This can rip them out of the story.

If you have many characters to introduce, consider spacing out their introductions if possible, rather than doing a mass intro in the same scene. Sometimes it helps to combine two characters into one.

Your assignment: Write roughly 250 words for your novel.

DAY 149

FIND THE CALM IN THE STORM

Perhaps danger fills your plot. Your characters are running for their lives, or saving a business. Amid their scheming to acquire their estranged father's millions or expose their ex as a creep with an agenda, you might want to consider introducing a moment of calm.

This moment can allow your main characters a chance to breathe, reflect, renew their hope or discover a well of strength they might not realize lay dormant inside them. It is within these moments of calm that your readers are able to learn more about your characters. Characters can introspect in their downtime, while their thoughts can be chaotic amid action.

Also, further action will have more impact the better your reader knows your character.

Your assignment: Double your daily word count! Write roughly 500 words for your novel.

DAY 150

JILL: This is one of my favorite stories about Gena. She and I met at our local RWA chapter in Oklahoma and dreamed of being published romance authors. She loves to send cards, and when she found out I was allergic to cats, all the notecards she sent me for a year were cute kitten ones. Even if I didn't recognize her chicken scratch handwriting (seriously her handwriting is the worst), the return address label always said: *New York Times* bestselling author, even though both of us were unpublished and querying at the time.

Gena knew her goal and spoke the words even before they happened. A few short years later, she was indeed a *New York Times* bestselling author!

GENA: I still do this kind of thing today. I focus on a goal, magnifying it in my thoughts, which then directs my every action until I triumph. I take it one step at a time. Baby steppin', baby!

Your assignment: Write roughly 250 words for your novel.

DAY 151

WHAT KEEPS THEM APART?

Whether you're writing a love story, have romantic elements or a buddy comedy, there's a strong connection between your main characters. What's keeping them apart?

Introduce their conflict early. Just when they think they can make their relationship work... remind them why they can't.

Don't feel like that reason has to remain the same throughout your entire novel. The reason can change throughout the book as their circumstances and mindsets change.

When one character is willing to make a go of the relationship but the other isn't because of reasons...what will it take to reverse their decisions so that the willing one is now unwilling and the unwilling one is now willing?

Your assignment: Write roughly 250 words for your novel.

MASLOW'S HIERARCHY OF NEEDS

You can't go through a managerial or education program without being introduced to Abraham Maslow's Hierarchy of Needs. Based on his groundbreaking paper "A Theory of Human Motivation" he attempted to describe the stages of growth and how these stages affect behavior.

Imagine a pyramid, and at the bottom is PHYSICAL NEEDS. Meaning, things like 'sleep' and 'food.' On the rung above it is SAFETY. The middle stage is THE FEELING OF LOVE and BELONGING. Above that is ESTEEM (respect and status) and finally at the very top is SELF-ACTUALIZATION–how the person feels about their parenting, if they're a good spouse, if they've contributed something to the world, etc.

The theory goes like this: You're not worrying about finding love, doing well at your job or contributing to society if you feel unsafe in your environment or don't have food to eat.

Where are your main characters on the pyramid? Figure it out to help you define their actions. Are they protecting themselves? Protecting their physical being, their emotions? Their family? Their beliefs?

Your assignment: Write roughly 250 words for your novel.

Maslow, A.H. (1943). "A theory of human motivation". *Psychological Review*.

DAY 153

CONFLICT IS NOT THE SAME AS ARGUING

Real, sustainable conflict between your characters goes much deeper than simple arguing. It cannot be solved with a conversation. Heck, it cannot be solved easily. Real conflict is the difference between *I overheard you call me a bad name on the phone...oh, you were speaking about my sister?* and *you lied to me, so I can never trust you again.*

How does the upset character know the hero referred to them specifically? Did the upset character simply assume? Does the conflict go away once a mistake has been pointed out or an explanation has been made?

This misunderstanding creates unsustainable conflict—conflict that cannot carry your story on its back—its legs break under the weight.

But, you can use arguments to advance your story and convey the emotions your characters are having trouble expressing. Have you ever argued about something other than the main issue because you didn't know how to share your true feelings?

Your assignment: Write roughly 250 words for your novel.

DAY 154

Write the stories you are the most passionate about. Your passion and enthusiasm for your writing is the one constant in the crazy, unpredictable business of publishing. So much of a book's success in the marketplace is out of an author's control, especially in traditional publishing, but the one thing that will remain is your love for what you do. Protect it at all costs. Write the stories you want to tell.

–Bestselling author Teri Wilson

DAY 155

REST IN PIECES

Don't be afraid to kill off a secondary character. While it's easy—well, easier—to savagely murder/gently kill a character with no real stake in the game, a death scene will have a greater emotional impact if the character is loved. And, once your reader knows you're willing to kill a beloved character, the tension should rise every time they flip a page. They'll wonder, *Who is next to go?*

Just make sure you give these secondary characters a death they deserve, or one that impacts your story. That doesn't mean you should or shouldn't kill them in the most heinous way possible; it only means the characters still breathing your fictional air need to feel grief or loss or *something*, depending on the relationship the two characters shared, and respond accordingly.

When you respect the sacrifice made by your characters, you make sure your readers' emotional investment has a worthy payoff. Killing a character for a simple reaction is never the goal.

Your assignment: Write roughly 250 words for your novel.

DAY 156

FLIRTING BEGINS: NEW BOOK SYNDROME

As you write one book, you might get an idea for another. One you are even more excited about. Many romance writers like to call this New Book Boyfriend Syndrome.

We know because we've soooo been there. *Look at all the pretty new book ideas. Surely they're better than the one I'm working on right now.* But. At this point, the allure of a new idea can be detrimental to your writing.

If you never finish writing book one, you'll never finish writing book two and three, either. So, whatever you do, finish your first book. Afterward, you can look back and say, *I did it! I can do it again!*

Have some authors published their first novel? Yes. Will *our* first manuscripts ever see the light of day? No. They suck. But we learned so much from the experience and the process. As we mentioned above, we also discovered we had the wherewithal to write a complete novel, and it gave us the confidence to finish the next and the next.

Once you have a full book under your belt, you'll have more confidence to judge what works and what doesn't, as well as what is a viable idea versus a pretty but useless one.

So how do you combat new book boyfriend syndrome? Get a notebook or open a new file and label it NEW IDEAS. As you are writing your first book, write any new ideas that come to you. Once you've finished *Book One*, you can review those new ideas and more confidently write your favorite.

Your writing assignment: Write roughly 250 words for your novel.

DAY 157

TRACK IT!

We love leaving editorial notes for ourselves in whatever word processing program we happen to be using. We leave these comments, questions, and ideas for ourselves in each of the four stages of our writing: rough draft, revising, line edit, and copy edit.

The rough draft is the first draft. Revising is what we call an overhaul of the rough draft, where we add other layers and fix any plot holes. A line edit focuses on writing style, while a copy edit focuses on style as well as grammar.

When we are editing for a publishing house, we also leave notes for our editors, and our editors even leave notes for us. But don't forget to remove any comment bubbles before sending to your editor or proofer.

JILL: One time I left a note for my editor as a track change. Somehow, between our conversations, my comment was inserted into the manuscript. We didn't realize it until the final read through when all of a sudden, in the middle of a description, was a personal note to my editor. I shudder at thinking the book could have been printed that way, but laugh about it now.

GENA: The same thing happened to me! My editor had written "Ha ha this is so funny!" in the margin, and at some point, someone inserted her comment into the actual book. Thank the Lord I caught the mistake before it made it to print. Now, I do an extra check for this type of thing.

Your assignment: Write roughly 250 words for your novel.

DAY 158

We are often asked which is more important, plot or character? This question is very much like the famous debate: *which came first—the chicken or the egg?* The truth is, both plot and character are integral to your book, but every author has a different method of developing their stories. Some start with the story itself, and work their way through the characters as they go. Others have a character in mind and design a story to match. But every author is different. Some prefer plot, some prefer character. Neither preference is wrong.

For instance, when Jill set up the original table of contents, she devoted a full eighteen days to character development at the beginning of the book. Another seven days devoted to setting came before she threw in a measly three days devoted to plot. She seemed genuinely stunned when Gena suggested the plot section come before characterization. See! Two different authors working on the same project, with two different methods of operation. Just remember: Loving one doesn't mean you should neglect the other. But it might mean you need to pay more attention to the other.

Your assignment: Write roughly 250 words for your novel.

Bonus assignment: Always be thinking. Plot holes–those pesky inconsistencies in the storyline–can creep up on your story. Like the time traveler who journeys into the past and hooks up with a local woman...but if you do the math, he's actually her great-great-great-great-great grandson.

DAY 159

GOD COMPLEX

In your story world, you are a god. You call the shots. You decide your character's world, history, and end.

- Do you need to blow up someone's entire world, your majesty?

- Should you be merciful today, oh kind one?

- How can your character's serve your endgame, oh great, dark overlord?

Remember, don't fall into the trap of adding something to the story just because you love it. Make sure it fits.

Your assignment: Double your daily word count! Write roughly 500 words for your novel.

DAY 160

How does today's scene advance your plot? If you don't yet know, consider doing a little scene blocking—writing a bullet point outline listing everything you need to accomplish in the scene. When you see it laid out, you might notice spots in need of tweaking.

GENA: Here's an example of one of my scene blocks, taken from the first chapter of *The Glass Queen*:

- Opens with Ashleigh as a little girl, crying at her mother's funeral. It's sunny and hot. Standing with her father, she remembers what led up to her mother's death and how she failed the woman.

- Explain the importance of glass coffins and a little about Ashleigh's heart condition.

- Locks gazes with the hero, Saxon. (His description.) He's glaring. She wonders why he's angry with her/what she did wrong.

- Father gets upset over her emotional reaction. Has her sent away, but she sneaks back.

- Caught by one of the story's villains, who disappears when Saxon arrives.

- Showdown between Ashleigh and Saxon. She passes out and the evil witch possessing her comes out to play—the witch is Saxon's greatest enemy. Saxon is hurt. This marks the start of a war between Ashleigh and Saxon.

As you can see, my scene blocks cover highlights, nothing more. So I guess that makes them "building blocks," because I have a lot to expand. Then, once I've written the scene, I'm able to go back with my list in mind and make sure I covered everything I mentioned.

Your assignment: Write roughly 250 words for your novel.

DAY 161

In a work of fiction, do not kill the dog. I had to learn that lesson the hard way.

−Anonymous

DAY 162

Are your characters acting in character? If not, make sure there's a logical reason.

Someone afraid of snakes wouldn't pick one up without a ~~good~~ great miraculous reason.

Someone who loves to run or exercise might prefer to take the stairs than an elevator.

Someone allergic to peanuts wouldn't eat a scoop of peanut butter without needing medication.

If you've mentioned your character has no sense of direction, show it! Prove it.

Your assignment: Write roughly 250 words for your novel.

DAY 163

Don't forget to keep a list of your overused words and phrases. Some of ours are:

All
As if
Then
Gritted
Growled
Finally
Just
Very
Already
Like

When you finish your rough draft, you can do a word search to find, replace or delete as needed.

Your assignment: Double your daily word count! Write roughly 500 words for your novel.

DAY 164

BE ON THE LOOKOUT!

Crafting rich descriptions in your novel can often take a backseat to plot and character development. But descriptions are a necessary part of storytelling.

If you find your descriptions are nonexistent or lacking, consider taking a field trip. When you go outside or visit a business establishment, take note of your surroundings. What details can you include in your book? Pay attention to scents and sounds. What kind of vibe did you pick up? Creepy or welcoming? How were the other patrons dressed? Did they speak in hushed tones or full volume? Did the other guests appear to be happy to be there or just going through their day?

Your assignment: Write roughly 250 words for your novel.

DAY 165

Highlight any real world facts you are even slightly unsure about for further research when you have time or after you finish your rough draft. It never hurts to double check. In fact, a double check could save you from an avalanche of reader email describing where you went wrong–aka regret.

Your assignment: Write roughly 250 words for your novel.

DAY 166

DO JUDGE A BOOK BY ITS COVER

There's a reason you've heard the phrase, "Don't judge a book by its cover." Because people do it all the time. If you plan to self-publish, monitoring the trends and covers in your genre of choice is part of your job. Be on the lookout for cover designers you love. They may have a sale or post a premade cover perfect for your story. Often your favorite authors will post who designed their cover, or whether they used an original photo by a specific photographer.

While an amazing cover isn't a guaranteed sale, it will never be a deterrent to one, or stop a reader from reading the blurb.

Your cover should give a clue to your reader of the sensuality level as can the title and series name.

Your assignment: Write roughly 250 words for your novel.

DAY 167

SHOW ME THE MONEY

"How much money do you make?"

If we had a dollar for every time someone asked us that question, we'd have made a lot more dollars. The thing is, no two authors are alike. There are too many variables to consider. The publisher. The state of the market. Timing. Trends. Ability to meet deadlines. Past sales. Idea. Competition. The list goes on and on.

You can make pennies or millions, something or nothing. You can even lose money, pouring cash into covers and content, by not making enough sales.

But here's the kicker: You won't know what you can make until you finish your book.

JILL: Whenever I'm asked, my go-to response is always the same. "Not as much as you would think."

Your assignment: Write roughly 250 words for your novel.

DAY 168

My advice is to write what you love. That sounds so simple, right? What I mean is that when an author writes they have to care about what they are putting on the page. If you don't care about whatever it is you're saying, how can you expect your readers to care? How can you expect your readers to be invested in the character or what your character is doing if you aren't? Sometimes authors write what they think will sell, but if whatever it is doesn't move them emotionally, that often times comes across in their story and causes it to fall flat.

–Bestselling author Janice Lynn

DAY 169

Are you waiting for your "muse" to strike? Is she late, late, late for a very important date? Well, inspire yourself! You have the tools. Stir up your creativity with music, art, a walk through nature, something! Anything! If ever something evoked strong emotions in you—the emotion you need for your story—revisit it and ponder. Plumb the depths.

Find the spark that sets your imagination on fire and let it burn!

Your assignment: Write roughly 250 words for your novel.

DAY 170

As you write, keep track of any sentences you can use for promotional teasers, also known as shareables—short, punchy one-liners or snippets that make someone want to know more or act as a hook. You can paste those sentences on stock photos and share them on your online properties.

Pro-tip: As you scroll through social media, make a note of shareables that grab your attention as well as those you want to pass right by. What made you like/dislike them? Was the font readable? Was the title or book cover lost?

Your assignment: Write roughly 250 words for your novel.

DAY 171

BUILD THE BRIDGE

To flow smoothly, your story will need transitional sentences, paragraphs, scenes and chapters. The bridge that brings your different thoughts, actions and emotions together.

I love my life. Writing is fun.

The two thoughts appear unrelated. But, we can connect them by adding a transitional sentence.

I love my life. I get to write! Writing is fun.

You can even vary the sentences, adding narrative between your statements, to give your bridges added flavor.

Dogs like to play in my backyard. I stepped in poop.

Dogs like to play in my backyard and crap. Oh, the smell! This morning I stepped in poop.

The same principle is true for the entirety of your novel. One thing should always lead to another. How is the scene you're working on connected to the scene that came before it? How will you connect today's scene with the next?

Your assignment: Write roughly 250 words for your novel.

DAY 172

PACING POINTERS

The pace of your novel is the speed with which your story unfolds for the reader. For example, urban fantasy may unveil its secrets at a much faster clip than an epic fantasy. And "slow-paced" does not mean boring, while "fast-paced" doesn't mean the story will always keep your reader engaged.

Once again, there is no right or wrong answer for the pace of your novel, but as you read, there will be visual clues that tell you if things need to pick up or slow down.

Clumps Aren't Just Bad In Gravy. Too much narrative clumped together can slow your book's pace to a crawl. And yes, this *can* be boring. Consider searching for places to add dialogue whenever you notice extended periods of thought and action.

Dialogue is often the quickest way to deliver information and backstory without needing to rely on exposition. But long stretches of one-sided conversation could indicate your dialogue is shifting to a monologue.

Additionally, dialogue can slow your pace if the reader is forced to slow down and figure out who is talking. Make sure to tag, add emotional reactions and physical reactions to the dialogue as needed.

Action scenes can be some of the most fun to write, showing conflict, encounters and dangers as they occur, all while moving the story forward. Inner thoughts and long, descriptive passages are kept at a minimum during these scenes. If you were running for your life or in the middle of an argument, you wouldn't stop to consider the weather or how someone's hat looks.

Going with non-stop action to keep things lively is a temptation, certainly, but like in life, your character will need a moment to breathe and reflect. So does your reader.

The length of your sentences, the depth in which you explore character emotion will slow or quicken the pace. If you need to slow your pace, you can craft longer sentences. To speed up your pace and convey action, consider writing shorter sentences.

Word choice can also affect pace. "Tropical" may convey relaxed, while "boiling" may feel more urgent, even though both words are synonyms for hot.

Your assignment: Write roughly 250 words for your novel.

DAY 173

Remember: If your plot can be solved with two characters having a simple conversation, their conflict is too weak. You can deepen any conflict in a number of ways. Here are three.

1. Up the emotional stakes. What do they have to lose?
2. Connect the conflict to a past event to deep the emotional responses.
3. Retool a character's motivation to have a hidden agenda.

Focus. Magnify. Accomplish. Triumph!

Your assignment: Write roughly 250 words for your novel.

DAY 174

THE TREES DID WHAT NOW?

Make sure your word choices match the tone of your scene. "Trees knifed toward the sky" might not convey the right tone in a romantic comedy, but it could work in an action adventure.

As you write, you can leave messages to yourself in the book itself, noting the mood you hope to convey in each individual scene. Then, when you go back to edit, you will automatically know to check whether your word choices fit that specific mood.

Your assignment: Write roughly 250 words for your novel.

DAY 175

Don't compare your career to anyone else's. Your writing schedule, your ideas, your highs and lows, are all for you. No one else can write your stories.

–A.C. Arthur

DAY 176

Challenge yourself to learn a new word today and use it in a scene. We'll help get you started. Are any of these words unfamiliar to you?

Dauntless
Alfresco
Satiated
Scarce
Render
Egregious
Abate
Complacent

Your assignment: Write roughly 250 words for your novel.

DAY 177

If you want to write a creepy scene, you can use your setting to freak out your reader. Think strange noises and shadows. Howling wind. A fetid scent. You can even use setting to foreshadow bad things to come. A murder took place in that spot centuries ago...and it's soon to happen again...

What setting related things have freaked *you* out in the course of your life?

Your assignment: Double your daily word count! Write roughly 500 words for your novel.

DAY 178

The more we get to know someone, the more beautiful or ugly they can become. You can apply that principle to your fiction, letting the reader see these types of personality/appearance changes through the eyes of your characters.

Your assignment: Write roughly 250 words for your novel.

DAY 179

If your character is not doing as you wish and you'd like a little payback, consider giving them exactly what they want—then taking it away. Fine! You can do this even if you love your character and just want to up the stakes.

GENA: I did this with a reader favorite character, Kat from the **White Rabbit Chronicles**. Throughout the series, she suffered from kidney disease. The same disease that killed her mother at a young age, in fact. (Foreshadowing!) All Kat wants is to get better. So, just when they find a way to cure her...she dies in a tragic accident. And no, I didn't kill her off because I wanted payback. I loved and adored this character. But the story had a lot of action, with fights taking place between slayers and zombies, as well as slayers and other slayers. There had to be consequences and casualties to these battles. I decided to kill two birds with one stone.

Your assignment: Write roughly 250 words for your novel.

DAY 180

To help you keep track of days within your story, write key events in a calendar. You can also track your days by writing chapter numbers in the calendar. If chapters 1 - 3 three take place on Monday, September 1st, mark September 1st with a 1. 2. 3. That way, you will know how much time has passed during any given scene.

JILL: Not keeping track of story days came back to haunt me in *At The Heart of Christmas*. I mentioned something that happened on the December Solstice...and then had one too many days between the Solstice and Christmas Eve. To fix it, I had to reorder a few scenes.

Your assignment: Write roughly 250 words for your novel.

DAY 181

When you lose your excitement for your story, consider taking a break to brainstorm new ways to elevate the tale.

Just like senior slump or post vacation letdown, that first brush of excitement with your manuscript can fade the more you work on it. This is completely normal. Double check that your hesitation to write has nothing to do with feeling like a pretend writer (imposter syndrome), a lack of research or fear of tackling an emotional scene. Take a breather. Then power through.

GENA: I recently lost all my excitement for a manuscript. I had to sit down with my critique partner—Jill!—and brainstorm changes I could make to spice up my storyline, ways I could torture my characters, and different roads those characters could travel. The possibilities sparked my imagination and suddenly I couldn't wait to work on the book again.

Your assignment: Write roughly 250 words for your novel.

DAY 182

The Strength of Personal Entertainment or
How To Recognize Good Storytelling

Judging your own writing can be very hard when you're a new writer. I'm not talking about the quality of your craft here, but rather the depth and stickiness of your storytelling. That X factor that makes a reader keep reading. This is the ultimate question of... Is this book *good*? While that sense improves with your maturity as a writer, the bottom line always comes down to what I like to call personal entertainment.

Basically, are you entertained by your own work? Do you want to keep writing to find out what happens? Are you looking forward to your next writing session? Have you laughed or cried or gotten angry while writing? (I laughed out loud a lot and even occasionally applauded the book when I was writing *The Vampire's Mail Order Bride*.) Emotions are a strong indicator that something "good" is happening in the writing. And there's a high probability that if you're entertained by your own words, readers will be too.

Sure, this method isn't foolproof. You might think your Great Aunt Bertha's tale about meeting your Great Uncle George at a swap meet is riveting, but that's because you're family. What we write has to be universally appealing, or at least appealing to our potential readership.

So how do you hone that sense of what works in the beginning? Read in the genre you want to write. Read everything. The good, the bad and the ugly. Ultimately, your capacity to know what's working and what's not will develop into one of your most useful tools.

Until then, don't hesitate to ask a friend. One who you know will tell the truth.

–Bestselling author Kristen Painter

DAY 183

THE FLUKES OF FATE

Coincidences can be a hard sell in fiction, because they come across as a convenience for the author. Two people accidentally arriving at the same place at the same time. Possible in real life. Too easy in fiction?

What about eavesdropping at the perfect moment? Or finding the perfect solution at the last minute just because someone else says or does the exact right thing?

If you write a coincidence in your story, make sure readers can suspend their disbelief. Is there a logical reason for this to happen? Two characters accidentally arrive at the same place at the same time...because they were both invited by different people within their group of friends. Eavesdropping at the perfect moment...because the character has been hiding under the bed, waiting and listening. Finding the perfect solution at the last minute...because they've been working and building to the moment.

Are there any coincidences in your story? Is there a logical reason for each one?

Your assignment: Write roughly 250 words for your novel.

DAY 184

AN INCONVENIENT CONVENIENCE

We talked about coincidences. Now we'll discuss conveniences. If you are amazed by an easy, convenient solution to a plot problem, that solution might lack excitement or complexity.

How can you shake things up? Should you keep thinking of possible solutions and go a more surprising route, letting your characters struggle for a bit?

Your assignment: Write roughly 250 words for your novel.

DAY 185

Be careful not to drop plot threads. If you introduce an element to your story, make sure:

- There's a reason for it.
- There's progress for it throughout the novel.
- There's a conclusion if it isn't going to be addressed in another book.

Otherwise it can come across as a mistake on your part.

Note: If you are writing a series, some plot threads may need to remain open to be solved in a later novel.

Your assignment: Write roughly 250 words for your novel.

DAY 186

Anytime you make a change in your manuscript, be on the lookout for the domino effect. How will that one teensy weensy change affect other aspects of your story? You might be shocked at the far reaching complications, so be sure to consider every angle of the change.

GENA: When writing *The Glass Queen*, I originally pictured the heroine Ashleigh with two sisters. Since she is the embodiment of Cinderella, I felt she needed to have two stepsisters in order stay true to the original fairy tale. As I progressed in the story, however, those sisters never came into play. And the fairy tale roles were not literal, so the evil stepsisters didn't have to be Ashleigh's actual stepsisters. With an already large cast of characters, I decided to cut her sisters and deleted every reference...

Or did I?

I forgot to check the reference she'd made about her family as a whole, and there were places where Ashleigh mentioned having a family of five when it should have been three.

The domino effect got me.

Your assignment: Write roughly 250 words for your novel.

DAY 187

If you aren't making time to write, your story isn't progressing. If your story isn't progressing, you won't be able to finish it. If you fail to finish it, you won't publish and possibly make money.

Have a notebook when you are in bed watching TV. Jot down any scenes that come to your head. In the car, you can use a voice recorder app to record as you speak out scenes or bits of thought and dialogue. Waiting in line? Write!

When you do block out time to write, look out for distractions. If you need to turn off your phone's ringer and/or shut off social media for a bit—do it!

Your assignment: Write roughly 250 words for your novel.

DAY 188

Are your main characters sympathetic in some way? Can readers relate to them, even the slightest bit?

Have you ever rooted for the bad guy to win? Maybe he had a more relatable backstory or motive than the hero. Readers don't have to like your characters, but it might be nice if they understand why your characters do what they do. That way, readers can root for them. That's why we try to give our most unlikable characters at least one redeeming quality.

A love for animals, perhaps, or kindness to children. Be creative. A ruthless assassin who always bakes his grandmother a cake on her birthday. A grumpy old man who secretly visits his wife's grave every day to tell her about his life. A mother who criticizes the appearance of others, but cries when she sees herself in the mirror.

How are your characters relatable to others?

Your assignment: Write roughly 250 words for your novel.

DAY 189

REFLECT AND CATCH UP

Just keep writing. Again, that's something I've heard said over and over. That's because it's true. I've now written over 40 stories that have been published. I have half a dozen or more that never sold, but that honed my craft. With each story, I like to think I get a little better, that I learned something new while writing the previous book that I can draw from on the new one. If you want to be a writer, you have to write. It's easy for life to take over, for doubts to take over, a writer has to make time and write. No matter what.

–Bestselling author Janice Lynn

DAY 190

WHAT'S THE BIG IDEA?

On Day 146, Gena shared a time she woke up to an email she sent to herself. That email simply stated, "Make paper dolls and pretend they are real." Ultimately, she opted not to run with that idea, which leads to the question—How do you know if you should pursue an idea or not. Here are some questions to ask yourself:

- Are you able to brainstorm a decision tree off of the idea? (Day 90)
- Can you layer, layer, layer, layer? (Day 96)
- Can you see or create the theme? (Day 6)
- Will you be able to develop a full RANGE for your characters? (Day 10)
- How about SEARCH? (Day 11)

Will this idea sustain your interest?

How much research will it take? Sometimes the amount of knowledge you must know to write this story might take the time you could spend writing another book. Maybe you can hire someone to do the research, or keep the idea on the back burner, letting it percolate until you're in a position to write it.

Lastly, discuss your new idea with your critique partner or someone who "gets" your writing. (But beware! Taking this step can also be a confidence killer, if you start before you're ready.)

Your assignment: Double your daily word count! Write roughly 500 words for your novel.

DAY 191

Sometimes it's fun to make your main character decide between a bad choice...and an even worse one. This is reminiscent of an ethics thought experience known as "the trolley problem."

The problem goes like this: A runaway trolley is heading down the tracks. Up ahead, five people are tied to the tracks. You have two options. 1) Pull a lever to divert the trolley to a second track... where only one person is tied down, but it's someone you love or 2) Do nothing and let the five people die.

Which option do you choose? Either way, someone dies, so you must decide between something horrible and something terrible.

Consider shaking up your story with an ethical dilemma for your characters!

Your assignment: Write roughly 250 words for your novel.

DAY 192

Is there an event you need to magnify and foreshadow?

As a reminder, "foreshadowing" is hinting at something major to come. Is today a good day to foreshadow danger or something wonderful?

Your assignment: Write roughly 250 words for your novel.

DAY 193

THIS WAY...NO, THAT WAY

Knowing all the answers isn't necessary to begin a book, a chapter, or even a scene. It's okay to figure things out as you move forward. Use whatever process works best for you.

GENA: I often change my mind as I'm writing a rough draft. I'll be headed in one direction and realize I don't like the destination, so I'll change tracks. This creates a domino effect, as we mentioned, which means I'll need to go back and make other changes to ensure the old direction properly leads to the new one. But I digress. By the end of the story, I'll have everything figured out. So, once I finish that draft, I sit down and figure out everything the new direction changes about the rest of the book, making notes along the way, then I go back to edit the book, making sure everything lines up.

Your assignment: Write roughly 250 words for your novel.

DAY 194

Sometimes the thought of writing a book can be overwhelming. When we get overwhelmed, we like to baby step, tackling our manuscripts one task at a time.

- Thought of writing a 500 page book? Yikes!

- Thought of writing a single scene? Doable!

- Thought of finishing a complete rough draft in 30 days? Yikes!

- Thought of finishing a single chapter today? Doable!

Accomplish and triumph!

Your assignment: Write roughly 250 words for your novel.

DAY 195

MAKE 'EM SMILE: CHALLENGE

Remember when we discussed adding a pop of humor to break the tension in your novel?

Think about things you've found humorous lately. What makes you laugh? How can you incorporate a moment of humor into your own writing?

Your assignment: Write roughly 250 words for your novel.

DAY 196

REFLECT AND CATCH UP

Is your story progressing the way you want? Have you realized you got off track at some point? Is something niggling at the back of your mind, telling you something is wrong...but you have no idea what?

When this happens to us, we like to go through the novel scene by scene to make a bullet point list of everything that has occurred. (Yes, we are big on lists.) That way, we can see the beating heart of the story. The highs and lows. Patterns might begin to emerge, allowing us to see what's missing, and where the problems first arose.

GENA: One day, Jill spent about 10 hours helping me do this. We were at a conference but working in our hotel room during our down time. I'd gotten stuck, so, I opened my work in progress and described everything that happened in each chapter, scene by scene. Along the way, she asked me plot and character questions that gave me insight I'd previously missed. She also helped me brainstorm ideas for sections in need of improvement. I made notes inside my draft of the book about what changes needed to occur where. That back-and-forth with Jill helped me craft one of my favorite stories to date!

DAY 197

CLICHÉS: A DIAMOND IN THE ROUGH?

Are clichés a diamond in the rough? Yes, no and maybe?

Clichés and idioms are overused phrases like "Plenty of fish in the sea," "A dime a dozen," and "Out of the box."

Clichés can take place in dialogue and narrative. They can be tired, but they can also give you some interesting insight into a character. Does your main character mix up clichés up by accident because their implanted translator needs an update?

Example: *You can't judge a book by its spine.*

Or maybe they're switching the words around by choice. Your risk-taking character might like to say: *Better sorry than safe.*

Maybe a character's dialogue is littered with depressing clichés: "Life's a bitch and then you die," "It could be worse" or "When it rains it pours." Then suddenly, they're spouting things like "The more the merrier" or "Take one for the team." Now you have a mystery for your other characters to solve.

Titles often play on clichés. Jill wrote *SEALed With A Kiss* and *SEALed and Delivered,* playing on a Navy SEAL twist.

Your assignment: Write roughly 250 words for your novel.

DAY 198

DISCIPLINE!

When it comes to writing your book, discipline is your friend. Get yourself in the habit of writing, no excuses. In any job, there's only one way to get paid—do your work.

Creating a regular routine for your writing can jumpstart your brain. "Now's the time we write."

Be sure to keep track of your word count. What time of the day was it? Were you more productive in the morning? More creative in the afternoon? Knowing your strengths and weaknesses will help you work with yourself not against.

If you formed a bad habit, you can also break it. Give yourself time to adjust to a new way of doing things.

Your assignment: Write roughly 250 words for your novel.

DAY 199

Is today a good day for your main character to make a mistake? Big or small, how does that mistake affect their life? Magnify it. Plant the seeds for how they triumph.

Your assignment: Write roughly 250 words for your novel.

DAY 200

WHEN TO RESEARCH AND WHEN TO...NOT

JILL: We've talked about when and when not to research. Here's and example. My freshman year of college, I took an anthropology class as a core requirement. I LOVED it. I loved learning about people all around the world, their customs and traditions and how we are connected by love.

In *Primal Instincts (soon to be rereleased as Sworn by Instinct),* I gave my love of learning about lore and ritual to my heroine, who was contracted to write a book about love and sex rites through time across the globe. Only, the writing was slow going for her. And me! Mostly me. There was a lot of research and—

Okay, I'm interrupting my retelling of the story right here, because it was at this point that Gena all but slapped me upside the head and reminded me that I was writing *fiction.* She asked why I was doing all this research when I could just make things up. Then I could be certain the facts were correct.

So yeah, I started making the sex rites lore. Needless to say, I had a lot of fun creating and writing that book!

Your assignment: Write roughly 250 words for your novel.

DAY 201

WIND UP THE SPRING

If you plan to add sexual encounters into your book, sexual tension is key. Sure, the characters noticed each other's overall appearance when they met. But now they've spent more time together. Have they begun to notice the little details ? A specific cluster of freckles that reminds him of the Milky Way? He has a different laugh for different types of humor? There's a fleck of blue in her green eyes?

What little things can your characters notice about each other?

GENA: On the topic of sexual tension, I will share some advice Jill gave me years ago. I was telling her about the story I was writing, and she stopped me to ask what make the hero and heroine different to each other. In other words, what set them apart from all the others they'd dated in the past? What made them "the one" for each other? I thought about it and realized I'd just relied on the old standby: He thinks she's the most beautiful...she think he's the hottest... Bottom line: It was a superficial connection. I had to think deeper, longer, harder—pun intended—to figure out what made these people special to each other and why no one else would do. They began to notice details that went beyond appearance. What can the hero give the heroine that no one else can and vice versa?

Your assignment: Write roughly 250 words for your novel.

NICKNAMES

In our group of friends, multiple people have nicknames. They have the same purpose as an inside joke—a means of showcasing the specialness of a relationship. Would a nickname work for any of your characters?

JILL: In *Sworn Enemies*, originally published as *Hitting the Mark*, the main character's name is Dani. She's spent time in juvenile detention, but she's out now and trying to live on the straight and narrow. Her father, a conman, has reappeared on the scene, using his nickname for her: Danibear. He wields her nickname as a weapon, attempting to use her emotions and love as leverage to lure her back into a new scheme.

GENA: The couples in my books LOVE to give each other nicknames. Sometimes they use the usual endearments. "Darling." "Pet." "Princess." "Baby." Other times they use the not so usual. Fox became "vixen," because another name for a female fox is, in fact, vixen. Belle became "Four Elements Girl," among a host of over fake superhero titles the hero teasingly gave her. Everly became "sorceress," at first an insult by the hero, then a declaration of his unconditional love. Sometimes the nick names work with their significant other's name. Ashleigh = Asha. William = Willy. Alice = Ali.

Your assignment: Write roughly 250 words for your novel.

DAY 203

My best advice is to trust your instincts. Whether it's in regard to a scene you're writing, a plot twist you're crafting, a career choice, or even just a particularly hard sentence. If your gut tells you something isn't working, chances are...you're right. So whatever your gut is telling you, do it. Do it and don't look back. Beginning writers often overlook advice that tells them to trust themselves, because they're still developing confidence in their own intuition and skills, but over the years of my career writing (and also teaching budding authors), I've learned that no matter how new you are to this, we're all innate storytellers, so if we just trust our instincts, we'll typically lead ourselves in the right direction.

–Award-winning and bestselling author Kait Ballenger

DAY 204

WHY DO YOU LOVE WHAT YOU LOVE?

Have you ever analyzed why you love certain books, movies or TV shows? What aspect of the stories holds you captive? The relationships? The characters? The mystery? The prose? The wit? The creep factor?

How did the author or director make that part of the book or show work? Lots of build up? Getting straight to the point? What made it stand out to you? Is there a trope you can add to your own story?

Your assignment: Write roughly 250 words for your novel.

DAY 205

You know everything there is to know about your main character. Do you have to tell your readers every little detail? No. Hinting about something and leaving a little mystery can be better at times.

"What did you do?" she demanded.
He scrubbed a hand down his face. "Something...nothing. It doesn't matter."
"Tell me!"
"I–you–" Lips pressed in a thin line, he stomped from the room.

Now we want to know what he did, right?
This type of shut-it-down reaction can work for narrative, too. People often cut off a troubling thought before it has time to fully form.

I wiped a tear from my cheek and forced my mind to blank. No way would I let myself consider—no! I wouldn't even think of her name.

What secrets do your characters want to keep from your readers, and what hints can you offer?

Your assignment: Write roughly 250 words for your novel.

DAY 206

BENCHMARK. DON'T COMPARE

There will be times you read someone else's work and feel inadequate. That is natural. We've said it before but it bears mentioning again. Your voice is unique and all yours, and that makes it special. There's not another like it. Keep going! The more you write, the more you'll learn about the process. Accomplish and triumph!

Your assignment: Double your daily word count! Write roughly 500 words for your novel.

DAY 207

You're probably far enough along in your story that you've written an argument scene or two. Can you see both character viewpoints and the validity of both sides? If the argument is purposely skewed in one direction, for whatever reason, have you proven your point? If it is accidentally skewed in one direction, consider revising to show both sides have merit.

Your assignment: Write roughly 250 words for your novel.

DAY 208

HAPPY HOLIDAYS!

Depending on the timing of your story, your characters might need to celebrate a holiday. If you are writing a fantasy or science fiction novel, it might be prudent to create a brand new holiday that fits within your new world.

Are you marking your fictional book days in a calendar? This can help you know what day it is in every scene, so you never lose track of time.

Your assignment: Write roughly 250 words for your novel.

DAY 209

GO AHEAD AND FIGHT

If you're having trouble with the physical aspects of a fight scene, try acting out the motions yourself. You might feel like a fool while you're doing it—we have!—but the end result is worth the means. If an action doesn't work for you, chances are good it won't work for your character. (Though we admit our characters are far more flexible than we are.)

Your assignment: Write roughly 250 words for your novel.

DAY 210

It sounds cheesy but...follow your heart! As a recent debut author, I had no idea what direction I wanted to go with my brand, series, and career as a whole. The plethora of possibilities was overwhelming, but I found that the most positive feedback I've gotten is about the aspects of my books that came from my heart, not from writing to fit a certain market. It's obviously important to write books that are going to sell, but it's equally important to create stories, characters, and themes that feel right in your heart and inspire you creatively as an artist. If you're only writing a certain plot, genre, or style because it's selling in a hot market – and not because you truly love it – the passion may be lost on the page. Ultimately, if you love your words, that will come across to readers, and they will love them too!

–Breezie Bennett

DAY 211

CRUTCH

JILL: I love my writing space. It's a desk and hutch where I'm surrounded by my favorite books, pictures and notes from readers. I'd share a photo, but it's covered with 3 notebooks, tax receipts and tons of loose papers I can't get rid of (have I mentioned my slight hoarding tendency?).

In the past, I used the state of my desk as an excuse not to write. Being creative writers, we can convince ourselves of anything. We call those our crutches.

I had this great professor in college, Deborah Chester, who advised us to get rid of our crutches. My desk was my crutch. Once I got rid of that crutch, I could write anywhere. Gena and I plotted *Dating the Undead* while I sat in my car on top of a canyon; the only place I could get cell reception while chaperoning at a youth camp. I wrote *Lord of Rage* in a cafeteria and edited *Naked Thrill* stuck in a tornado shelter.

Lack of time is the most popular crutch for not writing, and yet we can craft a scene anywhere. We're not tied to a desk or our electronics—grab a notebook and write while you're waiting for your kids to get out of school or practice. Write on the train to and from work. Write during lunch.

Key word: Write.

Your assignment: Write roughly 250 words for your novel.

Bonus assignment: Identify your writing crutches. Are you developing new ones?

DAY 212

If you're anything like us, you've thought, *Oh, the naughty things I can do to my characters...*

Go ahead. Get your god complex on again. Why not surprise a character and shake up your story world?

The loss of a job?
Food poisoning?
Alien toxin?
A dead body found?
The arrival of a long lost friend?
Fainting?
Car crash?
World-wide computer crash?
The return of an ex?
Win the lottery?

Your assignment: Double your daily word count! Write roughly 500 words for your novel.

DAY 213

MEAL TIME

Real people get real hungry. Don't forget to feed your characters; they need to eat, too. Unless they are a supernatural being of some kind. But even then, they'll have to consume *something* for nourishment.

In Kresley Cole's **Immortals After Dark** series, the valkyries consume lightning.

You don't have to describe every bite, or even every meal, but eating with others can add depth to the act. Also, behavior around the dinner table can set the tone of a scene. What are the emotional undercurrents? Are the diners at war? Or falling in love? Eating can also be one of the most sensual acts between characters...

Your assignment: Write roughly 250 words for your novel.

DAY 214

ADDING FLAVOR TO CHARACTER-SPEAK

Dialects can vary from town to town, city to city, state to state. Research common words and phrases for the location of your story.

Caution: Less can sometimes do more. Sometimes authors demonstrate their love of research here, but too much of a good thing can often overwhelm. We may love reading a good Scottish brogue or the lilt of a Cajun accent, but too much can take a reader out of a story or turn our characters into caricatures.

Your assignment: Write roughly 250 words for your novel.

DAY 215

PEDAL TO THE METAL

You've come so far. You are working to make your dream of becoming a published author a reality. This isn't the time to pump the brakes. Floor it! Keep going!

You should have around 200 pages of story written. That is a rough draft of about 50k words.

GENA: I've written a 60k word rough draft and turned it into a 100k novel. It just depends on how many scenes you are missing. I've also turned a 60k word rough draft into a 40k word novella, because I over-explained things.

If you've finished your rough draft, congrats! But this *still* isn't the time to pump the brakes. Think about any elements that might be missing from your story. Do you need to add scenes?

Remember to keep reading the daily lessons in *All Write Already,* though. We have tips to consider before you dive into the revision and editing process.

Your assignment: If you haven't finished your first draft, write roughly 250 words for your novel.

DAY 216

BE AWARE OF OLD STEREOTYPES

The human brain tends to sort things into patterns. That is how we learn both math and reading. We can also box *people* into patterns or stereotypes that come out in our writing. For example, the old lie that females are always catty to each other and they can never maintain a true friendship in real or fictional life. We prove that idea wrong every day.

GENA: As a teen, every book I read had girls being cruel to each other. That wasn't my personal experience, yet I began to believe that was the way things must be. When I started writing, I fell into that trap. I thought, *For excitement and entertainment, the girls must strike out at each other.* Then I read *Divine By Mistake* by PC Cast. The females were—gasp!—supportive of each other. In that moment, I realized I had perpetuated a stereotype. Now? Each of my heroines has a best friend who will never, ever betray her.

Characters can battle stereotypes, too. Let them appreciate the things that make another different while also discovering what they have in common. If they made assumptions about another character, how did that affect their relationship? How did they grow?

Sensitivity readers can help you identify stereotypes in your writing.

Your assignment: Write roughly 250 words for your novel.

DAY 217

Find Your People

Second-guessing, doubts, and uncertainty can be brutal in a field like ours where rejection plays a pivotal, yet unwelcome, role.

When negative thoughts get in our way or stop us from making headway with our work in progress (WIP), we can react in different ways. If you're like me, I'll be honest, there's probably some chocolate eating involved, maybe some ice cream or fro-yo binging. Or both. But, a chica can only eat so much, and I know what really helps is talking out the problem with writer friends and mentors who understand the industry's ups and downs and who often battle the same Imposter Syndrome beast.

You see, it doesn't matter if you're working on your first, your fifth or your fiftieth novel...odds are, you'll face this sneaky villain at some point. But good news, you *can* silence it, often thanks to a pep talk or kick in the pants from writing buddies.

That's why it's invaluable to find that group of people in Romancelandia who will celebrate good news, hold you accountable when you need it, brainstorm an idea, and "get" you when it seems like non-writers in your close circle don't. So, consider joining a professional writers' organization, look for a local or online chapter, seek out a local writers' group, hop onto social media and connect with fellow authors, attend writers' conferences or a NaNoWriMo event in your community. Make connections—doing so can help immensely, in both business and personal ways.

I'll be honest, a writer's life can be hair-pulling and emotion-wrought at times, but with the right people on your side, part of your community, it's also absolutely rewarding.

–*USA Today* Bestselling author Priscilla Oliveras

DAY 218

Language is always evolving and changing. The most popular dictionaries release a new version every year. Word nerds eagerly await the list of new words that have been added.

You're an author. You can invent words, or use old words in new ways. It's totally cake. You can even take common words and phrases and twist them for added flare.

Baby back ribs = baby back bitch
Vegetarian = pleasuretarian
Polka dots = poke-me dots

You can also turn a noun into a verb. Math = mathing.

Today, have fun with words and look for an opportunity to give an ordinary word new meaning.

Your assignment: Double your daily word count! Write roughly 500 words for your novel.

Bonus assignment: Create a new word for one of your characters to use. It doesn't have to end up in your final manuscript, but can give you new insights into your character while giving your creativity a boost.

DAY 219

DON'T DROP A DROPPED CLUE

If you drop a clue about something, don't forget to expand it at some point in the story.

Think of the movie *Dirty Dancing* and the oh, so famous lift between Johnny and Baby. How cheated would you feel if they hadn't executed the perfect lift at the end of the movie?

Your assignment: Write roughly 250 words for your novel.

Bonus assignment: Go through your manuscript, making note of every clue and loop you've crafted to ensure they've been closed.

DAY 220

Once you finish today's scene, spend some time thinking about what comes next, preparing your mind. Jot down ideas or make bullet points.

The next time you open your manuscript, you already have a blueprint for where to go next.

Your assignment: Write roughly 250 words for your novel.

DAY 221

He Nodded, She Nodded, They All Nodded

You might catch yourself reusing the same actions, facial expressions, and physical reactions. If you notice, readers will notice. Consider highlighting the repeats or keeping a list and fixing in editing.

Here are some of the most common overused actions, expressions and reactions we've noticed in our own writing, with a possible alternative:

Grated → Rasped
Growled → Rumbled
Swing (a sword) → Brandished
Frowned → Glowered
Scowled → Glared
Reeled → Lurched

Your assignment: Write roughly 250 words for your novel.

DAY 222

What does your main character have to lose? Is today the day to take it away? Magnify their pain. Plant the seeds for how they'll triumph.

Your assignment: Write roughly 250 words for your novel.

DAY 223

Keep going! You've got this! Forget about only writing what you know. Write whatever you can imagine!

A petting zoo, with humans in the cages?
A new way to fly?
A society that never touches due to fear of a mutant flu virus?
An otherworldly animal?
A sentient house?
A new currency?
The perfect drug?
If your story has a need for something that doesn't exist, invent it!

Your assignment: Write roughly 250 words for your novel.

DAY 224

As a new author I often heard, write what you know. It's so true. Write what you know. When I first sold to Harlequin, I sold a medical romance. By training, I'm a nurse practitioner, so pulling that knowledge and emotional experiences into my writing just made sense. When I sold to Hallmark, I'd gotten a couple of rejections from them, and when I sat down to write a new proposal, I went for emotion. What emotions does watching a Hallmark movie make me feel? How do they make me feel that way? Why do I like those emotions and keep going back for more? Then, I looked at what made me feel that way in my real life. I love to quilt and knew I wanted my heroine to be a quilter. My son was in the process of enlisting in the Army and the military was heavy on my heart. Thus, my military hero was born. I'd been to a quilt show several years before where quilts were made for and given to foster children. That program hit me deep inside. I always knew I'd use something along those lines in a book someday. Why not have my heroine's church group donate quilts to wounded warriors and my hero be one of those recipients? From there, I just kept brainstorming ideas on paper, trying to remember that I was going for emotions foremost. Every idea had to elicit an emotion. When I was through, I pulled my ideas together into a synopsis, sent it to my agent, and after revising a few things, *Wrapped Up in Christmas*, sold to Hallmark and became my first book to hit a major list.

–Bestselling author Janice Lynn

DAY 225

THE FLAWS COME OUT

Remember Day 29? We talked about flaws. Have you made sure to show/reveal flaws in your main and secondary characters, as well as at least one good characteristic about your villain/antagonist/monster? Magnify them!

Your assignment: Write roughly 250 words for your novel.

DAY 226

REALISTIC EXPECTATIONS

It is important to set realistic expectations for yourself. Many writers dream of hitting bestseller lists and seeing their books made into movies. But it wasn't until Gena's 7th book, *The Nymph King*, that she hit the *New York Times*. Jill was over ten years into her writing career before *Naked Pursuit* was produced as a TV movie for Lifetime Movie Network.

To put it succinctly, it can take years to be an overnight success. Give yourself time. Create logical and achievable benchmarks of accomplishment that are in your control. Movie options and bestseller lists have variables you can't plan for or anticipate.

- Is the quality of your writing continuing to improve?
- Are you doing your best, not just what's good enough?
- Are you gaining new readers and keeping the ones you have (aside from some natural attrition)?
- Are you losing money by self-publishing?
- Are you getting requests from agents and editors to edit and resubmit?
- Are agents and editors giving you an invitation to submit additional work?
- Is your self-publishing income providing enough to hire cover designers, editors and personal assistants?

If you need to make adjustments, make adjustments. If you just need more time to take off, patience is your best friend.

Focus. Magnify. Accomplish. Triumph!

Your assignment: Write roughly 250 words for your novel.

DAY 227

MAKE THE CONNECTION!

Did you mention something in an earlier scene but it hasn't come up again? You could have a dropped thread on your hands.

GENA: In *The Glass Queen*, the heroine unwittingly strokes her dead mother's ring for comfort. The more I wrote, the more I forgot to have her stroke the stupid thing LOL I either needed to remove it or go through the book and look for places to organically mention. Since I planned to use the ring as a plot point at the end, I ended up putting in the extra work and adding the mentions.

Your assignment: Write roughly 250 words for your novel.

DAY 228

No one makes the correct decision every time. People make mistakes. Is today a good day for your character to screw up?

Here are some questions to keep in mind while crafting a scene with a screw up:

- Did your character know they were making a bad choice and continued with their decision anyway?
- Do they blame themselves or others?
- How does this mistake reflect their growth?
- What have they learned?
- Does the opportunity to make a similar choice appear later in the book?
- How will they react knowing what they've learned?

Your assignment: Double your daily word count! Write roughly 500 words for your novel.

DAY 229

RED HERRING

A red herring is a clue meant to mislead your readers.

Have you ever read a story and been 100 percent certain you'd figured out the big secret? Were you right or wrong? Did you fall for a red herring?

Adding a red herring is a way to keep your readers surprised when the big reveal of truth happens. Both M. Night Shyamalan's *The Sixth Sense* and Christopher McQuarrie's *The Usual Suspects* give us multiple red herrings to keep us guessing throughout the movie until the surprise ending.

You can use red herrings in any genre, not just murder mystery and suspense. A switch from one romantic lead to another can throw both your character and reader off balance.

Misleading readers is one of the perks of the job. Have fun with it!

Your assignment: Write roughly 250 words for your novel.

DAY 230

Some days you will love your book. Other days you will hate it. These feelings are normal and happen to writers at almost every stage in their career. In fact, writing can sometimes feel like you are shoving a hook into your brain in an attempt to fish out every little word and idea. And a good portion of those words and ideas should be thrown back!

Don't worry, most of us feel that way at some point. Press on. You're closing in on the reward!

JILL: After that first blush of romance with a new story fades, the real work begins. The work of staying seated in my chair. The work of not firing up my favorite social media pages. The work of digging deep in my emotional well. Holding that finished book in your hands or scrolling through the words on my iPad make the extra effort worth it.

You can't have the days you love it without dealing with the days you hate it. Just remember, emotions can be fleeting, and they are always subject to change.

Your assignment: Write roughly 250 words for your novel.

Things I wished I'd known when I first started writing...

1) I would start to predict endings to TV shows, movies, and books.

2) Writing is addictive! The more I write, the more I want, nay, need to write.

3) How many amazing friends I'd make along the way.

4) The exhilaration of starting and publishing every book.

5) The good feeling I'd get when readers find hope and happiness between the pages of my books.

6) The thankfulness and gratitude I have for everyone who supports my work.

7) How indebted I feel to all who are excited for the next book.

The naysayers don't matter. What truly matters is what I feel inspired to write, and do. It amazes me how people love books I write that I think won't go over well.

Honestly, I never thought I'd be a writer, but now that I am, I don't want any other occupation. Being a mom is my greatest privilege. Being a daughter of the Most High King is beyond words. I'm thankful for every book, and never want to take what I get to do for granted.

–Acclaimed author Cathy Jackson

DAY 232

We began writing before self-publishing was an accepted thing, so we had to find other ways to get our names in front of publishing professionals. Often we opted to go with three chapter writing contests, because editors and agents would judge the final round. In fact, Jill's first published novel, *Never Naughty Enough*, was purchased by the editor who read her manuscript in the final round of a contest.

If we happened to win the contests we entered, we had the added bonus of padding our writing resumes.

However, one phenomenon emerged from the contest trend. New writers would polish and revise the first three chapters of their novel over and over again, making them perfect for the contest, yet never actually finish writing the book.

JILL: The first book I wrote will NEVER see the light of day. But I finished that sucker and the one after that. Each story I completed put me one step closer to learning about the craft of writing and what works best for me. That doesn't mean you should finish every novel you begin. But the first one? Yes. You will learn so much by completing your first novel. How to push through to the end. How to build a bridge between your beginning, middle and end. How to transition between each individual scene. When to add emotion or delete narrative. When to quicken or slow the pace. So finish the first manuscript and learn what you need to know to begin the second.

Your assignment: Write roughly 250 words for your novel.

DAY 233

Think about the scene you are writing today and ask yourself these questions:

- How does this advance my plot?
- Does this raise the stakes?
- Does this impact my characters in some way?
- If I remove the scene, will my story flow better or will there be a hole?

Make sure the scene is important, advances the plot or develops a character. Also make sure it is layered with description and emotion.

Your assignment: Write roughly 250 words for your novel.

DAY 234

READY TO THROW IN THE TOWEL?

As we mentioned, there will be days you hate your book, your characters and every word you've written. We understand. We've been there!

We challenge you to press on, anyway. If you stop now, all your hard work would be for nothing. Keep going! You can do this! Focus. Magnify. Accomplish. Triumph!

Your assignment: Write roughly 250 words for your novel.

RETHINK SETTING YOUR WORLD IN A REAL PLACE?

People know their facts. Medical workers will know when you mess up medical details. Historians will know when you mess up historical information.

If you haven't spoken to a professional or researched the job, disease or site—or a multitude of other things—you might want to make something up instead.

Similarly, we live in Oklahoma, so we know the weather patterns, the streets, when traffic is bad, and a thousand other things. If someone gets the facts wrong, we—always—know.

Using a maps app can help, but it won't provide the little details. That is one of the reasons we prefer to create fictional towns/realms.

GENA: In my **Original Heartbreakers** series, I created Strawberry Valley. For **The Forest of Good and Evil**, I created the magical kingdom of Enchantia. In my **Lords of the Underworld** series, there's a made-up realm in practically every book. I make up jobs, holidays, superpowers and more—heck, I make up everything I can!

Your assignment: Double your daily word count! Write roughly 500 words for your novel.

DAY 236

Don't be afraid to reach out to professionals in the same field as your characters to ask questions.

GENA: I once rode in a two-seater plane for research, and I hated to fly! I was writing a hero who flew those types of planes, and I needed to know what he experienced up in the air. I got to sit in the cockpit and speak with the pilot who sat right next to me. It was fun. It was terrifying. But mostly, it was informative. And terrifying. Did I mention terrifying? Oh, the things we do for our characters.

Your assignment: Write roughly 20 words for your novel.

DAY 237

Remember, just because *you* know something story-wise doesn't mean your character should know it.

You might recognize a Rembrandt on sight, but should the character who's never seen one?

Cooking might come naturally to you, but should your character have those same skills?

Someone who's never worked on a car might not know the name of the part or tools.

Give your character a reason for knowing what they know!

Your assignment: Write roughly 250 words for your novel.

DAY 238

As you've written more and more pages of your story, you've learned more about your process as an author. It's time to ask yourself some hard-hitting questions.

- What will you do differently for your second book?
- What feels easier?
- What do you think you still have left to learn?
- How will you handle your pre-writing?
- What to focus on and magnify?

USE YOUR PET PEEVES TO YOUR ADVANTAGE

You have a story to tell which makes us think you were a reader first. Do you recall any pet peeves you had with other works? Make sure those same annoyances aren't making their way into your novel!

JILL: My grandma had grocery sacks filled with romance novels that I would take home and read. Those books were like a microcosm of the sexual revolution. In the earliest ones, the heroines took pride in their virginity until marriage, which happened some time after the book ended.

As I moved through the books, they got steamier. The virginal heroine would have sex on the page with the hero, but usually only with a lot of guilt. In the next round, the heroine was no longer a virgin, but in no way shape or form did she enjoy the sex previous to meeting the hero of the book. And that's where my pet peeve came into play. It may be hard to believe, but even just ten years ago it was controversial to write women characters with fully realized sexually satisfying pasts. Now, women and all their various life experiences are shown on the page.

Your assignment: Write roughly 250 words for your novel.

DAY 240

Try not to overuse run-on sentences and sentence fragments. Too many can be distracting, like, seriously distracting, I mean, run-on sentences just go on and on and on, and they never seem to stop, and all you want them to do is make them stop stop stop stop dang it. Right? Your readers. Might want. To pull out. YOUR hair. (See! Distracting! And annoying.)

However, when used in moderation these tools can be highly effective. Seriously!

Your assignment: Double your daily word count! Write roughly 500 words for your novel.

DAY 241

If an object means the world to your character, what would it take to make them sell it? Or give it away?

One favorite example is *The Gift of the Magi* by O. Henry. Both characters will gladly part with their most cherished possession to make the other happy.

The more your character loves the item, the more emotional the giving of it will be for the reader.

Your assignment: Write roughly 250 words for your novel.

DAY 242

Before you started writing, you were a reader. At least, that is our best guess, considering your desire to become an author. Between the writing of your books, be sure to read, read, read. Note and look up any words you don't understand and grow your vocabulary.

Did one of your favorite stories evoke certain emotions that spoke to you? Consider rereading it to study the author's style and word-craft. How did they do what they did? Can you consciously or unconsciously pick up the rhythm of their plotting?

Also, it's important to study the genre you plan to write in even after you've taken the plunge. Notice the tropes and themes. What resonates with you most? What leaves you cold?

Your assignment: Write roughly 250 words for your novel.

DAY 243

If you've invented a new world or society, the citizens might not know common words and phrases we use in everyday life, like 'Heaven' and 'Hell.' Is there an afterlife in your fictional world? Religion? If not, using "hell" as an expletive might not work.

For the people of your new world, you might need to create an original set of curses for them.

GENA: In the **Everlife** series, the heroine is obsessed with numbers. So, a curse for her is "zero." In the **Forest of Good and Evil** series, one of the heroines is from a land that blooms with roses all year. A curse to the citizens is "withering roses" or "weeds!" On the other hand, a proclamation of delight could be "blooming roses!" In the **White Rabbit Chronicles**, the heroine doesn't want to curse, so she uses the phrase "good glory."

Think about your characters and your world. Are there any specific words or phrases that would work as a curse or an exclamation of delight?

Your assignment: Write roughly 250 words for your novel.

DAY 244

GIVE IT EVERYTHING

Many writers worry about being the best author ever. Stop! To some, you will amaze and delight. Others you'll never make happy, no matter what or how you write it. All you can do is your best. Just write!

GENA: For the longest time, I had no idea what I wanted to do with my life career-wise. I dropped out of college three times. I worked for my mother—and got voted worst employee ever multiple years in a row. (Trust me, I earned the title!) I would start projects, then stop them halfway. Nothing was a ~~great good~~ half way decent fit for me. Then, I started writing. In my stories, I found my passion. Love what you do, and it can love you back!

Your assignment: Write roughly 250 words for your novel.

DAY 245

REFLECT AND CATCH UP

I thought it would get easier. When I say "it" I mean everything relating to writing and my writing career. Almost fourteen years in, the books would be easier to write. I wouldn't be worried all the time about sales or being dropped by my publisher. I would feel secure and the words would flow...and, wow, was I wrong.

This career stays hard and frustrating. It toys with your insecurities regardless if you're new or have been in this game for forty books, whether your sales sputter along or you're a bestseller. But there's a good thing. Not really good, I guess, but something that should make it bearable: You are not alone. You will feel like you are. You will think everyone else has an easier time setting goals, writing, selling and sleeping at night.

Wrong!

A lot of us (most of us?) feel those prickly doubts and worries. The idea that "it" gets easier, you'll be able to write for X hours a day no matter what disaster hits and you'll sell every idea—Nope. That is a lot of pressure and since so much of this career happens in silence, in our own spaces with limited contact with others, we feel alone.

You're not alone and once you realize that, the other uncontrollables won't seem so daunting.

–HelenKay Dimon

DAY 246

There's a popular saying: Write what you want to read! Is there something you've always wanted to read, but no one has written anything similar? Consider writing it yourself. You may kick-start a new subgenre that others didn't know they needed.

Or, the book could just be the "book of your heart" that only a handful of people will read. Success is how you define it. Maybe you needed to get that one story idea out of your head, and now you're done. Each time we finish a new manuscript, we're stretching our creativity and hopefully learning more about the craft of creating fiction.

Often writers will take the book of their heart and later add in tropes and themes that will make their book more commercial and appeal to a wider audience of readers. Whether the book goes public or gets shoved under your bed, you've accomplished something. Be proud of your triumph, we are!

Your assignment: Double your daily word count! Write roughly 250 words for your novel.

Whatever your field of business, you probably use unique words only your coworkers understand. The publishing world is no different. Here's a list of common words and terms used by authors and editors:

ARC: This stands for Advance Reader Copy. (Sometimes mistakenly referred to as Advanced Reader Copy.) These are copies of the book, often uncorrected proofs, given to reviewers and book promoters. These can be both bound/ printed copies or electronic. Traditional publishing houses usually handle distribution, while also giving a limited number of copies to the author.

ARC Team: A team of readers organized by the author or author's assistant who are given an advanced reader copy in exchange for voluntarily leaving a review.

Back Matter: The pages after the last word of your story. This includes endnotes, a list of your other works, invitations to join your newsletter or follow you on social media.

Backlist: The books you published before your newest release.

Blurb: The blurb refers to the back cover copy on the back of the book or on the online bookseller's website. There are several wonderful books out there about blurb writing, so we won't delve deep here—that comes later—but it can be one of the most important aspects of publishing because these few words can sell your book to readers or drive them away.

Distribution, aka Wide Versus Exclusive: When you self publish, you have the option to go exclusive with one platform (such as Kindle

Unlimited) or wide on any and all platforms available to you. This is a very personal choice. Going wide may fit your marketing plans at one time and later you may change your mind–self-publishing allows you the flexibility. Read your terms of service carefully.

Front Matter: The pages before your story begins, including dedication, acknowledgements, copyright notices, table of contents, etc.

ISBN: This is short for International Standard Book Number which is usually 13 digits long. It's used by bookstores, libraries and publishers to track inventory etc. It is your responsibility as an author to understand when and how to apply for an ISBN.

ASIN: The Amazon Standard Identification Number.

Piracy: When someone posts your book online without your permission, allowing others to read it for free. It is theft of your intellectual property and a violation of your copyright.

Your assignment: Write roughly 250 words for your novel.

DAY 248

Yesterday we discussed jargon for writers. Today we'll discuss jargon for the publication of your novel.

Advance: An advance is actually an advance against royalties. Meaning, a traditional publishing house will give the author money up front, an amount based on what they think the book will earn back. If your book does not earn its full advance, authors are usually not expected to pay that money back. But, your next advance might be lower.

JILL: On the topic of advances, I want to share the best piece of advice I ever received: Think of that advance as the only money you'll ever be paid. That is the money you can live on, using it to pay your taxes and maintain your business. When—if—you receive royalties, well, that money is icing!

Galley: A printed copy of your manuscript used for editing purposes.

Mass market: Small, printed paperback books.

Option: If you sell your book to a publisher, your contract will probably ensure that the publisher has the right to read and buy your next book before anyone else.

Print on Demand (POD): Print on demand has changed the landscape of self-publishing by allowing authors to publish books as needed at more reasonable costs.

Proofs or Page Proofs: A copy of your book before publication, usually at the final stage when you are only hunting for typos.

Query letter: A letter you send to editors or agents, telling them a little about your book and asking if they'd like to read more. Think of this as the blurb for yourself and your project.

Rights: The manuscript you have crafted is your intellectual property. You sell your publishing rights when you contract with a publishing house. They might also acquire your film, audio, gaming, foreign markets rights, as well as mediums we don't even know of yet. You can negotiate your own contract, hire a lawyer for contract review or work with an agent. We cannot stress this enough—Selling your rights is serious business, so always read the contract. You do not want to rue the day you agreed to the terms.

Reversion of Rights: The rights to your intellectual property can be returned to you. The terms should be spelled out once your rights have been returned, you are free to do with them whatever you choose. You can sell them again or publish them yourself. Please Note: Often a new publisher or distributor will ask for proof that your rights have been returned to you.

Royalty: When you contract with a publisher, you are giving them the rights to sell your book. They pay you a portion of the money they earned, which is your royalty. If the publisher gave you an advance, that money must be earned before you're paid royalties. Typically, traditional publishing houses pay twice a year. The terms of payment should be spelled out clearly in your negotiated contract.

STET: Let it stand. This word is used during the editing process to indicate a change should be ignored.

Your assignment: Write roughly 250 words for your novel.

DAY 249

JILL: This is one of the oldest pieces of advice I have ever received and it's still true today. *Don't have your character look into a mirror to relay their description to the reader.*

This tactic has been played out. Allow the details of your character's attire to come out naturally though dialogue, narrative, or someone else's point of view (POV.)

There are exceptions, of course. A good example would be a main character who hates their appearance; they can't stop staring at themselves, lamenting every feature. Or a plot that revolves around beauty.

If you do decide to avoid the self-mirror-exam, there are other ways to show readers what your characters look like or what they are wearing.

Does a main character hate ties, but wears one to visit his grandmother? Show him adjusting it with a little thought about Granny.

Are your heroine's clothes designer, hand sewn or from the thrift store? Ill-fitting? Itchy? Let her adjust and think about why.

Is there a contrast between skin/hair/eye color and a color found nearby the character? Does their hair or eye color remind your narrator of something?

Your assignment: Write roughly 250 words for your novel.

DAY 250

WANT OR NEED?

What your characters want isn't always what they need. They can crave something, obtain it, and realize they were wrong, that this new job or move will never fix all their problems.

We love to surprise the main characters with what they *really* need, dropping clues for the reader along the way.

GENA: In *The Glass Queen*, the heroine is desperate to obtain her father's approval. She thinks if she works hard enough, she can earn his love. Over the course of the book, however, she learns that love isn't earned but freely given, and that she doesn't need someone else's approval to be worthy of anything.

JILL: In *Fun & Games*, the hero believes he wants revenge on his absent father. By going after his father, however, he ends up pushing everyone away, and realizes his real need is to accept that he himself is worthy of someone else's love.

Your assignment: Write roughly 250 words for your novel.

DAY 251

I JUST DIDN'T LOVE IT

JILL: A few years ago, a friend of mine shared a rejection letter she received. The agent wrote, "I just didn't love it."

Ouch!

But what does that mean?

As someone who trained as a journalist, I feel the burning frustration of that question. Was it the writing? Was it the characterization? Problems with the plot, perhaps? Those, I can fix. Not loving something... not so much.

Everything about a book can be perfect—the plot, grammar, and characterization, etc.—but none of that matters if the writing is passionless. I know I'm not alone in watching a movie or beginning a new series that should hit every one of my hot buttons, but it just left me with a sense of meh. So, I started a list of things that have the power to take us away from the creative passion found in our storytelling.

- Ruthless self-editing can make your prose tight, but is your aim for perfection also deleting your enthusiasm?
- Avoiding risks and following writing "rules" in an effort to make your work rejection proof. (An example of this is hearing a "rule," even a wrong rule, and considering it gospel. Like: *Never use the word "was." It's passive.* Wrong! Sometimes a sentence needs "was," and that's that.)
- Listening to your inner editor and allowing self doubt to keep you from writing the way you want to write.
- Writing everything but what you love.

Your assignment: Write roughly 250 words for your novel.

DAY 252

So you want to write a novel but you're having a hard time starting. You've read books on plotting and craft. You've joined writer groups and soaked up the nuggets of advice, but you're still not sure what to do. Am I a panster? Am I a plotter? You have no clue what you are. My advice is to just write. Sit down in a comfy place, open up your laptop and just start typing stream of consciousness. Don't worry about where it fits into the plot. Don't start at chapter one if you have a certain scene in mind. Maybe just put down on paper a few minutes of dialogue between two characters. Whatever it is, just start typing. And don't stop. Don't bother to correct your spelling, your spacing or your grammar. Just keep going. Let it flow. Spit it all out and don't stop until you draw a blank. There you go... you've started writing your book. This may sound flip, but sometimes the biggest block we have in writing is having confidence that we can do it and that can have you staring at a blank screen for hours. You have to just push past that initial fear and jump into the deep end. You might be surprised that what comes out is really good. It might be garbage, but if it is, learn from it and correct it. Start writing again. Eventually, you will learn what you are... a plotter or a pantser or something in between, and you can develop your style as you grow in confidence and skill. But you have to start!!!!!

–*New York Times* bestselling author Sawyer Bennett

DAY 253

Remember when we asked you to write a scene showing a shared experience between your main characters? Have you included it in your story? Is today an opportunity to create one with the antagonist and a main character?

If you're having trouble coming up with a shared experience, we'll jumpstart a brainstorming session with three possible ideas:

- Lock two enemies in a confined space to force them to work together, building bonds that can be tested later.

- Have two friends head into battle against an enemy, solidifying an already established bond.

- Show two opposites in the same scene, dealing with the same problem, how it affects them differently, and their varying reactions, as well as how it affects them similarly.

Your assignment: Write roughly 250 words for your novel.

DAY 254

Passive Voice Versus Active Voice

As you write, it helps to be aware of passive versus active voice.

Active voice: Subject + Verb (action) + Object (the receiver of the action)

Jill and Gena are going to write a book today.

Subject—Jill and Gena
Action—write
Object—book

In passive voice, the verb emphasizes the action rather than the subject.

Example: Today, a book is going to be written by Jill and Gena.
    Active can invite a reader into your story, while passive can tell a story to the reader. Both have their purpose and place.

Your assignment: Write roughly 250 words for your novel.

Bonus assignment: Keep an eye out for passive voice as you write, but especially as you edit.

DAY 255

The word "lied" has only one meaning: To tell an untruth. It is never the past tense of "lie down."

You wouldn't say: I lied down. He lied down. She lied down. We all lied down.

The word "lie," however, is a different story. But would you use "lie" or "lay," that is the question?

When referencing the action of reclining in a horizontal position, "lie/lying" works.

If you are putting something else down, you would go with "lay/laying."

"Lay" needs an object for the action. The something else you're laying down. "Lie" does not need an object for the action, because you—or whoever—is performing the act of reclining.

Your assignment: Double your daily word count! Write roughly 500 words for your novel.

DAY 256

Wondering whether or not to write with a pen name? That is a personal decision, and you'll have to make it sooner rather than later. There are pros and cons to both options.

We're going to explore the reasons to use one.

The first benefit is the ability to keep professional identities separate. For instance, if you're an elementary school teacher but also a horror writer, you may not want your two worlds colliding.

GENA: I opted not to go with a pen name. (Blaze Champagne, anyone?) When I first started writing with a goal of publication, I had two little babies. By the time my first book hit bookstores, both kids were in elementary school. Because I write sexy romance novels, a handful of moms decided I "worked in the porn industry," and their children were not allowed to play with mine. I attended a field trip and oh man, if those moms could have stoned me, they would have done it. I guess their snide insults were enough, though. By that point, I had toughened up. A windfall of negative reviews will do that to you. And you *will* get negative reviews. Everyone does, even your favorite authors. But that's a lesson for another day. When my kids got older, other kids took my books to school to read the sexiest passages aloud in front of everyone. If I could go back, I would use a pen name simply to spare my children the teasing.

A second benefit is helping you maintain your privacy. A true blessing! A five second search on the internet can yield the names of your family members, as well as where you work and live. For your sense of safety, you want fans to make contact on your terms.

Also, in some genres, males sell better. That's just a fact. In other genres, women sell better. Some writers will give themselves a more masculine or feminine name, depending on their needs. Some will give themselves a neutral name.

Just be aware: When using a pen name, your two worlds can accidentally blur together. Double check that contracts and tax information reflect your LEGAL name. Otherwise, consider using your pen name in all other communication. Sometimes editors and professional acquaintances will slip up and say your legal name on social media or public gatherings.

Your assignment: Write roughly 250 words for your novel.

DAY 257

Something we are asked quite a bit is how to format dialogue tags. Here are examples of common mistakes.

Wrong: "I'm writing a book." She said.
Wrong: "I'm writing a book." she said.
Correct: "I'm writing a book," she said.

When adding a dialogue tag, end your dialogue with a comma, a quote mark, *then* the tag. You only use a period if you are not adding a tag.

Wrong: "Are you writing a book?" She asked.
Correct: "Are you writing a book?" she asked.

When using a question mark, do not capitalize the speaker's pronoun.

Your assignment: Write roughly 250 words for your novel.

DAY 258

JILL: To tell you the truth, this was going to be a much longer entry. I had written a lot of stuff (in my mind) about watching my children overcoming procrastination or discussing regret for the things left undone.

But really, what are you and I both waiting for?

Write.

Now.

Write now, right now! Tomorrow, we'll both look back at yesterday and smile.

Your assignment: Write roughly 250 words for your novel.

DAY 259

REFLECT AND CATCH UP

There are a million ways to write a book and a million ways people will tell you how to do it. The best advice I ever got was to listen to everyone, then take what parts I liked to try to use for myself. If they worked, great. If they didn't, look for something else. Because at the end of the day, there's no *right* way to write a book. There's only *your* way. I've written over a hundred books without plotting a single detail. That's what works for me.

I sit down every day and write. I used to have a quota of pages— 20 a day. Writing 5 days a week, that's 100 pages in a week. I did that for over a decade with great results. However, recently I switched to meeting word count instead, and I'm actually getting more writing done each day. So my second piece of advice is to not get too set in your ways. Always be willing to try something new, be it writing a new genre or just changing up how you write slightly, because you never know what kind of rewards it can bring.

–New York Times bestselling author Donna Grant

DAY 260

In the first weeks of *All Write Already*, we challenged you to write different events that have affected your main character in the past. Have you included parts of that backstory? Have you connected it throughout the story, showing how it affects him/her?

Did you change your mind as you got deeper into the story and developed a new backstory as you wrote your tale? Is this new backstory reflected in the beginning of the book? If not, write yourself a note, so you'll remember to fix it later.

If you are writing a standalone novel, remember to resolve any remaining backstory issues by the end of the book. If resolution is your goal, of course.

Your assignment: Double your daily word count! Write roughly 500 words for your novel.

DAY 261
WILL I HAVE TO DO THIS EVERY TIME?

Reading about RANGE and SEARCH and character interviews and world building, you may worry that you must do this kind of detailed pre-writing for absolutely every book. Don't. Like all other skills, the more you write the better you'll become. Most likely you'll internalize themes and tropes. Soon, you may be riffing ideas like an accountant cranks numbers, the skills to have your characters arguing and battling against hard choices at your fingertips.

The more you write, the more you'll notice your strengths and weaknesses as an author. Are readers loving the banter you create? Did your editor suggest adding more depth to your world building? With more books written, you'll have a better understanding about where to focus your learning.

The number one way humans learn is through repeated exposure. (We'll talk more about learning styles in the weeks to come.) But humans should also be lifelong learners. Always challenge yourself to keep your skills fresh. Learn when to listen to others about your story and when to ignore their suggestions. What will make your story better and what is merely their personal preference? Tastes change, styles change, we change.

Your assignment: Write roughly 250 words for your novel.

DAY 262

What is the difference between "show" and "tell," and how do you fix it if you've got a problem?

Showing is when you let your readers see/experience events as they unfold. Readers are in the moment with the characters, feeling what they feel, seeing what they see. Telling is when you explain something that happened or is happening.

There is a time for showing and a time for telling. For example, if you're wanting to convey a quickness of time, you could say "Three weeks later." No one wants to read about three weeks of boring stuff as they wait for the action to start. If you are writing an action scene, you'll lose a sense of immediacy and urgency if you tell it rather than show it.

Usually the time for showing occurs more often than the time for telling. (Or should.).

Telling: I'd never been hurt so badly.
Showing: Hurt seared me.

Stated emotion is often a sign of telling instead of showing.

Your assignment: Write roughly 250 words for your novel.

DAY 263

When used as a verb, the choice is usually 'affect,' which means to influence, impact or change.

Effect is most often a noun, and points to the thing that was influenced, impacted or changed.

How did *All Write Already* affect your writing?

What effect did *All Write Already* have on you?

If you can't recall which to use, see if "impact" "influence" or "change" work in your sentence.

Your assignment: Write roughly 250 words for your novel.

DAY 264

We've all done it. We've written a sentence only to pause and wonder whether we're supposed to use "which" or "that."

The short and sweet answer: The clause preceding "which" or "that" is the determining factor.

The basic rule: If the clause clarifies the meaning of your sentence, use "that." If the clause can be deleted and the meaning of the sentence remains the same, use "which."

Your assignment: Write roughly 250 words for your novel.

DAY 265

WRITE LIKE A CHAMPION

JILL: I grew up watching sports (not playing—yuck) and you can't find better motivational sayings than the ones in athletics. The advertisements around sports can be pretty amazing, too.

Of course, you need a ton of motivation when there's a good chance you're going to fail. Two teams meet; one will win, one will lose. Those are terrible odds. Only one team takes home the championship trophy after March Madness. The rest have a sad ride home. With those kinds of stats, self-doubt creeps in, so coaches and players need some stellar motivation.

Both the University of Oklahoma and Notre Dame have a sign in their locker room that they take to away games. It simply states—Play Like A Champion Today. Players touch (or often smack) the sign on their way out to the field to remind them why they are there.

I have never met a writer (or anyone for that matter) who doesn't have at least a little self-doubt. When you first begin writing, phrases like "You'll never be as good as XX" or "Do you really think anyone will ever want to read this?" float through your mind the moment you pick up the pen. As you become more seasoned, you might experience the always pleasant "This will probably get rejected, too".

It doesn't stop when you become published. Then it's "This won't be as good as your last book" and "Your agent will drop you." Every 1 or 2 star review or bad comment you stumble upon will add fuel to the fire.

And that's your internal editor acting up again, being the worst kind of jerk. I used to get up at 5:30 every morning because I believed the internal editor just wasn't awake that early.

Why does self-doubt have to creep into everything? Cobbled together from dozens of articles I've read over time, my personal view is insecurity is survival at its most basic. Your mind is preparing you for all that can go wrong so you can be aware, plan, prepare and survive. (Thank you, self doubt!) You've seen the danger, now it's fight-or-flight time.

Only our project isn't a charging mastodon, so sometimes that fight-or-flight instinct doesn't engage and we're stuck in self-doubt. Here are a few things that have worked for me:

1. Recognize doubt for what it is–part of the process–and move on.

2. Remember what made you excited about your project in the first place, harness that joy.

3. Create a motivational ritual.

Now normally, I'm against having writing rites because we can use them as excuses. "Oh, I can't write today because I didn't drink my special coffee." But I have a little sign near my computer that says 'Write Like A Champion.' If I'm writing in a notebook, I usually jot it down somewhere. *Today I will fight the mastodon. I will write like a champion.*

Now go WRITE LIKE A CHAMPION!!!

Your assignment: Write roughly 250 words for your novel.

DAY 266

If You Build It, Will They Come?

- If you are constructing a whole new otherworld, you can utilize SEARCH and RANGE to help, by treating the world like a main character. Because it is!
- Ask yourself questions about the world. Create a detailed history. Wars, famines, trials and tribulations coupled with celebrations, victories, and holidays. Relatable events, both good and bad.
- Think beyond the physical and what is seen. What is the beating heart of this world?
- Currency? Dress? What is revered? What is despised?

DAY 267

Earlier in *All Write Already*, we challenged you to create hard choices for your characters. Let's do a checklist.

- Have you given your main characters a choice?
- What about the villain/antagonist/monster?
- Did you show the ramifications of those choices?

Your assignment: Write roughly 250 words for your novel.

DAY 268

THE BODY FUNCTIONS

Bodily functions are real, y'all!

Characters need to brush their teeth and shower just as much as they need to eat. But how much do you tell/show and how much do you leave out? A lot of times, a simple mention will do.

GENA: One of my personal pet peeves—characters who kiss when they first wake up, without brushing their teeth. Yuck! The thought of morning breath can rip me out of a story faster than anything. I mean, I know what my mouth tastes like, and I would NEVER share it with another. In my books, if there's a reason the characters can't brush their teeth before I need them to kiss, I come up with a method for pre-cleaning their mouths. Magic. An immortal ability. A hero and heroine who got out of bed an hour before to sneak brush their teeth. There are many ways to circumvent a pet peeve and remain in the story.

JILL: In *The Wrong Bed: Naked Pursuit* my characters wake up hand-cuffed together with no memory of what happened. I wrote a fairly elaborate scene on how they went to the bathroom while bound. My editor suggested I touch on it briefly instead and then move on. She was right. If I hadn't moved on, my readers would have wondered how they were jumping over railings and running down the sidewalk, rather than staying in the scene. It didn't have to be a whole big thing.

Your assignment: Double your daily word count! Write roughly 500 words for your novel.

DAY 269

How can you tell if a scene you've written is boring? We have some tried-and-true tips!

- After you write the scene, read over it. Did you want to gloss over anything as you read? If so, take another look and see if those snippets can be cut.
- Did you expound on a topic that has no real bearing on your plot or characters? Consider cutting.
- Have you repeated the same information in several places? Which references can you cut or shorten?
- Does the scene further the plot? Does it teach the characters anything? What about teaching the reader anything about the characters?
- Was the dialogue stilted and boring and mirror elevator conversation. "Good morning." "How are you?"
- Did you over-share? While we need details to set the scene, knowing if the characters had eggs or cereal for breakfast might not be a necessary one.
- Don't be afraid to cut or trim when necessary.

Your assignment: Write roughly 250 words for your novel.

DAY 270

EMOTIONS AFFECT PRODUCTIVITY

A quick internet search yields dozens of articles on how emotions affect performance in the workplace. Feeling unsupported or anxious can make writing more difficult, decreasing your productivity.

Identify who or what is toxic for you and your writing.

Consider creating a writing nook, a private space where you can decompress and focus. For some, this is a completely clean surface. For others it involves pictures and scattered mementoes.

Your feelings and emotions are important. Celebrate the good stuff and be sad about the disappointing stuff. Seek professional help when needed.

When you can, use your emotions to your advantage. Experienced road rage on the drive home? Now's the perfect time to dictate that argument scene. Just watched a commercial with puppies that made you cry? Grab that notebook and jot down how your skin felt, how your body reacted, and what you did to quiet or encourage the emotion. This is why writing can be so emotionally wrenching.

JILL: I wrote *SEALed and Delivered* (soon to be rereleased as *Sworn to Duty*) during one of the most difficult times of my adult life. To this day, whenever I look at the cover, all those emotions come crashing back. Yet, readers tell me it's the book that made them pick up the next.

Your assignment: Write roughly 250 words for your novel.

DAY 271

Buy your domain name as soon as possible.

JILL: I actually have two domain names: jillmonroebooks.com and jillmonroe.com. When I first began writing, someone had already purchased jillmonroe.com and kept it parked for several years while doing nothing with it. Eventually it went up for sale and I grabbed it as soon as possible.

Purchasing your domain name means you have money in the game now. Things just got real. Well, realer. Finish your book and don't let that money go to waste!

GENA: Start posting now to help build your audience reach. Post updates about your writing progress. When you finish a rough draft, slap up a picture of the words "The End" on Instagram. That's inspiration for another writer! Make connections now.

Use hashtags such as #amwriting and #amwritingromance (or whichever genre you're writing).

Don't forget about possible pen names. Grab your social media pages there, too.

Your assignment: Write roughly 250 words for your novel.

DAY 272

Have you ever been on a picnic when someone says, "Good thing it's not raining?" Argh! Why would they tempt fate that way? It's for sure going to rain now. That's just science.

Fate loves to twist and intervene, right? That's why we have phrases like "As fate would have it" and "Don't tempt fate."

Have your characters tempted fate yet? Should they?

Have they left something to fate? Should they?

Do they believe something is a fate worse than death? Should you give that something to them?

In real life, no one's fate is sealed...should your character's?

Your assignment: Write roughly 250 words for your novel.

DAY 273

REFLECT AND CATCH UP

Signing up for Instagram, Twitter, and Facebook I expected. Creating author accounts on Bookbub and Goodreads I forgot about until a reviewer reminded me. Don't make my mistake.

–Molly Jarrett

DAY 274

JILL: As a former educator, I'm fascinated by learning styles. While research is mixed, there is some belief that identifying and understanding a child's learning style helps them excel in the classroom. Touching base with your own style may create an environment that helps you get words on the page.

According to Howard Gardner of Harvard College, there are 7 learning styles. Most of us use a combination of them, but usually end up favoring one over the others. There are many online quizzes you can take to determine your style, but for our purposes, ask yourself these questions:

- Do I get inspiration from looking at images online or out of a magazine? Do I create collages of my characters? (Visual)
- Do I create a playlist that inspires my scenes and/or characters? Do I like music playing in the background as I write or must it be completely silent? (Auditory)
- Do I speak aloud as I write? Does overhearing a conversation spark ideas for me? (Verbal)
- Must I touch everything? Do I like to feel the silk before I can write about it? Or physically visit the park or museum to fill in the gaps? (Physical)
- Do I enjoy creating elaborate storyboards, breaking down and piecing together every part of the story with loads of research, grids, character charts and outlines? (Logical)
- Do I prefer collaborating with others, bouncing ideas off a partner and working together to produce a project? (Social)
- At my core, do I believe alone time is the best time, and I'm at my most productive by myself? (Solitary)

You can read more about the theory of multiple intelligences in Howard Gardner's *Frames of Mind: The Theory of Multiple Intelligences.*

Your assignment: Double your daily word count! Write roughly 500 words for your novel.

DAY 275

If you are a visual learner, you probably prefer your office area to be attractive, neat and clean. You might also really enjoy color-coding things like plot and characterization as an organizational tool. White boards and highlighters are your friends.

When setting a scene, describing objects by sight and color may be easiest for you. Challenge yourself to describe the texture of an object, too. Instead of focusing on the brilliant blues of a flower, try to notice how your other senses respond, such as scent and touch.

As descriptive imagery might be most important to you, be sure to pay attention to your character's internal thoughts and narrative, and balance your descriptions with characterization and plot. Index cards can act as visual reminders for these things.

If you're trying to conquer a new-to-you concept like marketing or world building, you might be better served seeking a video to reinforce what you've read.

When you are not a visual learner: Collect color descriptions by looking at the names of paint colors on swatches at the paint store. You can get clothing ideas from catalogues. Online photos might spark the perfect words to describe your character's physical appearance.

Your assignment: Write roughly 250 words for your novel.

DAY 276

Reading your manuscript aloud, especially the dialogue, might be your favorite thing to do. You may also catch things more easily if your computer is the one to read back your words. Music might help you get in touch with your emotions more easily than simply thinking about it. Keep a running list of songs that put you in a happy mood or remind you of that broken heart so when you need to dig in a particular well, the titles are at your disposal.

On the flip side, you may need total quiet or a fan to block out distracting noise.

If you are trying to learn a new-to-you writing or career concept, listening to a podcast might be the fastest way you digest the information.

You probably love titles and playing around with words in fun and unique ways. Alliteration? Pile that on! If you come across a plot problem, consider removing that plot device altogether.

When you are not an auditory learner: The tone of a character's voice conveys a lot of information to the reader. Remember to describe voices and the sounds around your character when they first enter a scene. Pay attention if you've accidentally written sentences that rhyme.

Your assignment: Write roughly 250 words for your novel.

DAY 277

VERBAL LEARNER

For you, speaking out loud as you write might be the key to getting words on the page. When learning a new concept for your hobby or career, listening to an audio book or talking to a professional might be best for you. Jotting down the concepts in your own words or creating outlines will help. Teaching someone else the material might seal the idea in your mind.

Like an auditory learner, if you come across a plot problem, try removing that plot thread from your story. Does the book work without it? Tell yourself all about your characterization and plot: the main character goes to the bank and *this* happens and *then this* happens.

Dialogue might be your favorite thing to write, so make sure you take time to add any necessary speech tags and physicality into your scene. When editing your manuscript, remember to include description and narrative. Clothing and quiet moments might not be important to you, but they can be to certain readers. You love words, but sometimes your vocabulary can be arresting. Make sure your word choices enhance the story and never draw the reader back to reality. *Sangfroid?* Uh, what the what?

When you're not a verbal learner: Look for the white space on the page. Are there long stretches of narrative and introspection rarely broken up by dialogue?

Your assignment: Write roughly 250 words for your novel.

DAY 278

Have a variety of tactile objects around that help you describe how things feel to your touch. This also keeps your fingers active when you're thinking. Having a wooden, posable model found in art stores may help you capture the exact phrasing you need to describe an action. Speaking of action, don't forget to describe the quiet times, too.

Learning new concepts may require you to leave your house. Go to the park or museum to get actively involved in what you're describing. If you're drafting a police procedural, sign up for a ride along. Visit the rodeo if you're penning a western. The best part of this writing gig is that your job might require field trips!

Sitting for long periods of time might hamper your creativity. A treaddesk or standing desk might be a great investment for you, or try to write at the kitchen counter. Maybe one of those bouncy desk ball chairs will work for you.

If you're stuck on a plot idea, take a walk. Although flashcards might not be your thing, the physical act of writing them might. If anyone told you to be still, stop rocking or popping your gum while you worked—they were wrong.

When you're not a physical learner: It's still really important to stand and move around for your health. Get up and move around, shake out your hands, roll your neck and stretch your back.

Your assignment: Write roughly 250 words for your novel.

DAY 279

To challenge yourself, you might enjoy writing courtroom dramas, mysteries and suspense. Your characters might be engineers or gamers and your plots filled with abstract concepts. Now is the time to indulge in those grids and diagrams of your characters' traits. Storyboard your plot.

You may always be in pursuit of the perfect procedure for your writing. Breaking up a novel into to-do lists could be helpful. Jotting down theme and character mottos to display around your desk might keep the understanding of your characters first in your mind.

Because you're so logical, you may want to overanalyze and dwell on certain aspects of your writing or story, so think of each component—character, plot, editing—as part of a whole and that each one plays an important part of the book. If you find you're not getting words on the page, analyze how you are spending your time. You may want to make a sign: *Write it and move on.*

You understand algorithms and enjoy searching out keywords and phrases, so marketing and promotional activities could tempt you to take too much time away from your writing. All your friends might ask you to help them with their projects.

You probably love facts and figures, but don't be afraid to challenge your reader to think critically. Just remember they will need moments to breathe, to reflect. To feel. Don't cheat them by glossing over the emotion.

When you're not a logical learner: You may want to rethink plots and characters that require tons of research. You'll also want to do a double-check for plot holes. Keep a map of your world handy to help keep your world details straight. Added bonus: if you wish, you can offer the map to your readers as a free download or story extra.

Your assignment: Write roughly 250 words for your novel.

DAY 280

While you're working hard to become an author, life happens and your viewpoint will change. What you write at twenty-five will be very different from what you'll feel compelled to write at thirty-five, forty-five and so on. Stay fresh. Remain true to who you are. Don't cling to a project, rewriting, endlessly tweaking, entering contests, subbing to agents and editors, searching for validation. When a project no longer sings, let it go and move on to the next. I promise she will grab your imagination and sing just as beautifully. The ones you let go weren't written for no reason; aren't a waste of time. They become part of who you are as a writer.

–Award-winning author Stephanie Feagan

DAY 281

SOCIAL LEARNER

Writing can be a solitary profession, so you might want to seek out opportunities to connect with others. What about joining a local writers group? Perhaps consider writing with a co-author. Your critique group or beta readers may take on a special role in your life. Bounce ideas off other people. You may spend your downtime researching and ranking editors and proofers or agonizing over a decision. Social media might be your jam, but remember writing and publishing books is your ultimate goal.

You learn new concepts by attending lectures and other social events, but you can also listen to your favorite podcasters on your commute.

Decorate your office with pictures and gifts from friends and loved ones to remind you that you're loved.

You might tend to create a large cast of characters and give your main character a wide range of friends, so think about crafting your books into a series and spinning off secondary characters for their own stories. When working through your plot, envision your characters on stage, playing a role. How do they move and interact with others on the stage? See and hear through their eyes and ears.

When you're not a social learner: At some point you will need input from others. Reaching out and asking for a beta reader or securing a proofreader or editor will be something you shouldn't put off until the last minute. Make sure your main characters have a friend. Keep non-verbal communication in mind when constructing scenes.

Your assignment: Write roughly 250 words for your novel.

DAY 282

SOLITARY LEARNER

Secondary characters are more difficult for you. Promotion may be more difficult, too, because social media is not your favorite thing. Consider picking one rather than spreading yourself thin over several. When you can, delegate social media to a trusted assistant or family member.

Give yourself time to think things over. While writing in a coffee shop or library may seem like the hip thing to do, setting yourself up in a quiet place with few distractions might be your best bet.

Incorporate your personal hobbies into your work. If you love to sew or woodwork, give that same trait to a character you're not connecting as much as others.

When creating a character's RANGE, you must decide why certain things matter. Print out the results and post them where you can see them or refer to them as you write. Your characters may be prone to long paragraphs of thinking and sifting through options. Challenge yourself to balance narrative with action and dialogue. You may also be attracted to the backstory of every character. Backstory, while important, should not be your main focus; otherwise your book would have started there.

Creating and devising your own study plan is a great way for you to learn new things. You may find yourself gravitating to the self-help section of the bookstore. To motivate yourself, envision the outcome rather than the process. Create plans of action for yourself and your characters and post your goals.

Respect your own process. You may be tempted to change, thinking, "I should be able to do things this way."

Visualize that you have already written the book. Get inside your character's head the way you get into yours. Make sure you're adding in body language in dialogue scenes.

Because you tend to spend a lot of your time alone, you may know yourself and values really well.

When you're not a solitary learner: Give your main characters some alone time to think and reflect. Create a situation where their friends scatter, how will your character react to being alone? Your characters may not be as set on their goals.

Your assignment: Write roughly 250 words for your novel.

DAY 283
GO AHEAD AND STARE

Don't let anyone tell you staring off into space isn't part of your work day. We're thinking, dang it! Thinking!

Your assignment: Write roughly 250 words for your novel.

DAY 284

We all know that one person who comes into your life, workplace, or conversation and blows it up with their drama. Should this happen to your main characters? How will they react?

Perhaps the hero or heroine is the one creating all the drama and angst in the first place. Maybe they realize that they are their own worst enemy. But how will you show that kind of drama in your manuscript?

If you need help, try following these 3 steps.

1. Establish what triggers the drama earlier in the manuscript. (Unless this a new aspect to the character and will surprise him/her.)
2. Trigger it.
3. Show the ensuing chaos.

Your assignment: Double your daily word count! Write roughly 500 words for your novel.

DAY 285

Have you ever read a book that explains the mechanics of the story world page after page...after page? Information you didn't really need is given all at once. Well, that is what's called an info dump. A lot of readers will skip or skim info dumps. How do we know? Because we do it, too.

Save your readers the trouble and aggravation. Ask yourself: *What information is vital in this scene? What can be parsed out as the story progresses?*

Your assignment: Write roughly 250 words for your novel.

DAY 286

You can link character emotion to different parts of your novel.

Setting: A place they love or hate, for whatever reason.

Memories: The good, the bad and the ugly.

Conflict: Readers can relate to being at odds with someone else.

Other characters: Again, the good, the bad and the ugly.

You can link your character's emotion to anything, really. Emotions draw your reader in, connecting them to your characters and story, keeping them involved and invested until the very last word. Readers like to see beloved characters succeed. On the other hand, they want to see despised characters punished.

Your assignment: Write roughly 250 words for your novel.

DAY 287

REFLECT AND CATCH UP

I wish I had taken more time off. Writing is hard work. This business is so competitive and there's so much pressure to get books out there. After a while it takes a toll. Don't feel compelled to write every day. Take time to enjoy life. Take vacations, take naps, hang out with friends and family or just stare up at the ceiling. Time away from the work refills the creative well. The writing will be better—and more enjoyable—if you do.

–New York Times bestselling author Jaci Burton

DAY 288

THANK YOU FOR THIS FAILURE

There's a million quotes about learning from failure, always persevering, and getting back on the horse. But it still sucks to fail. You can only make it suck less.

The reality of this job is that you will face failure no matter where you are in your career. Be forewarned. There will be rejections and bad reviews and editors asking for complete rewrites.

So, to circle back, here's what you can learn from failure:

Creativity: *How can I turn this failure into a success?*

Determination: *I'm gonna show them!*

Reveals your depths: *Wow, I can do this. I can do anything.*

Wisdom: *Okay, now I know that didn't work. I'll try something else.*

Acknowledge the failure, glean what you can from it, and keep writing. Each failure is a stepping stone on the path to success.

Your assignment: Double your daily word count! Write roughly 500 words for your novel.

DAY 289

PLAGIARISM

Lifting words straight from another writer to pass off as your own is theft. Almost every year a new plagiarism scandal breaks out. It's not fun to realize someone has siphoned off of your hard word to sell as their own. Respect the labor of others.

(Please note that Gena and Jill are not lawyers. They can only offer opinions. If you have questions about plagiarism, seek professional guidance from an attorney.)

Some writers allow other authors to dabble in the worlds they've created. This is a type of fanfiction, but the original author is always agreeable and paid.

Roxanne St. Claire's **Barefoot Bay** series is a perfect example of this. Contracts had to be signed, and contractual obligations had to be met. Not all authors or publishers allow this, however. Do your homework before writing in another author's world!

Also, don't allow your non-fiction research to slip into your fiction book. Just like in high school, you must process this information and write in your own words. Specific research should be credited in an author's note.

We'll use Gena's **Lords of the Underworld** series as an example. If you took her first book from the series, *The Darkest Night*, then changed the character names, jobs and physical description to fit your characters, that's plagiarism.

Now, you can be inspired by ideas within *The Darkest Night,* and that's wonderful. You may really like the "band of brothers" aspect or possession by demons, and that's totally fine. Gena did not invent either trope, nor is she the only one to use it. Feel free to run with it!

When *can* you retell someone else's story? When that story is in public domain. Retelling classic stories based on folktales, fairy tales, myths and legends is not considered plagiarism. But you cannot take someone's unique idea and tell it in your own words. You cannot take someone else's characters, craft your own story, and sell it either. That violates the other author's copyright.

Many authors stop reading all together so they won't accidentally lift an idea or passage, and that's a shame because most likely reading is one of your favorite pastimes, or you wouldn't be writing. When it comes to inspiration, keep these words in mind: Deliberate, Unique and Original.

Are you deliberately copying from someone else's worlds, characters and words? Are you presenting your world, characters and words in unique and original ways?

Your assignment: Write roughly 250 words for your novel.

GRAMMAR BASICS: NOUNS

JILL: Gena and I met while working on a writing contest sponsored by our local RWA chapter. I think between the two of us, we've read hundreds of first chapters. We've also talked with editors and agents about their grammatical pet peeves. While we are not giving grammar lessons here, we *are* sharing pitfalls writers can avoid.

Think of grammar as the first impression you make on a reader, whether that reader is an editor or a customer who purchased your novel.

Like it or not, grammar is something you must conquer either by learning (or relearning) it yourself or hiring someone to read your manuscript for you. Readers will report your book to online retailers for grammatical mistakes and typos.

Here are the basics:

- A noun is a person, place or thing.

- An apostrophe "s" does not make a noun plural.

- Pronouns take the place of a noun (antecedent).

- Double check that pronouns are connected to the proper antecedent. Example: Gena and Jill wrote a book. She loved it. (Great, but which she loved? One? Both?)

- Prepositions take the objective form of the pronoun. 'Between you and me' is correct. 'Between you and I' is not.

Add the word "it" to your list of words to check and replace when you're editing. Sometimes "it" can be replaced by a more powerful noun.

Your assignment: Write roughly 250 words for your novel.

DAY 291

Writing and journaling may have been your fun, creative outlet before you started working to publish, but the two fail to excite you now. That's because writing is no longer a hobby but a job. Jobs can come with stresses. You might even lose your passion for creating. Why not find a new hobby to help fill your creative well and make writing a joy again?

GENA: I foster and play with dogs and cats in my free time. They bring me such incredible joy, they've become my new passion. In fact, one of my favorite things to do is write one of my animals into a story. I look forward to delving into my book and finding places to add their shenanigans.

Your assignment: Write roughly 250 words for your novel.

DAY 292

CREATE YOUR OWN DEADLINE

Why do we procrastinate? We don't know, but we'll research it later.

We kid, we kid. There's actually quite a bit of research into why humans need deadlines. We don't necessarily love them, but different online studies suggest our productivity usually increases if we have one. Some people believe deadlines kick up our fight-or-flight response while others believe they increase the impact of scarcity.

Some writers will intentionally trigger those responses by putting a book up for pre-order long before it's done, or schedule a proofreader or editor.

In this book, we've given you a deadline—one year—with one assignment a day. Each assignment is a stepping stone to help you meet your deadline.

So, go ahead. Give yourself mini-deadlines designed to help you reach your ultimate goal.

Note: If you become overwhelmed, the deadline has become a detriment, and your productivity could go down. At that point, it's time to make a hard choice. Just admitting that you're at this point is difficult. It feels like a failure, but chances are, the quality of your writing is suffering. Consider rescheduling with an outside editor, proofreader or asking for a deadline extension from your publisher.

Your assignment: Write roughly 250 words for your novel.

DAY 293

THE BUSINESS BEHIND THE WRITING

This is not a business or marketing book. But. We've seen too many friends and colleagues run into financial problems because they didn't know what they didn't know. So, we're going to share what we have learned. Just remember, we are not financial advisors or lawyers. If you need help, please seek guidance from professionals.

The following are tips we've picked up along our publishing journey:

- When you begin making money, think about putting aside 25% of that for taxes. Unlike other jobs, the taxes do not come out of your check automatically. Truly, the cost of self-employment taxes can be high and shocking.
- Designate a file both physical and electronic for business expense receipts. Keeping these handy and in one place will save you time and stress come tax time.
- Make a note of your car's mileage on January 1st. If you use your car to drive to conferences or other business related excursions, you may be able to count mileage on your taxes. Note dates, and trip miles as well.
- One general business thought is to sink roughly 10% of profits back into your business, covering websites, postage, domain name registrations, promotional costs, etc.
- Treat yourself upon occasion.
- Know that book money is never guaranteed money. You can never predict how much you'll make with any given release, because there are too many outside variables. Paying off debt when you can and saving for a dry spell is often lifesaving. Most financial advisers will advise paying down debt before anything else.

- Consider creating an LLC. The laws vary from state to state.

Once again, we want to remind you that we are not financial advisors or lawyers. If you have questions on this topic, seek professional counsel.

Your assignment: Write roughly 250 words for your novel.

If you want to be a professional author you need to approach the career like you would any other job. Research the writing profession. You can begin by reading: *Bird by Bird* by Anne Lamott, *How to Get Happily Published* by Judith Appelbaum, and *The Writer's Market*. Ignore the romanticized idea that says being an author is something magical and mystical – that you lounge around waiting for your Muse to whisper in your ear, or for your dreams to coalesce, and then you're simply the vessel through which all the stories flow. Being an author is a job. Writing is work. Treat the career with the respect it deserves. Period.

–*New York Times* bestselling author PC Cast

DAY 295

EPILOGUES: ARE THEY NECESSARY?

We are reaching the end of our writing days. How much of your rough draft is written? Have you finished? Do you think the story will require an epilogue?

If you ask ten writers about their opinion on epilogues, you'll get twenty different answers. Some people love them, because they can offer one more note of happiness to the ever after. Some hate them, suggesting that the writer should have proven there's a happily ever after or a happily for now, or tied up every loose end and subplot by the last chapter. Others believe they are unnecessary unless you are teasing readers with a glimpse of the next book.

As the author of your tale, you must decide whether or not an epilogue is necessary. Our stories have both had and not had epilogues. It always depend on the story.

Before you write an epilogue, ask yourself two questions:

1. Should this information be incorporated into earlier chapters?

2. Would your time be better served moving onto the next book? If the answer to those questions is yes, then you might want to rethink the epilogue.

Your assignment: Write the required number of words to finish your book within the next 6 days. To do this, you must first figure out how many scenes you have left to write. So, instead of worrying about word count, you're going to write by scene for the next 6 days. You'll need to divide the number of scenes by 6 in order to know how many scenes you need to write each of the next 6 days.

You can use this week as practice for meeting publication deadlines!

DAY 296

An adjective describes a noun. Most native English speakers don't consciously realize it, but there is an order to how we use our adjectives. The order can get really refined, and if you're curious, we encourage you to research further. For our purposes, the order of adjectives go before a noun. Like this:

Amount/ Size /Age /Shape /Color /Noun

Beware of stacking too many adjectives in a row, however. When adjectives are lumped together, they can lose impact.

Your assignment: Write your required daily word count.

DAY 297

PROFESSIONAL JEALOUSY

At some point, you will probably think another author is better than you. Or maybe you'll wonder why so and so has all these amazing things happening to them. They might even be living your dream, while you're still struggling. It happens to all of us.

The thing to remember is that another author's success can lead to more sales for you. When *Twilight* and *Fifty Shades of Grey* hit it big, the sale of other vampire and BDSM books skyrocketed!

JILL: I prefer to look at the careers of other authors as benchmarks. Am I where I should be in my career relative to other writers? How many series do I have in comparison? Are we promoting ourselves at the same level with blogs or reader events? Are they foregoing social media to write more words? Should I?

The fact is, you and I can't write all the books. There must be others. Think of it like adding a new pet to the household. You don't stop loving your old pets. No, your love grows to include the new addition. Along the same vein, your readers have a place in their heart for a multitude of authors.

At the end of the day, when I stop focusing on others, magnifying what they're doing, how their careers are progressing, if they're deserving, etc., and start focusing on my own journey, I'm much more productive and happier with my place in life. Am I the person I want to be? Am I doing everything in my power to succeed? That's where my satisfaction originates.

Your assignment: Write your required daily scene(s).

DAY 298

Sometimes you can include backstory or a company's history in dialogue. This can help prevent an information dump.

JILL: In *Share the Darkness (soon to rereleased as Sworn to Protect)*, I wanted to convey that my character Hannah hadn't put down roots or bothered to make her workspace personal. Her reasons for needing distance become clear later in the book, but here is how I used dialogue to share this info. Below is a snippet:

> "Take a peek at your office. Where are the pictures? Where's the dead plant? You don't have a single doodad on your desk. You're also the only person who's left all those silly inspirational sayings on the wall."

> "I kind of like them."

Your assignment: Write your required daily word count.

If we had to guess, we'd say proofreaders and editors wished authors knew more about misplaced modifiers and dangling participles.

The noun is the life of the party, err, participle.

Participles are modifiers. Like adjectives, they need to modify a noun. A dangling participle is a participle that has no noun to modify.

Sometimes it's not a good time to dangle.

A modifier describes or clarifies a detail about something in your sentence. A dangling modifier means that something is not modified clearly in the sentence, usually because that something—the subject—is left out. Dangling modifiers are not your friend.

Wrong: Writing the book, a cat sat on my laptop. (Who wrote the book? Not the cat. The one writing the book is missing from the sentence.).

Right: A cat sat on my laptop as I wrote the book.

Your assignment: Write your required daily word count.

DAY 300

THE END

If you haven't finished your draft already, chances are good you are far enough along to finish today, even if you have to do a series of writing sprints—writing for short bursts of time, allowing zero distractions, then taking a break before writing again.

Just remember, the end of your novel is just as important as the beginning. The end can help set up your next book, or leave your readers dying for more or—yikes!—ruin the entire story.

- Have you tied up every loose plot thread?
- Have you addressed every issue you brought up?
- Did you stay true to your theme?

And what about your last line? It is as much a hook as your chapter enders?

Your assignment: Finish your rough draft!

Bonus assignment: Brainstorm 3 alternate last lines for your book.

DAY 301

REFLECT AND CATCH UP

Congratulations! You have finished your rough draft. Today is a day for celebration. And sleep. You have accomplished an incredible feat!

Focus. Magnify. Accomplish. Triumph!

RENEW Day 1

Congratulations, guys! You have completed your first draft! This is a major accomplishment, and we are so proud of you. We hope *you* are proud of you, too. Not many people understand how difficult it can be to complete an entire manuscript, but we do, so take a bow.

Now. What's the first thing you do after you type *The End*?

Answer: RENEW!

R - Review and Release Stress
E - Enjoy
N - Need
E - Engage
W - Wakeup

GENA: Once I finish a book, I like to set up a "nest." I gather all the things I require: alkaline water, snacks, my iPad, my laptop, a notebook, pen, my phone, and a crapton of dogs and cats. We all pile into bed and I read, play ridiculous games, and binge all the shows I missed while I lived in my office, chained to my computer and remember what it's like to feel human.

JILL: Without question, the first thing I do is take a nap! During that last push to finish my manuscript, I'm often working until the wee hours of the night and going on very little sleep. I have "rewarded" myself with a nap since college, and it's something my family expects.

Let's break down RENEW.

R – Review and Release Stress. While you worked on your manuscript, chores, errands and other things may have piled up. These little details build and nag, creating a stressful background. Now's the time to catch up. Make that phone call, research whether to change streaming services, throw out the expired food in the fridge. Whatever you've put off, get those off your to-do list now, so you'll go into the editing stage of your manuscript with nothing else to worry about.

E – Enjoy. You've buckled down and used your entertainment time to work. Why not have a little fun? You can catch up on your favorite show, hang out with your friends, or window-shop. Whatever you prefer! Maybe you like to reward yourself with cheesecake or maybe you've been living off junk food and need to reintroduce veggies to your diet. This is a great time to treat yourself.

N – Need, both physical and emotional. Take a look at what you need. Even if you achieved eight hours of sleep a night, writing a novel is still physically and mentally taxing, so take a moment to consider what you require going forward. You have probably been sitting for hours at a time, every single day. Consider going for a walk or taking a swim, or even just stretching out your tired muscles before catching up on your sleep.

It's as important to emotionally recharge as it is to take care of your physical needs. Check in with your emotions. Completing a novel is a major accomplishment, and you could be ecstatic, disappointed or simply drained by the end result.

E – Engage. You've been hunkered down in your writing cave, but now metaphorical spring has arrived, and you can take your bearish self out into the sunshine to reconnect. If you've been writing during your lunch hour, maybe it's time for drinks after work. Or go on that special playdate with your child or romantic date with your significant other. If you've fallen behind, you can catch up on calls, emails, texts and social media.

W – Wakeup. You've been in a book fog for months. Now it's time to challenge your thoughts in a different way. Read a book. Visit a museum to appreciate art or sculpture. We highly recommend reading *The Artist's Way* by Julia Cameron.

Your assignment: Don't feel like you have to take on every aspect of RENEW today. Over the rest of this week, we'll give you ideas and suggestions to help return balance to your life. For now, grab a piece of paper and draft a side-by-side column. Column one is for things you put off and need to get done. The second column is a list of things you enjoy, but missed because you were writing.

Note: Between the completion and revision of our manuscript, we like to give ourselves a few days rest. That way, we can return to it with fresh eyes. This might not suit your current wants/needs. People are different, and everyone works in different ways. What aids one may not aid another. If you'd rather wait and RENEW after the revision process and final readthrough, that's perfectly fine. Just don't forget to look over this daily guide for tips and tricks.

RENEW Day 2

Ready to RENEW? The next five assignments will follow the days of R-E-N-E-W in letter order, the method we prefer for ourselves. But. You can tackle the R-E-N-E-W days in any order you desire. Whatever works best! You can even do a little of each all five days. There are no rules.

When we complete a novel, the first thing we do is catch up on calls, emails, texts and social media. (Hopefully not *too* many calls. Shudder.) To keep ourselves from becoming overwhelmed, we ignore the total number of responses and replies that are due and just tackle them one email, one text, one online property at a time. Baby steps all the way to the end!

Bonus: The more tasks you complete before revising your rough draft, the less your brain can use as fodder for procrastination. By now you might have a love-hate relationship with writing. Sometimes we'd rather clean our bathrooms for the sixth time than draft another scene.

JILL: I like doing the easiest tasks first. There's something about successfully crossing something off my list that spurs me on to complete more. Don't be afraid to break up bigger assignments into smaller ones that are easier to handle. Make one or two of your tasks fun! Build in things you look forward to in your to-do list so you aren't tempted to trash it.

GENA: I'm the opposite of Jill. I do the most difficult tasks first, just to get them over with. (I also eat the crust before I eat the sandwich, saving the best for last.) Setting up a reward system hasn't really worked for me. After telling myself I could have a cookie when I finished writing my scene, I spent the next hour thinking, "I want that cookie. Man, that cookie is going to taste so good." I got nothing done. So, I ate the cookie while working on my scene and magic happened...which means I reward myself as I work. That. That is the method I recommend for anyone like me.

Your assignment: (If you choose to accept it.) Look at Column One from yesterday's project. Focusing on one task at a time, complete as many sub-tasks as possible.

DAY 304

RENEW Day 3

What do you enjoy doing? What makes you happy? Reading works by other authors? Binging a beloved TV show? Nature walk? Going out to eat?

GENA: One of my favorite things to do is send my family to the restaurant of my choice, so they can enjoy a nice meal together...and carry out my order. It's win/win for everyone. They get quality time together and good food, and I get to remain in the comfort of my home and bond through text. I love dining at home...in my PJ's...while my dogs stare. It's a reward tucked inside a prize, sprinkled with a whole lot of win.

JILL: One word—CHOCOLATE.

Your assignment: Keep recharging! Today might be a good day to eat your favorite foods or catch up on a TV show. Pamper yourself with a pedicure, facial or take a long, relaxing soak in the bathtub.

RENEW Day 4

There's never a bad time to take care of yourself physically and emotionally. Did you put off scheduling a yearly wellness exam? Your muscles may be cramping and your back aching from hours of sitting. Maybe your wrists are irritated and dictation looms in your future.

Our physical well-being often plays into the emotional. Don't forget to assess how you're feeling inside and out. You could be ecstatic, but also drained or even let down. You just accomplished a major goal and lifelong dream...but now you're wondering why you're not happier?

Authors often explore their own heartbreak and pain to bring those emotions to life on the page. That's very powerful. While it can be cathartic for some, it can be unsettling for others. Respect your emotions and don't be afraid to talk to someone, a friend or a therapist.

JILL: I try to take a low-impact walk everyday. But, if I'm bumping up against a deadline, I'll ditch the walk. Problem is, my body is never happy when that happens. Every time I feel sunshine on my face and breathe in fresh air, I remember how much I love that walk, how much I *need* it. Usually the relief of completing a novel doesn't hit me until a day or two later.

GENA: To help me physically and emotionally simultaneously, I'll sometimes volunteer at a shelter and walk dogs. (As I'm typing this, I'm wondering why I haven't volunteered to nap with cats. An-n-n-nd yes. Now there's a new item on my to-do list.) Not only is walking dogs good for me and the canine, petting those goofy furballs injects rainbows straight into my heart. I *may* have even brought a dog home once or twice. I said may!

Your assignment: Pamper yourself physically and do whatever you need to do to aid your emotions.

RENEW Day 5

This is the time we like to engage with those who gave us space while we were writing.

This is the second book we've written together, so we've communicated about the book's development from start to finish. Usually, we write on our own and when we're both done, we meet for lunch and order a feast, then tell each other all about the characters and plot. We won't mention the number of times we'd had to rewrite a book because the other one picked up a plot hole.

Don't forget to engage with your readers, either. Even if you haven't published a book yet, future readers are out there! You can start building your readership now, even before the release of your book, by posting updates about your progress and snippets from the book itself.

If you plan to self-publish and hope to book a freelance editor, you might want to contact one to set up a time ASAP. Check out the online pages and book dedications of your favorite indie authors–they might mention their editor by name.

Your assignment: Keep renewing! Engage! Meetings don't have to be face-to-face. Skype or have a Facetime call. There's nothing like seeing another's smile to lift your spirits.

RENEW Day 6

Is today a good day to glean inspiration from other sources? Several art galleries and museums have virtual tours available. Try that recipe that's been tempting you. Like to work with your hands? Maybe woodworking or knitting is more your style. Take a class or watch instructional videos. Turn on some music and dance. Work a puzzle or play a video game. Active play and learning gets your brain ready to tackle the revising to come!

JILL: This is the time where I'm ready to explore a new hobby. So far I've tried making candles, embroidery, scrapbooking, sewing and gardening.

GENA: My hobbies include cutting split ends, bird watching from my window, and playing a ridiculous, never-ending merging dragons game. For me, these mindless activities open the door for new ideas.

Your assignment: Renew your mind with other activities and keep recharging with active fun!

DAY 308

REFLECT AND CATCH UP

Tomorrow, we begin 30 days of editing your manuscript, tackling at least one chapter a day. Have more than 30 chapters? You might need to double up some days, doing two chapters at a time. Be sure to plan accordingly!

DAY 309

INTRODUCTION TO EDITING

We prefer to edit one chapter a day. If you edit less, you can miss repeated phrases within the same scene, inconsistencies in your plot and character growth.

All Write Already gives you enough time to edit a 100k book using the one chapter a day method. If your book is on the shorter side, this back half of work will be less intense for you, but still necessary.

After you've gone through your book chapter by chapter, then we'll have you do one final read-through. After that, your book could be ready to send out for submission–if you wish to go with traditional publishing. Or, if you plan to self-publish, your book could be ready for beta readers/proofers/formatters.

This editing stage is the time to get brutal with your words. You are no longer the artist who is simply getting your thoughts on paper. No, you are the savage curator deciding which words should stay and which get axed. Eliminate pride and rethink your love of certain phrases. From this moment forward, you should read each word with a critical eye.

We like to conduct the first pass of our draft directly at the computer with a notebook nearby.

Jill prefers to make easy changes first. She changes tenses and words as she goes, then comes back to larger items later. In a notebook, she jots down the manuscript's page number and what she needs to fix/research, gaining a special satisfaction in crossing off things she's completed.

Gena prefers to focus on the big picture items first. She writes down every major change she plans to make—and why—considers the domino effect and other changes she'll need to make to ensure the new storyline works, then makes ALL CAP notes for herself throughout the manuscript. Then she goes back to the beginning to read one chapter at a time.

So grab a notebook and pen and let's get to work!

Your assignment: Let's do a little planning first. How many chapters does your book have? For the next 30 working/writing days, we are going to ask you to edit a chapter a day. If you have over 30 chapters, however, be sure to double or triple the amount of work you do as many days as needed.

Read and edit the PROLOGUE (if you have one) and CHAPTER ONE of your novel with these questions in mind:

1. Is this word/phrase/scene important to the story?
2. Does this word/phrase/scene move it forward?
3. Will this phrasing seem awkward and rip the reader from the story?
4. What can I add or subtract to make this the best it can be?
5. Did you show instead of tell?
6. Have you created an info dump?
7. Did you catch the reader's attention and make them want to know more?
8. Is your ending hook in place?

DAY 310

GO BACK TO THEME

Every chapter should somehow reiterate the theme of your novel, even in the smallest of ways. As a reminder, the theme is the underlying message you wish to convey to your readers. It's part of your big idea, and the passion that drives you to finish.

Do what your character say and think support the point you are trying to make?

Your assignment: Read and edit CHAPTER TWO of your manuscript.

Bonus assignment: Reread the list of themes you created. Did you convey your theme all the way through your book? Did you change your theme in the middle of your story?

DAY 311

Your draft is written. You know more about the idiosyncrasies and quirks of your characters, the story world and a million more details than you did when you started. Did the setting change? Around "Chapter Three" did a much-needed sister arrive on the scene...but your main character is an only child in the beginning?

Chapter One, heck, the first paragraph, can be make or break for many readers. There are many amazing books out there, so make sure your opening grabs a reader's attention from the very first word.

Your assignment: Read and edit CHAPTER THREE of your novel. As you work, be on the lookout for repetitious was/were/are sentence construction, as well as our quick words to reconsider, then challenge yourself to find more dynamic wording. Remember to PRESS but not OBSESS.

DAY 312

SHOW VERSUS TELL: THE CHALLENGE

Did you do more telling than showing? Be on the lookout for scenes in need of showing. Take your writing to a deeper level. Show action. Show emotion. Show relationship. Don't always tell.

Tell: I felt the wind and it left me cold.

Show: The wind brushed icy fingers against my skin.

Your assignment: Read and edit CHAPTER FOUR of your novel. As you work, look for places you've told rather than shown and consider revising. Challenge yourself to use character thoughts, the five senses and dialogue to eliminate unnecessary telling.

DAY 313

Homophones are words that sound alike but have completely different meanings.

There — They're —Their

There is the store. (As in, look over there!)
    They're going to the store. (They are going.)
    The store is theirs. (It belongs to them.)

    Your — You're
    It's — Its
    Then — Than

This is your book. (You own it)
You're such an amazing author! (You are)

It's mine! (It is mine. It belongs to me.)
This book is on its 232nd day. ("Its" references the book)

Let's go then. (Emphasizes a references)
I'd rather write than watch TV. (Compares two things)

    Peek — Peak — Pique

I took a peek at his butt. (I looked.)
He stood atop the peak. (The highest point.)
He piqued my curiosity. (He roused my curiosity.)

Your assignment: Read and edit CHAPTER FIVE of your novel.

DAY 314

DEUS EX MACHINA

Deus Ex Machina is a Latin phrase that basically means an "act of God" saved your plot. This is not to say a Deus Ex Machina won't work. In a favorite movie, *The Wizard of Oz*, The Wicked Witch of the West melts from water–a surprise to absolutely everyone. But it is Oz, so it all works. Readers are more forgiving and willing to suspend disbelief. Editors, not so much.

Your Assignment: Read and edit CHAPTER SIX of your novel.

Bonus assignment: Re-examine your plot. Have you solved plot points through an act of God? You can still make this work, go through your manuscript and plant seeds, so when the solution is presented, readers aren't getting whiplash wondering where *that* came from.

DAY 315

REFLECT AND CATCH UP

You haven't written your best book yet. A while ago, I said this to another author. I vaguely remember doing so, but I say a lot of nonsense, so the words came out of my mouth and I totally forgot about them. Then, a year or so later, she posted a picture of those words on her office wall and a short caption about how she reminds herself of this before she starts each book and thanked me for the piece of advice that I had forgotten about. But seeing the picture, I realized this, at least for me, is one of the best pieces of advice to operate by. Why? Because every single time you sit down to write another book, it's an opportunity to write your best book—an opportunity to do better, to go further than, to enthrall yourself and readers, and to always, always improve. It's an opportunity to make every book your best book.

–New York Times bestselling author Jennifer L. Armentrout

DAY 316

Character GROWth CharIn real life, characters grow emotionally. They should grow in fiction, too. Well, some of them. Probably most of them.

G—gain
R—reasoning
O—or
W—wither

It is when characters grow that they earn their happily ever after.

Example: Hero starts of bitter and closed off–> by middle he's softening–> by the end he's open to love

Your assignment: Read and edit CHAPTER SEVEN of your novel.

Bonus assignment: Create a growth chart for your main characters. How do they start out in the story? How do they feel and act in the middle? How do they feel and behave by the end?

DAY 317

Look for places with longer than average paragraphs within your pages, as well as multiple pages with introspection and no dialogue. Have you provided too much information there? Can that information be chopped up, bits and pieces moved around and pasted elsewhere?

Your assignment: Read and edit CHAPTER EIGHT of your novel.

DAY 318

SAY IT LOUD!

At the revision and final edit stage of a manuscript, read the whole book out loud. Anything that trips you up or makes you pause needs to be reevaluated.

Your Assignment: Read and edit CHAPTER NINE of your novel.

Bonus assignment: Search how your word processing program can dictate your book. Play around to see what works for you. Read from the screen as the manuscript words are spoken. Maybe you can do some mundane tasks like folding towels while your computer reads your book to you. Whether this approach works for you, always always always read your dialogue out loud. If your characters are speaking in ways that no living, breathing human being would, your reader will notice. (Computers and aliens are exceptions to the rule, of course.)

DAY 319

Search And Replace Or Search And Destroy?

Your book might have a word that you've used over and over again. In Jill's book, *At the Heart of Christmas*, her editor pointed out that she'd used the word "door" over a hundred times. In Gena's book, *The Darkest King*, it was "as if." Often you don't even realize you're doing it. A critique partner, editor and/or software programs can help you find yours.

As you write more frequently, you'll discover other phrases that somehow manage to slip into each of your books without conscious thought. For Jill, it's "manage to." For Gena, it's "catapult." *A catapult of feminine fury. A catapult of lust. A catapult of frustration.*

These shorthand-phrases help you get your words on the page as quickly as possible. They are words you don't have to think about. You'll begin to recognize your shorthand-phrases, which means you can fix them as you go or highlight to fix later, as we've advised in the past. That way, you can continue to put your words on the page.

Below, we give you a list of words to rethink. Sometimes you can find a more dynamic word to use in its place. Other times you can cut the word completely. Or, you might decide that word everyone hates is actually beautiful and leave it as is. The one thing to always keep in mind: YOU ARE THE WRITER. This book is your vision and your story, and only your name will be on the cover. **You** must be happy with what's inside it. Just don't dig your heels in too deep. We all need editing, and no one can see every mistake they've made. We get too close to the story sometimes.

Note: When editing, remember dialogue is a different beast than prose. Regionalisms and quirky words—they can be necessary in dialogue, and removing them completely may make the conversation stilted and unnatural, or even flavorless.

Quick List for Words To Reconsider:
That
Just
Began to
Very
Pick up
Sit down
About to
Fixing to

Now, let's look at the word "was" for a moment and analyze its place in your manuscript.

'Was' can be a very useful verb, but not a dynamic one. Often it can be replaced with something more vivid.

But Jill and Gena, sometimes a thing just was.

You're absolutely right! That's why our advice is to PRESS but not OBSESS. When you can replace it with something stronger, do. If it works in the sentence and conveys the message you want, don't. And don't spend hours and hours trying to find a way to replace a word your readers will spend a millisecond reading.

We were writing. → We wrote.

Not a big difference, right? But what happens when the was/were -ing construction is prevalent throughout your entire manuscript? You can lose a sense of immediacy and action.

Your assignment: Read and edit CHAPTER TEN of your novel.s

The title of your book is important. A good title can spur the imagination of readers and garner sells before anyone even knows what the book is about. And if not, it enhances your cover or your killer tagline. (More on taglines later!)

GENA: One of my most memorable and beloved titles is *Alice In Zombieland*. With the title alone, readers are able to guess what kind of story they'll be getting: a paranormal/zombie tale inspired by *Alice's Adventures in Wonderland* by Lewis Carroll. But I also have titles like *The Darkest Night*. Not the most original title, and it doesn't tell you much about the story (except that it's dark) yet it works because it fits within a series name that *does* tell you the kind of story you're getting: Lords of the Underworld.

JILL: Sometimes it's just a tweak to a title that makes a difference. At first, Sharing the Darkness was the title given to my second Harlequin Blaze, but taking off the "ing" felt more right and *Share The Darkness* it became (soon to be rereleased as *Sworn to Protect*).

There might come a point where you'll need to tweak a title to fit a season. My first book *Never Naughty Enough* was originally titled *When She Was Bad*, but when the publication date moved to December, my editor suggested I brainstorm titles with the word "naughty" in it.

Your assignment: Red and edit CHAPTER ELEVEN of your novel.

Bonus assignment: Make a list of 5 titles for your book—at least!—ensuring each one reflects a different aspect of your novel. In the end, you'll only acquire one title, yes, but sometimes it takes work to come up with THE ONE. When you give yourself multiple options, you can mix and match different parts of them until you find your winner.

Some book covers have taglines while others display blurbs from bestselling authors. For new authors, snagging a blurb from a best seller might be difficult. A tagline of your own might be your best bet. The thing to remember? A tagline serves a single purpose: to tempt the reader into picking up or out your book.

These taglines should be short and punchy and fit the tone of your book. Think about your hooks, tropes and themes. What is the WOW factor that sells your book? Build your tagline around it.

GENA: In my opinion, one of my best taglines is on the cover of *The Evil Queen*. It is: *Mirror, mirror on the wall, who will perish when I call?*

Since the book is a *Little Snow White* retelling, I twisted the infamous line about the "mirror on the wall" to fit my equally twisted story.

JILL: Both *The Naked Truth* and *Naked Pursuit* were part of the *Wrong Bed* series from *Harlequin Blaze*. Wrong Bed tells you everything.

Your assignment: Read and edit CHAPTER TWELVE of your novel.

Bonus assignment: Write 5 possible taglines for your book.

DAY 322

REFLECT AND CATCH UP

Words matter. I know this seems obvious, but after as many books as I've written, I still find myself reaching for the easy and lazy (yes, I said lazy) adjective instead of something that relates to the story, that brings it alive. Words that mean something to those characters in that situation. Don't be generic!!

–Bestselling author Alison Kent

GRAMMAR BASICS: DYNAMIC VERBS

There are two kinds of verbs. (1) Dynamic—the action verbs. They are the things we do, or things that happen, and they can be used in simple, perfect or progressive forms. And (2) stative—the non-action verbs, in an unchanging state, and they can be used in simple and perfect form only.

Dynamic:

> The cat is biting my hand. (progressive)
> The cat bites my hand. (simple)
> The cat bit my hand. (perfect)

Stative:

> I love you.
> I recognize your face.
> I own a stable of book boyfriends.

Verbs can be present or past tense. Just make sure you don't accidentally shift tenses in your narrative.

Example: Gena typed her book and bows.

Typed is past tense. Bows is present tense.

The is/was/are/were sentence construction is popular because it can be easy, but too many of these in the narrative can come off sounding vague and boring. This can be a hint that you need to rewrite using more dynamic verbs.

Your assignment: Read and edit CHAPTER SIXTEEN of your novel.

DAY 324

The word "said" can be an awesome dialogue tag, because it's often invisible to readers. "At the same time, it tells them who is speaking, without interrupting the flow of your story," Gena said.

But, sometimes the word "said" doesn't convey the proper emotion, and you need to go a different route. Here are some options:

Rasped
Croaked
Whispered
Lamented
Vowed/Pleaded/Begged
Screamed/Bellowed/Yelled/Shouted
Snapped
Snarled
Growled
Babbled
Blurted

Your assignment: Read and edit CHAPTER FOURTEEN of your novel.

DAY 325

NO NEED TO RHYME ALL THE TIME

Rhymes can be distracting in fiction, especially if you are a poet and didn't even know it.

She walked out the door, her muscles sore.

He bought a pack of cards to play in his yard.

They ate a steak, and it was great.

Personally, we prefer to keep rhyming sentences to a minimum.

Your assignment: Read and edit CHAPTER FIFTEEN of your novel.

Bonus assignment: As you edit, take a second look at any sentences that rhyme. Reading your manuscript out loud or having your computer read it really helps with this task.

GRAMMAR BASICS: ADVERBS

Adverbs get a bad rap, but shouldn't. Just don't overuse them, and you'll be fine. And always double check to make sure you aren't using your adverbs as shortcuts to tell your story versus show the action. Let the reader experience the tale alongside the characters.

Using an adverb: She walked quietly.
Using a stronger verb: She tiptoed. She crept. She skirted.

Tiptoed, crept and skirted are much stronger images.
However, a more dynamic verb is not always needed or necessary. Sometimes, they can weaken or dilute the message behind your sentence.

She sang her songs with a beautiful voice. Versus: *She sang beautifully.*

He skittered his fingers over the lace. Versus: *He lightly traced the lace.*

Always ask yourself if a change improves your writing, or complicates it. On the other hand, it never hurts to vary the very.
If you've used the word "very," consider tweaking the sentence to remove.

Very quiet = silent
Very fast = warp speed
Very hot = sexy

Other likely culprits in need of adjusting include "really," "exactly," and "finally." When needed, challenge yourself to find more a dynamic verb to replace a verb/adverb combination.

Your assignment: Read and edit CHAPTER THIRTEEN of your manuscript.

DAY 327

Make sure your subject and verb agree in number. If the subject is singular, then the verb must be.

Example:

The cats purr. (Plural)
The cat purrs. (Singular)

Your assignment: Read and edit CHAPTER SEVENTEEN of your novel.

DAY 328

Some say there should be one space after a period (Jill.). Some people are correct and say two spaces after a period. (Gena.)

GENA: Jill would be right if she wasn't completely wrong. Fine! When my publisher reformats my books, they always delete one of the spaces after my periods. But I was taught to put two spaces, and now when I type the muscle memory in my fingers forces me to add the spaces without conscious thought. I'm helpless to change it. Helpless, I tell you!

Your assignment: Read and edit CHAPTER EIGHTEEN of your novel. Do you need to double up your chapters to finish your first round of editing within the next 12 days?

Note from Jill: Please notice how many spaces come after the periods in this novel. Jill right, Gena wrong.

DAY 329

Grow thick skin. There, likely, will be rejections. Lots of them. Even if you are that rare gifted and lucky author who writes a masterpiece the first time you put pen to paper and it immediately sells, there will be reviews. Taste is subjective. One reader's 5 star manna is another reader's 1 star no thanks. Sometimes the comments can border on almost being cruel or leave you wondering if they even read your book as what they're saying doesn't mesh with what you wrote. Rejects? Bad reviews? Just keep writing those emotion-filled stories and moving forward one word after the next. Keep putting yourself out there and listen to advice, take what will make you a better writer, and chuck what tears your voice down. Did I mention to just keep writing?

–Bestselling author Janice Lynn

DAY 330

FRAGMENTS AND RUN-ONS

Fragments. They are...incomplete. Incomplete thoughts.

Run-on sentences go on and on and on and on, much like this sentence is doing right now, and I bet you would rather be doing anything else than reading more of this nonsense that just won't stop. Both serve a purpose. Yep. They do. Just don't forget that they usually work best in moderation.

Your assignment: Read and edit CHAPTER NINETEEN of your novel.

DAY 331

Most fiction writers use ellipses (...) to indicate a trailing thought or dialogue. In the past, this was formatted with a space . . . and another space, but ebooks changed things. Typically, ellipses are now formatted with no space, as if it's all one thought—

I couldn't believe it...I just couldn't.

—or a space after the ellipses when the next sentence is a different thought.

I couldn't believe it... No. I wouldn't think about it.

Most writers we know love em dashes (—). Em dashes take the place of a comma when the author wants a stronger break.

Sometimes people will confuse the em dash and the en dash (-). An en dash is a replacement for the word "through," like when you are using dates.

Example: January 1-31, 2025 will be the time to focus.

Your assignment: Read and edit CHAPTER TWENTY of your novel. Only ten more to go after this, unless you have more than 30 chapters and need to double up.

DAY 332

NEXT TIME

Now that you've finished a rough draft, you should have the confidence to do it again. And again. And again.

What writing exercises worked for you? How can you apply those skills to your second novel?

For that matter, have you begun to think about what you'll write about next? A sequel or a standalone? Do you want to try a different genre now?

Your assignment: Read and edit CHAPTER TWENTY-ONE of your novel.

DAY 333

MAKE THIS FUNNIER

GENA: "Make this funnier" is a comment I've received during the editing process. Jill, too. It forces us to take another look at a comedic line and polish it until it sparkles.

Are there any lines in your story that you need to make funnier?

Your assignment: Read and edit CHAPTER TWENTY-TWO of your novel.

DAY 334

DIG DEEPER

Double check your emotion driven scenes. Do the emotions crackle off the page? Can you feel what your characters feel, or do you need to dig deeper into your well? Did you kill a character at the end? Make sure the death resonates.

GENA: I've killed off a lot of characters. What? I like to make readers cry. I use reminders of words and actions from past scenes to deepen the sense of loss. I also add reminders about something the character wanted but will now never receive.

Example: In *The Evil Queen*, the heroine and her sister enjoy playing the anti-joke game.

What is blue and smells like paint? Blue paint.

The novel is peppered with these anti-jokes. As the sister is dying, she tells the heroine, "How do you know I lived a good life? Because I lived it with you."

That bit of dialogue harkened back to their favorite game, reminding readers of their incredible bond. It deepened the loss. Evil? Yes. But also fun.

Your assignment: Read and edit CHAPTER TWENTY-THREE of your novel.

DAY 335

ANTICLIMACTIC

Ever read a book or watched a movie, your excitement building... then you reach the moment where everything comes together and you just feel let down? Chances are good the climax didn't live up to the series of events that lead up to it.

As you are reading the ending scenes of your novel, remember how your story began, the main characters' SEARCH and RANGE, and make sure the climax is worthy of them. Only then will it be satisfying.

Your assignment: Read and edit CHAPTER TWENTY-FOUR of your novel.

DAY 336

I made this goal that I'd be published by the time I was thirty. Looking back now, I realize I'd set myself up for failure because that dream wasn't fully in my hands.

This was before the wonderful rise of self-publishing, so I could put myself in the position to be published, but not truly make it happen.

I'm not sure why I latched onto thirty, but I do know it became my safety net—if I didn't get published by 30, I had an excuse to quit trying.

Have you worked up a safety net excuse? See if one of these fits:

- I don't have the skills.
- I don't know how to start.
- No one believes in me.
- It's too late.

With *All Write Already*, our goal was to help you battle against those excuses. It will never be too late. Toni Morrison didn't publish her first book, *The Bluest Eye*, until she was forty, and later won a Nobel and Pulitzer Prize. Julia Child didn't pen her cookbook until the age of fifty.

Goals can change over time, but please don't let your dream of holding your book in your hands die before giving it a shot!

–Bestselling Author Jill Monroe

DAY 337

You've written a satisfying climax. Your characters have faced and conquered their fears. Does your ending stay true to genre expectations, or do you have a logical reason for going a different route?

GENA: If I haven't overshot my word count goal and I don't plan on writing an epilogue, I like to prove my characters can sustain a happily ever after before the big climax. That way, if the story is strongest ending right after the climax, I can end it right after the climax.

Your assignment: Read and edit CHAPTER TWENTY-FIVE of your novel.

DAY 338

COLON VERSUS SEMICOLON

A colon is used when something is meant to follow it: a list, a quote etc.

We use a semicolon to join two complete thoughts; usually your word processing program will give you a hint on when to use a semicolon, so thank you, technology!

Did you notice our examples? (Wink!)

JILL: When this guy I knew used a semicolon correctly, I definitely gave him a second look. And then I married him. Punctuation is sexy!

Your assignment: Read and edit CHAPTER TWENTY-SIX of your novel.

COMMA, COMMA, COMMA

In school, you may have learned that commas are placed whenever there is a pause in a sentence. While that can usually get you by, it's not a true rule.

The most common use of commas is to separate a group of items. We'll use this sentence from *The Darkest Assassin*. See how the commas separate the colors.

His irises contained hints of blue, green, gold, and red.

Note: The Oxford comma is the comma used after the next to the last item in a list. The one before "and." In the sentence above, it is gold.

Some people use it, some people don't.

When typesetting was done by hand, this last comma was omitted in newspapers and books to save on time, money and labor. There is a huge debate in the writing community on the Oxford comma. We will not take a position, just know that either is acceptable even if not preferred. (If you happened to notice that some days use the Oxford comma and some do not, that is because one author of this book uses them and the others does not.)

If you have two independent clauses (meaning they can stand by themselves) and use the conjunction "and," "but," "for," "nor" and "yet," you'll need a comma before the conjunction.

Money was her source of life, and she always wanted more.

A comma can also follow a dependent clause—a statement that cannot stand on its own—if the dependent clause comes before the independent one.

When her friend tipped her over, the change fell out of her pockets.

The change fell out of her pockets when her friend tipped her over.

No comma needed in that second sentence because the independent clause came before the dependent one.

Finally, if your sentence begins with an adverb, use a comma. (Did you see what we did there? An example in the same sentence as the tip.)

Use commas before a proper name, the word "too" if it is used for emphasis to denote a shift in thought, and "also" if it is used at the beginning of a sentence, and after "yes" and "no" if they come at the beginning of a sentence and the following thought supports the affirmation or negation.

Commas matter:

I'm going to eat, Bob.
I'm going to eat Bob.

A comma splice is when you join two independent clauses together with a comma. This is usually done to elicit a certain tone.

Both of these clauses can and should stand alone:

She'd been a child, he'd saved her from a life on the streets.

She'd been a child. He'd saved her from a life on the streets.

The two examples convey the same message. Do they convey the same tone to you?

What if you use a semicolon?

She'd been a child; he'd saved her from a life on the streets.

Or use a conjunction?

She'd been a child, and he'd saved her from a life on the streets.

Does one incarnation of the sentence convey a stronger message to you?

Your assignment: Read and edit CHAPTER TWENTY-SEVEN of your manuscript.

Verbs, Adjectives and Their Hyphens

Phrasal Verb: This is when you tack an adverb or preposition onto a verb. "Turn down." "Log in." This phrase won't typically make sense without the context clues in the sentence. No hyphen is needed.

Compound adjective: When two or more adjectives are grouped together and come before the noun. You do use a hyphen.

His cold-blooded heart leaks hatred.

His heart is cold blooded and leaks hatred.

Similarly, ages as adjectives are hyphenated:

Age as adjective: The seven-year-dog is a lab mix.

Versus: My dog Zoey is seven years old.

A hyphen is also used with prefixes when two vowels might meet. Example: 'reenter' becomes 're-enter.'

Other hyphenated prefixes include "ex," "self" or when the meaning is changed. "Recover" is different from "re-cover."

Note: The reference standard in US publishing is the Merriam-Webster Dictionary.

JILL: When I'm really stuck, Mignon Fogarty aka Grammar Girl usually has the answer.

Your assignment: Read and edit CHAPTER TWENTY-EIGHT of your novel. We are so close to being done with our first round of editing!

DAY 341

RESEARCH: FIND AND REPLACE

Remember when you were in the writing flow and didn't stop to do research and instead just wrote RESEARCH in twenty-two point font? Or as Gena likes to do, leave a crapton of "????" everywhere, then run a search/find. Now it's time to find those spots!

Your assignment: Read and edit CHAPTER TWENTY-NINE of your novel. We finish this round of editing tomorrow, if you haven't already.

Bonus assignment: Search your document for any capitalized messages or symbols you left for yourself, fill in any missing details and conduct any last-minute research you may have forgotten. Remember, it's okay to create new things as long as they are believable. This is fiction, after all.

DAY 342

Often you may want to change a character name, town, or job. Our word processors make this incredibly easy, but we have a word of caution for you. You might ruin other words if you use "replace all."

JILL: Once I named a character Ian, but later changed my mind and went with Riley. Thanks to the handy "replace all," that task was completed in seconds. It wasn't until later that I discovered just how many words had the same three letters in a row.

Giant became Grileyt
Piano became PRileyo
Radiant became RadRileyt
Defiant became DefRileyt

Searching and fixing all of those was so not fun.

Your assignment: Read and edit the last chapter(s) of your novel. When you finish, you will have completed the first full read-through of your novel. Congrats!

DAY 343
REFLECT AND CATCH UP

Comparing yourself to others is a great way to quickly suck the joy out of doing what you love. Don't worry about what other people are writing/getting/doing. Concentrate on you and what you're writing/getting/doing and you'll not only be much happier, but much more productive as well.

–Author Kate Kessler

DAY 344

SEVER YOUR EMOTIONAL TIES WITH YOUR BOOK

JILL: In college, one of my professors invited a guest speaker, someone who worked in our field of study. This person spoke about the realities of the job. After his lecture, we got to spend the rest of class asking questions.

This is *our* time to talk about the realities of the job with *you*.

Sever the emotional ties you have with your book. Once you put it out in the wild, it is open to review. Expect it. Some feedback will be great, some terrible. Some of it will hurt your heart. Expect that, too.

It's perfectly okay to write for your own enjoyment. You are still an author. Once you publish your book, either through self-publishing or with a publishing house, you become a professional writer. There are responsibilities that come along with being a professional.

Our first suggestion is easy—Don't respond to reviews. You, the author, will never come out looking good. I know this may seem unfair, but this is one of the realities of the job. Just like elementary teachers must put up with germs and veterinarians must examine dog poop under a microscope, you have to deal with poor comments about your work. As a teacher you get loaded up with candles on the last day of school, and vets get pets and tail wags. **You** get the enjoyment of seeing your words printed on a page or pixelated on a screen, a dream many have but not everyone realizes.

Secondly, we like to caution authors not to read their reviews. Yes, it's wonderful to see lovely things written about the world you created and your talent, but you can't please every reader with every book. Is stumbling onto a soul-crushing review that will haunt you as you write your next book worth a possible pat on the back?

Okay, so you looked at the review, anyway. We'll pretend you didn't go searching for it, and that you were tagged in it (which does happen, so be prepared for that, too). This is where your author friend group can come into play. Lean on those people, commiserate with them, and keep it amongst yourselves.

Your assignment: Take some time to go over any problematic chapters that you haven't been able to get out of your mind. If you need to add new scenes to your manuscript, go for it!

DAY 345

IS OUTSIDE EDITING FOR YOU?

Have we published a lot of books? Yes.

Do we believe in editors? YES! We can become blind to our own mistakes. We can get tired of reading the same story over and over to hunt for those mistakes, our eyes seeing what we want/expect to see. Some type of outside help could take your work to the next level!

There are usually three types of editing for a book. (1) Developmental, (2) line editing and (3) copyediting.

A developmental edit looks for problems and inconsistencies with your plot and characters, but doesn't really focus on problems within your prose.

A line edit focuses mainly on the style of your prose.

Copyediting focuses on style as well as the mechanics of your text.

Depending on your budget, you may not be able to afford all three. You may not be able to afford any. Here are some alternatives.

First, there are several excellent books on self-editing. For example: *How to Polish Your Manuscript in 10 Days* by Anne Victory.

Secondly, find a critique partner or barter services. For instance, Jill will format Gena's self-published books in an electronic format, and Gena will create fun shareables for Jill to post on Instagram.

Third, computer programs such as Pro-Writing Aid and Grammarly. They come with a cost, but they can help!

How to find an editor? Look at the dedication page of books you've enjoyed. Ads in industry magazines. Good editors are often booked up in advance. It's best to get on their schedule long before you think you'll be done. It will spur you on to meeting a deadline and make sure you're not scrambling when your book is ready for an edit and your pre-order date is looming.

Your assignment: Examine your budget and the state of your manuscript, then determine how many rounds of editing you'll need. Decide what you'll hire out, what you'll skip and what you'll try to swap for.

Proofreader: Yes or No?

Our answer is short and sweet: Yes!

The reason is simple. We are extremely close to our characters and stories, and we can't always see our mistakes. Also, our minds sometimes see what they expect to see, not what is actually there.

YOU AR3 R34D1NG 7H15, R1GH7?

Here's an example of this very thing: The cover for this book had a typo for weeks that we simply did not see. That typo? A misspelling of Gena's last name. Did Gena herself catch this? NO.

By the way, we put a handful of typos and errors in this book to help awaken your internal editor. Because we're givers. And we care. Those mistakes have nothing to do with our own internal editors sleeping on the job. Honest! Maybe?

Your assignment: Research and book a proofreader if you decide to go that route. Good ones fill up fast, so you'll want to book one as soon as possible, while keeping a realistic deadline in mind.

DAY 347

JILL: In school, other students asked me to read their papers and check for spelling and grammar errors. Of course, my grammar isn't perfect. No one has perfect grammar. But I've been using ProWriting Aid for a while now and it has taught me to remain humble. We all make mistakes, and those mistakes can become invisible to us, as we've mentioned.

Also, proper grammar just "feels" wrong sometimes. For instance, "between you and me" is correct. However, most everyone will say "between you and I." Heck, even Shakespeare used this improper phrasing in *The Merchant of Venice*.

Another example of something that feels wrong is the phrase "bury the lede." Lede is correct, but many think it's lead. If you write lede, however, someone will ding you for it.

Now, when people ask me what to do when the grammar is correct but feels wrong my advice is simple. "Just write it differently." (This advice actually disappointed my husband because he wanted to know the actual rule.) The main idea is to not draw the reader out of your book and focus on your grammar. So, if you're worried about the grammar, discover conflicting "rules" or something doesn't feel right —just write it differently.

Your assignment: Do you have any last minute changes for your novel? Today is the day to make them! Tomorrow we begin the second round of editing, and we will move at a much faster pace.

DAY 348

This may seem obvious, but you've made a lot of changes while editing. Go ahead and run your spell check one more time before completing that final read through.

Your assignment: Read and edit the first 5 chapters of your manuscript, checking for flow and consistency. Hopefully, you are doing more reading than editing at this stage. If the opposite is true, don't worry. Gena edits heavily at every stage, too. Do what is best for your story!

Your Final Checklist:

- All subjects agree with their verbs.
- All sentences end with proper punctuation.?!
- All "quotations" have both opening and closing marks.
- You've checked for overused words.
- Did you end every chapter with a great hook?
- Have you answered every story questions that needed answering?
- Possessives are possessives and plurals are plurals?
- You've double checked for any kind of domino effect after making a change?

Your assignment: Read and edit chapters 6 - 10 of your manuscript, checking for flow and consistency.

DAY 350

It's okay to ignore a reader who contacts you personally. The customer isn't always right.

Look, opinions are subjective. Personal bias can make someone hate a good story. You'll get emails telling you there's too much sex, not enough sex, your book belongs in the trash, oh, and you're trash, too. Don't despair. Rejoice! You struck a nerve and made an impact. That's a good thing and far better than the dreaded *meh*.

You don't have to apologize because someone hates your work, and I hope you don't let it stop you from living your dream. Just stick with your vision and keep writing the best book you can. What's that saying? *One man's trash is another man's treasure.*

–Anonymous

DAY 351
REJECTION

At some point in your writing career, you will face rejection. Someone will decline to publish you, readers will post scathing reviews, and emails calling you a hack will trickle into your mailbox. It is the nature of the business. Authors are often considered products, like their books.

Accept it now: Not everyone is going to love your work. Not everyone will love the greatest book ever written, either.

The great thing about writing is that you can always reinvent yourself if one stream of work doesn't pay off. Write a new series. Try a new pen name. Go wide if you've been exclusive or vice versa. Use different promo. What about a new cover and back blurb?

Utilize your hooks and play up your strengths.

Your assignment: Read and edit chapters 11 - 15 of your manuscript, checking for flow and consistency.

DAY 352

SCAMS

If you aim to be traditionally published, know that money does not flow from the creator—you—to the publisher. They might or might not pay you an advance, but they should absolutely pay your royalties.

In self-publishing, you are the project manager and you are the one to hire contractors as editors, cover artists, etc. but the profits of your labor STILL flows back to you.

There are some really unscrupulous people out there who would love to steal your money. Be careful who you trust. Before giving anyone in the business money, ask around, research, and read reports from other authors. It might save your wallet.

Your assignment: Read and edit chapters 16 - 20 of your manuscript, checking for flow and consistency.

DAY 353
THE MERCH

Keep a running list of anything you make up in your stories. Yep, we're still big on lists.

- Funny sayings
- Town mottos
- Original T-shirts your characters wear
- Anything any of your characters are famous for within the pages of your books
- An animal who shows up in a scene

This will make promo easier. You can put your funny sayings on T-shirts and coffee mugs to give or sell. You can make or commission artwork, posters, shareables, teasers and so much more, to promote your book online. The animal in your book can have his own Instagram page with pictures...and probably a million more followers than you.

Basically, if you make it up, try to find a way to use it for some type of promo.

Your assignment: Read and edit chapters 21 - 25, checking for flow and consistency.

DAY 354

Your personal brand is, well, *you* the author. Your established readers will identify you by name and know what type of book you write at a glance. New readers need to get to know you.

A tagline can help! It acts as a short, punchy line—like the tagline on a book cover, only you are selling yourself as an author rather than a specific book.

Example: There's a list on Goodreads titled "Romance with bite." With that one tagline, you can probably guess they are referring to vampire romances.

JILL: Don't be afraid to change your brand tagline from time to time. Because I write in a variety of sensuality levels now, I use: Sweet or Spicy?

GENA: I write in multiple subgenres within romance—paranormal, contemporary, fantasy, retellings, and young adult—with a wide range of tones–dark, light, funny, serious, violent, sweetish, sexy–so I use taglines for my series rather than myself.
Enter the dark world of Atlantis...
Dare to open Pandora's box...
Original heartbreakers...original sin.
Love, laughter and sexy men!

Need a tagline to describe you and/or your writing as a whole? Well, first you'll need to nail down the basics about your work. Sexy, sweet? Fast-paced? Emotional? Fantastical? Quirky? Light? Dark? Snarky? Edgy? Black and white, or with lots of gray? What are your themes? What do you like best about your book(s)?

Make a list of the descriptive words that intrigue you most. Then, play around with them. Put them together. Come up with short sentences. Mix and match.

Your assignment: Read and edit chapters 26 - 30 of your manuscript.

Bonus assignment: Did you read a quote from other authors mentioned in *All Write Already*? Visit their websites and check out their taglines.

DAY 355

A TRICK TO INCREASE PRODUCTIVITY

First of all, congrats! Yesterday, you finished a second read-through of your novel. Another amazing accomplishment!

Did you enjoy your novel more or less this time? Anything left to fix?

Second, you're one step closer to beginning your second novel. We have a pro-tip to help hopefully increase your productivity. Whenever we begin writing a book, we pretend someone else has come up with the same idea and only one of us can publish it. This helps light a fire under us to get it done. And you know what? A few times, someone else has, in fact, had a similar idea around the same time.

GENA: I lost my first book deal this way. Three days after I'd sold my first two books, told everyone I knew, and announced online, the deal fell through because another publishing house had just bought a different author with a similar idea.

Never take your ideas for granted.

Focus. Magnify. Accomplish. Triumph!

Your assignment: Fix any remaining problems with your manuscript.

DAY 356

AGENTS

With the rise of self-publishing, fewer authors are seeking literary agents. To determine whether you need one, examine your options and decide which publishing path works best for you.

Usually, agents charge 15% of every dollar you make. They contact publishing houses on your behalf. They submit your manuscript to editors. Some agents maintain relationships with those editors and always know what they prefer. Agents also handle problems with the publisher if one should occur.

Plan to submit to publishing houses? You might need an agent. Some publishers do not accept unagented manuscripts. If they do, those unagented manuscripts can be transferred into "the slush pile," where manuscripts go to die. Though many books have been discovered in the slush pile, expect a long wait.

Want to know how to find an agent? Ask around. Look at the careers of authors you'd use as a benchmark. Read their book dedications. Is an agent listed? Now you know who to query. Are you affiliated with a professional organization? Often they keep records of complaints filed against them.

Follow agents on Twitter. Often they will put a call out for what they'd like to represent. Participate in #pitmad (a pitch opportunity on Twitter) and follow the rules. If PitMad is running an #OwnVoices session, and this doesn't apply to you, read and learn so you're ready for the next session that *does* apply to you.

Please note: A good agent will not charge you until they've made a sale.

Your assignment: Begin a final read through of your novel. Read the first 10 chapters. Does everything flow?

DAY 357

REFLECT AND CATCH UP

Merline Lovelace is a mentor to us both. She has always been there with encouragement and friendly advice since before we were published. With over 100 books to her name, we couldn't be more excited to share some of the wisdom she has given us over the years.
—Jill and Gena

Don't get so lost in the creative side of writing that you lose sight of the fact that publishing is a stone cold business. Treat it as such even before you put those first, brilliant words on paper. So I highly recommend that you: 1 - track every expense, from mileage to laptops to ink cartridges, organization dues and more, then deduct those expenses in your taxes. (Check out Peter Jason Riley's excellent New Tax Guide for Writers, Artists, Performers, and Other Creative People, available on Amazon). And 2 - sell yourself as well as your story. Publishers want to invest their time and dollars in writers who have more than one book in them, can meet deadlines, and won't be drama queens when it comes to edits and/or revisions. I always added a one-page bio detailing my professional background with each submission or included the information in the query letter.

–Bestselling Author Merline Lovelace

DAY 358

BACK COVER BLURB

A back cover blurb serves one purpose: to hook readers. This isn't the place for extraneous details. This isn't a place to explain anything other than why people should want to read your book. Your job? Hook them with your tropes and theme(s).

We tend to write three paragraph blurbs. One paragraph to make the reader want to learn more about the hero, one to make the reader want to learn more about the heroine, and one hinting at the plot driving them forward, ending with a hook. Always end with a hook.

JILL: I like to pack the first sentence with as much detail as possible or go with a tantalizing hook. In traditional publishing, your editor will often write the blurb with their house style. In self-publishing, you can hire someone to write it for you or write it yourself. Seek input from a trusted reader or author. Here's the back cover blurb Gena and I crafted for *Fun & Games*:

The woman who has sworn off romance finds herself trapped inside a romance novel...

Some think fate rules their lives. Others by chance. But Annalise Morrison knows who crafts her destiny–an interfering author hag. If Annalise ever finds that meddling writer, she is going to shove that keyboard down her throat. No one is going to tell her who to date, but grrr...why must Theo Griffin be so hot?

The man who's only looking for a little fun and games finds a whole lot of trouble...

Theo Griffin's down to play hero to Annalise's heroine. He's all in for any kind of action between the sheets this novel requires. That's what the hero does in these kinds of books, right? But this sexy woman entices him to ditch his plans and tempts him to give more of himself than he ever thought possible. Will he turn his back on love... or surrender?

It's fun and games until the emotions turn real...

GENA: One of my favorite back cover blurbs is from *The Darkest Warrior*. When I wrote it, I used the three paragraph structure:

He is ice...

Puck the Undefeated, host of the demon of Indifference, cannot experience emotion without punishment, so he allows himself to feel nothing. Until *her*. According to ancient prophecy, she is the key to avenging his past, saving his realm and ruling as king. All he must do? Steal her from the man she loves—and marry her.

She is fire...

Gillian Shaw has suffered many tragedies in her too-short life, but nothing could have prepared the fragile human for her transition into immortality. To survive, she must wed a horned monster who both intrigues and frightens her...and become the warrior queen she was born to be.

Together they burn.

As a rising sense of possession and obsession overtake Puck, so does insatiable lust. The more he learns about his clever, resourceful wife, the more he craves her. And the more time Gillian spends with her protective husband, the more she aches for him. But the prophecy also predicts an unhappily-ever-after. Can Puck defeat fate itself to keep the woman who brought his deadened heart back to life? Or will they succumb to destiny, losing each other...and everything they've been fighting for?

Your assignment: Read the next 10 chapters of your novel.

Bonus assignment: Read the blurbs for your favorite books. Dissect them. Study their word choices. The layout. Now, draft your book's blurb. Do you recognize tropes and themes?

DAY 359

CRAFTING YOUR ELEVATOR PITCH

Let's stay you're or stuck in an elevator with the editor of your dreams. She asks you about your story. You know you have two sentences to wow her. So what do you say? That is your elevator pitch. A short and sweet description of your book meant to hook a reader hard and fast.

GENA: My elevator pitch for my book *The Darkest Night* was: "An immortal warrior is murdered every night, only to awaken the next morning knowing he has to die again."

And here's the elevator pitch for one of my newer books, *The Darkest Assassin*: "What happens when a ruthless warrior angel falls in love with the demon-possessed beauty he's been ordered to kill?"

I used the word "ruthless" to describe the hero because it lets my target audience know he's an alpha, which is a popular trope in romance. My hook is the idea that a hardened man who might not love easily falls for the one person he cannot have, so what's his next move gonna be?

JILL: My elevator pitch for *Naked Thrill* and *Naked Pursuit* was: The Lost Weekend Series. Two couples. One very long night. Some people just can't handle dating. I followed it up with quotes from all four characters:

"If I had a dollar for every time I woke up with a naked man stretched out on the floor next to my bed, I'd have... a dollar. And who's giving out this dollar anyway, and with inflation, shouldn't it be more like five? Seriously, I really need the money!"

~Hayden Taylor, recent grad with a ton of debt

"My credit card, car keys and phone are all missing. But considering a gorgeous, naked woman just woke me up – I'll call it a win!"

~Anthony Garcia, documentary filmmaker

"Sure, I'm willing to try the whole mild bondage and handcuffs thing as much as the next girl... I'd just prefer not to do it when I'm running for my life."

~Stella Holbrook, med student

"I had my chief's orders: nothing but rest and relaxation or my sorry ass would be out of a job. But waking up in a bathtub with a gorgeous woman's head in my lap just might be the biggest rush of my life, and I'm not ready for it to end."

~Owen Perkins, smokejumper

Your assignment: Read the final 10 chapters of your manuscript.

Bonus assignment: Write an elevator pitch for your story.

DAY 360

Save your deleted scenes. You can offer them as bonus material for newsletter subscribers or prizes for contests. You can even retool them and add them to a different book.

JILL: I'm a bit of a hoarder. I admit it. I have saved every scene I have ever cut from a book. I always think I will recycle this scene into a later book. Have I? I don't think so, but there's something about deleting a scene wholesale that hurts my heart.

GENA: I've used deleted scenes as bonus material in the backs of books. I've also compiled different scenes I've written and packaged them together in a bonus book. (*Down the Rabbit Hole*, and *Kat in Zombieland*.)

That way, your work is never wasted!

Your assignment: You've now done two complete read-throughs of your book. Decide whether you are ready for the next stage. Or, does your story require more changes?

DAY 361

CREATING A BOOK BIBLE

Maybe you hope to write a trilogy, or even a long-running series. Maybe you're writing a stand-alone novel.

What if your readers fall in love with the world and want more, and you decided to turn your stand-alone into a series?

You might want to create a series bible. A document with every detail you've written about your world and your characters, including major events and outstanding questions yet to answer.

The more you write, the easier it is to forget a character's eye color, job or backstory. Details and scenes blend together, and what's original writing versus what's been added later. A series bible is an easy access fast-pass when you are writing a new novel in your series.

Your assignment: If necessary, write any outstanding scenes for your novel.

Bonus assignment: Create a list of everything you'll need to track within your book. Add the details you've already written. What a great start!

HOW TO CRAFT A SYNOPSIS

The purpose of the synopsis is to "sell" your idea to an agent or editor. Many publishers require this step with the understanding that the final version novel may stray. A synopsis will also keep you focused on the story as you move forward. Some authors prefer to write their synopsis before the book, so they have a detailed roadmap of their story. Some prefer to write it after.

JILL: I usually will stop after the first chapter or the word vomit stage to examine my idea—will it sustain a full manuscript? Am I still interested in it? How much research will it require? I may let my Internal Editor out just to put her toe in the water, not a full dive. If I want to move forward, I write a loose synopsis, lock the IE away and get right back into frenzied first draft mode.

Regardless of the tense you chose in the manuscript, synopses are written in the present. In length, the old standard was one page for every 10,000 words. However, many editors prefer a much shorter synopsis now, around five pages and even less.

JILL: I begin my synopsis with what you'd typically see as the first line of the back cover blurb. For *At the Heart of Christmas* it was:

> Hiring him could be her best idea.
> Or her worst mistake.

Next, you introduce the characters, including their RANGE and plot using what you used with the SEARCH assignment. Keep in mind tone, theme and level of sensuality within your synopsis, it should mirror your manuscript.

You'll need to mention what the characters want and need, the climax of the story, and how the book ends.

Your assignment: Begin crafting a synopsis for your story. Try to get the bare bones down. If you need an example, jump ahead to tomorrow's lesson, Day 363.

DAY 363

GENA: Because I was selling a new series and I hadn't yet written book 1, my publisher wanted to know where I planned to take the story. So, I wrote a detailed synopsis with highs and lows I expected to write about. And, while the below synopsis is how I thought I'd write the book, I ended up going a different route in the end. So, if you've read *Alice in Zombieland*, you'll find many differences between this synopsis and the actual story.

I decided to include it as an example because I wanted you to know it's okay to change your story at any point. If something you envision doesn't work, come up with something that does!

Sixteen-year-old Alice Randall is beautiful, a little shy despite the self-defense training her dad has drilled into her head, and has always felt distanced from life, as if she were merely walking around in someone else's dream. On the outside, her family appears normal. Her dad is a computer software tech whose hobbies are working out and boxing, her mom is a lawyer, and her little sister Emma is a wannabe ballerina. But her family hides a dark secret. Sometimes when her dad drinks, he rants about seeing zombies. He's always been afraid of the dark, and never ventures out at night.

Until one fateful Friday evening when Alice and her mother do the impossible and convince him to attend Emma's dance recital. All goes well until the drive home. He hasn't been drinking, but he begins to rave about the monsters on the road. The girls try to calm him down – they see no monsters – but the car spins out of control, flips, and crashes.

Alice awakens, bleeding, and manages to drag her little sister into nearby trees. She's about to go back for her mom and dad – until she sees the monsters surrounding the car, clawing and biting to get inside. She keeps her sis quiet and hidden, fighting to stay conscious herself, and help finally arrives, car headlights scaring the monsters away. Later, she wakes up in the hospital and learns her mom, dad and sis are dead.

For the first time in her life, she experiences strong emotions. No longer is she distanced. She feels *everything*. She also tastes and smells in a way she never has before, as if she had been asleep all her life, but the crash finally woke her up. She doesn't understand the change, but doesn't care. Along with her sadness and anger, she feels guilty for allowing fear to prevent her from trying to save her parents.

A few months pass while she recuperates physically, and her future is decided. Ultimately, she's sent to live with her aunt and uncle (her mom's brother). They have no children of their own, and never wanted any. The aunt sees her as a burden, and the uncle is rarely home, but because of the hefty life-insurance payout—which now belongs to Alice's guardians—they agree to keep her.

A new life begins, and with it, Alice must start a new school. She's nervous – until she walks into school for the first time and catches the eye of a boy her age. He's tall, muscled and clearly hanging with a rough crowd, but the instant their gazes meet, she sees a flash inside her mind. A flash where they are kissing. Everything around her fades, that flash becoming all that she sees, all she can think about. Until someone walks between them and the world around her kicks back into gear and she sees his friends drag him away.

She learns his name is Noah Hatter, and she sees him periodically throughout the day, but the flash never happens again. Still, she's attracted and drawn to him in a way she doesn't understand.

The next morning, he's in the same place, with the same kids, and their eyes meet. To her surprise, she has another mind-flash of kissing. Once again, someone has to walk between them to stop the vision. Before his friends can drag him away again, she looks down and continues walking to class, more confused than ever about what's happening. Is she hallucinating like her dad?

At lunch, Noah asks her if they can talk. She agrees and they head to a private corner outside. They introduce themselves, and she realizes that talking to him only intensifies the attraction she feels. This leaves her fluttery and unsure, and after several taunt pauses, where they are both staring at the other's lips and breathing heavily—standing far too close for two strangers—he asks if she's noticed anything weird when they look at each other. For some reason, he is angry when he asks this.

Does he see the kissing flashes, too? She admits that, yes, something weird always happens, but she doesn't tell him what, and she doesn't let him tell her what's weird to him. She's afraid that they won't believe each other if one goes first and the other simply says, "Ditto." So she tells him to write down what he sees on a note, and she will do the same, then they will exchange notes after last period.

After that last class, Noah is waiting outside her door. He walks her to her locker and then to her bus. Before she boards, they exchange notes. She trembles in her seat as she unfolds the paper and sees he wrote the word. *Kissing.* She isn't hallucinating, then, and her relief is overwhelming, but she wonders what's going on. How are they having those visions? *Why* are they having them?

Noah talks to his friends about what's happening with Alice. They are immediately suspicious about who she is and what she plans. They are zombie slayers, and they have to be careful. If anyone were to find out, they would be locked away and they know it. It's happened before. They've lost friends that way. So they wonder if Alice is some kind of spy. It is decided that Noah, their leader, will get close to her and find out the truth.

Noah's ex-girlfriend, Maddison Love – "Love" to her friends – is a part of the group, and she still hopes to win him back. She wants to beat Alice to a pulp rather than watch Noah spend time with her. But Noah commands everyone to leave Alice alone until he gets the answers they want. He's never been so protective of anyone, and Love suspects it's because he's falling for the stupid girl.

The next morning, Noah waits for Alice to arrive at school. He is desperate to see her. There's another kissing mind-flash. He doesn't understand how she's doing that to him, and he's determined to find out. But he doesn't talk to her right then, since there are so many people around. He heads to class and then waits for lunch. There, he approaches her once again. They go to their hidden spot outside and he asks her if she knows how the flashes are happening. She says no. They talk, the attraction deepening despite his suspicions and soon he has her backed up against a tree, his hands on her waist.

"Maybe we should see if reality is the same," he rasps.

"But . . . I don't know you, and I've never . . ."

His eyes widen. "You've never kissed anyone?"

She shakes her head. "I might be bad at it."

They kiss passionately. Noah's friends, who stayed close just in case they were needed, wonder what's going on and approach. The couple has no idea the others are there. Noah and Alice are only aware of each other. And when the friends reveal their presence, Noah fights them, reacting purely on instinct. *Protect Alice.*

Without Noah acting as her anchor, Alice falls. Seeing him fighting his friends, who are shocked because he doesn't seem to recognize them, she manages to pull herself from the fog around her brain – a fog focused solely on Noah, and stands. One touch to his arm, and he settles down. But she realizes she is now surrounded by his rough-looking friends and a pretty brunette whose glare is almost enough to kill her. Alice can't believe what just happened. She'd only meant to kiss Noah, to see if those tantalizing mind-flashes meant anything, but she'd lost track of her purpose the second his lips touched hers.

Shaking, she gathers her bag and whispers, "I'm sorry. I didn't mean . . ." She tries to leave it at that, but Noah pushes his friends aside and catches up to her. She wants to pull away, so afraid of touching him in public, but as he tenderly cups her jaw and asks her if she's okay, she can't. She likes his touch.

"We can't do that again," she tells him.

"Why?"

"I don't know you, and I would have let you . . . you know . . . right against that tree. At school! Anyone could have walked past us. And did!"

He agrees that he won't kiss her again—until they get to know each other. Then all bets are off. Alice likes this teasing side of him, and when he asks her on a date, she immediately says yes. Noah opens his mouth to say something else, but the tardy bell rings, forcing them apart.

He's waiting after her last class and offers to give her a ride home so they can talk some more. In the car, Alice – who has been plagued by thoughts of that earth-shattering kiss all day, says, "So. . . since you want to see me again, I'm guessing the kiss was . . .good for you?" He smiles slowly, and her heart flutters. They talk about the fact that neither of them have ever experienced anything like that kiss and he asks her questions about her family.

Alice is vague, and that rouses Noah's suspicion again. But he is curious about her – for himself, even though he knows he should be doing so for his friends and their safety. Ever since the kiss, his protective urges toward her have been deepening, so he doesn't push for more information. He's got to get himself under control. When his friends had distracted him from the kiss, he hadn't recognized them, and had wanted to kill them. Now he's ashamed of himself, but he can't imagine hurting Alice, even for answers. How has she reduced him to this poor state?

They see each other throughout the rest of the week, though he doesn't talk to her because he's trying to fortify himself against her appeal. His friends tell him that he's a fool for going on a date with her. That "getting to know him" must be a ploy to learn about his zombie slaying. But he doesn't change his plans. Every time their eyes meet for the first time at the start of a new day, he has a new kissing flash. And he likes it.

Alice is glad he stays away from her, too afraid of throwing herself at him and begging him to kiss her again, but she can't deny she's eager for the weekend to arrive. Even though she hears stories about how Noah and his friends are the bullies of the school, that they sleep during class, and are "losers." But she doesn't buy it. The boy who kissed her isn't a loser with no future. He's fierce, honest, and loyal.

Finally, Friday arrives. Noah picks her up and takes her out to eat. At first, he's abrupt because he's afraid his friends were right, that Alice will only want to know about his supernatural ability – every zombie slayer leader has one—and his past. Except, her questions are all about his likes and dislikes. What's his favorite color? What three items would he take to a deserted island? They talk and laugh and begin to learn about each other, and they like what they discover. He knows he should regret that he learns nothing to help his friends, but can't. He loves spending time with her. In a lifetime of war against flesh-hungry fiends, she is a light in darkness. She is soothing balm.

He drives her home. After he helps her out of the car, they both want to kiss goodbye, but can't risk losing track of the world. In the dark, bad things happen... He says he wants to see her again, and she agrees. They part, excited about the future. But when he gets home, his ex is waiting for him in his bedroom. She asks how his date went and if he got any answers. He says no and she yells at him, accusing him of liking Alice and putting everyone at risk. Then, she kisses him. He's so keyed up because of Alice that he kisses back—at first. But the kiss doesn't feel right. His desire is actually cooling, and he pushes her away. She leaves angry and jealous.

Monday morning, Love waits at the back door of the school, where the kids who ride the buses enter, and drags Alice into a hidden corner and punches her. She threatens to hurt Alice if Alice goes near "her boyfriend" again or if she tells him about the punch, then stomps away. Alice isn't afraid or intimidated – not after the fighting lessons her dad gave her—but when Love's skin touched Alice's during the punch, Alice has a mind-flash. In it, she sees Noah kissing the ex—and wearing the exact same clothes he'd worn on his date with Alice. She isn't sure how or why she had the vision, she just knows bone-deep that he kissed Love after his date with Alice. She thinks he lied about having a girlfriend, hoping to date Alice while sleeping with someone else. She thinks he's a cheater.

When she enters the school and sees him waiting in his usual play, a smile on his lips, there is no kissing mind-flash. She tries to convince herself she's glad about that and walks away. But he chases her down, concerned by her split lip. She brushes his hands away and says, "Tell your girlfriend I'm not afraid of her, and if she ever touches me again, *I'll* kill *her*."

"*Love* did this?"

"Funny. She didn't like the fact that her boyfriend was seeing someone behind her back."

"She's not my girlfriend, not anymore. I'm so sorry she hit you. I swear to you, Alice, that will never happen again. I'll take care of it."

He sounds determined and angry, but she doesn't let that sway her. "It doesn't matter." Then she laughs bitterly. "You already know I'm weird, so I don't mind telling you that I saw you kiss her. In my mind, another flash. I saw you kiss her *after* our date. And since the whole purpose of that date was for me to learn about you, I think it's safe to say that I don't like you or want anything else to do with you." She leaves him in her dust.

She's so hurt, near tears, and torn up inside. Since the accident, Noah was the one bright light in her life.

Noah approaches her at lunch with Love at his side and the rest of his friends behind him. Alice is eating her sack lunch in a hidden corner outside, and can't get away. To her surprise, Love grudgingly apologizes. Instead of replying, Alice punches her in the nose. Tit for tat. Love jumps up to attack her, but the friends hold her back. Noah dismisses them, telling them not to come back, and they reluctantly go away. He then tells Alice that since she saw the kiss through Love's eyes, would she give him a chance to show her what happened through *his* eyes? She doesn't know how either of them can control a mind-flash, but agrees to try.

They talk to figure out how she had the vision, and decide it was skin-to-skin contact. So they clasp each other's hands—but nothing happens.

"Maybe you need to hit me," she says.

"I'm not hitting you, not even to prove I didn't like kissing Love." He closes his eyes and tries to shove the kissing memory into her mind. This actually opens his mind to hers and hers to him. Finally she sees the kiss through his eyes, and realizes how much he wants her, Alice. Unbeknownst to her, however, he sees the accident she endured with her family and realizes she's exactly who and what she claims to be. She's no spy.

Hours later, the friends have to pull them apart. Neither Alice nor Noah realize how much time has passed. School is now out and she missed the bus. He drives her home, and along the way, he asks, "Do you like me again?"

She tells him she knows they are only dating, but seeing him kiss another girl hurt. He swears it won't ever happen again and they agree that even though they are "only dating" they won't see other people. They reach her house; Noah parks in the driveway and broaches the topic of the accident, telling her that he saw her in his mind. She gives him the details and admits how guilty she feels for leaving her parents inside that car while she hallucinated about monsters.

He asks her if she's seen the monsters since. She says she's now afraid of the dark and the only time she's been outside since the accident was on her date with him, but she only saw *him* that night.

Before he can explain that she has nothing to feel guilty about, the aunt comes storming out and demanding she get in there and do her chores. He says he wants to see her that night, she says her aunt won't let her go out on a school night, but that she will leave her window unlocked and he can sneak into her room around 9, when she's expected to shut herself in her room and study. Only, she gets stuck with dinner cleanup on her own—again. All the while, Alice fears Noah will leave.

Before heading to Alice's house, Noah calls his group together and tells them Alice is legit and they are to be nice to her. If anyone hurts her, he'll kick them out of the group. He reaches Alice's room a little before nine and since she's not there, quietly explores, impressed with how she turned the little attack room into a home. They tease and talk for a little while before he brings up her dad again. He explains that her dad was a zombie slayer and the moment he died, the abilities transferred to her.

Alice doesn't believe him and makes him leave, wondering if Noah is as messed up as her dad. The next day at school, he tries to talk to her, but again, she won't listen. Except, as the day passes, and she thinks about what he said and all that her father said over the years, and some part of her begins to accept.

After school *she* is waiting for *him*, and tells him she'd like to know more. He agrees to pick her up later that night, sneak her out, and show her the world he's lived in for the last five years.

And when he does as promised, the whole group is with him, loaded up in a van. They take her to a local cemetery. Alice and Noah sit in the back and he explains more about the zombie world. Zombies are ghosts that have taken corporal form. They resemble their decaying bodies and they are hungry for living flesh from slayers and energy from non-slayers. These zombies only come out at night, and they only attack—and eat—humans who can see them. But they drain the life force from humans who can't see them, killing those humans, so they are dangerous to everyone. And the only way to kill them is to cut off their heads.

The leader of a zombie slaying pack always has a gift, supernatural abilities, and Noah's is the ability to start a fire with his mind. With Alice's mind-flashing ability, he begins to wonder if she's supposed to be the leader of her own pack—or co-leader with him.

Alice learns that most of the kids in Noah's group grew up together, knowing about this stuff because their parents were slayers and fought together. So they were taught how to fight early on. At the cemetery, Noah shows her a few ways to track the living dead. When the group comes upon a nest of zombies, the fight is on, but Noah stays back with Alice, watching, explaining, protecting. She almost can't believe the violence. These are the same type of monsters she saw the night of the accident. Her dad wasn't crazy. And these . . . *things* were responsible for his death. The fury she feels is overwhelming and before she can stop herself, she launches into the battle, picking up a sword and hacking.

As new to it as she is, she is unprepared and soon overcome by their strength and easily subdued. Thankfully the other slayers save her. After the battle is won with only minor injuries for their group, Noah takes her home. He helps her sneak back into her room, and they kiss. He backs off before they can do anything more, still wanting to give her the time she needs and not wanting her to ever regret anything they do.

The next morning, she tells him that she wants to join their group. She wants to learn how to hunt and slay zombies. And so, finally, Alice's true training begins.

Your assignment: Finish writing your synopsis.

DAY 364

Be Kind About Your First Effort

GENA: When I sat down to write my first book, I'd never had so much fun. Finally, I was doing what I loved. I poured myself into every scene and lovingly considered every word...and it turned out to be a pile of garbage. I jumped around with tenses and scenes. I also put everything I thought was funny or moving in it, even if it didn't fit. This became *Heaven's Fury*, named after my heroine–Heaven.

JILL: My senior year of college, part of my internship was to attend and record the governor's weekly press conference. Now, I'm not saying that the governor's junior press secretary was hot or anything, but my first ever book centered on a governor's press secretary. The icing on the top was the title - *A Political Affair* - because if there's one thing romance readers are (not) clamoring for, it's politically themed books with affairs. Actually, the real icing was the 4 different points of view in the first scene, including one by a random guy opening a door who we never see again.

While the world will never read these brilliant works, they taught us something about the art of writing and gave us the confidence we needed to keep going. Does this mean your first book is/will be a steaming pile? No, absolutely not. Many authors have sold their first manuscript. Just don't beat yourself up if the book doesn't turn out the way you picture in your head. You can get there. Keep going!

DAY 365

YOUR FINAL READ THROUGH

Let's be honest. By this point, you've read your book so many times, the idea of reading it ONE MORE TIME is exhausting. Or, maybe you're raring to go and can't wait to gaze upon your words again. Maybe you're somewhere in between. However you feel, don't skip this step. This is that one last look before you upload the manuscript for publishing or zip it off for submission to an agent, editor, or after the proofer so make it count.

You can print the book and read it on paper. You can listen as your computer dictates it. You can read it backward. Yes, some people do, in fact, read their book backward—starting with the last chapter and working their way back one chapter at a time—to trick their mind and help them more easily see any mistakes. Find what works best for you and tweak as you go.

Our main suggestion is to approach this final reading with a different process from how you wrote and edited the book. You're defeating muscle memory before it attempts to kick in.

GENA: I tend to edit heavily at every stage—which I do not recommend, because domino effect–so I switch up formatting for my final read through. For the first time, I read it formatted like a published novel. Do you know how many times I've kick myself for missing so many errors? Enough to bruise!

JILL: I prefer to send the manuscript to my tablet and read as if I'm pleasure-reading. I stop and correct mistakes as I find them. Sometimes I don't always understand my hastily jotted down notes to myself, so I fix the mistake and get back to reading.

Your assignment: Block off several hours to read through your book one last time—all the way from beginning to end–looking for any typos or confusing sentences you might have missed.

DAY 366

Congrats, baby!

You did it. You really did it. You had an idea, you put in the work, and now you have a finished product ready for the next step.

You've accomplished something incredible, and this is a day of celebration. Focus. Magnify. Accomplish. Triumph!

Thank you so much for taking this journey with us. We hope you enjoyed the process, and we wish you all the best in your future literary endeavors. We'd love to keep in touch!

You can join our exclusive group, secret word: **Triumph**

https://www.facebook.com/groups/AllWriteAlready/

Your assignment: Celebrate!

AUTHOR ACKNOWLEDGEMENTS

A special thanks to the authors who so generously participated by giving up their advice. Please visit their websites and show them some love!

Jennifer L. Armentrout
AC Arthur
Kait Ballenger
Breezie Bennett
Sawyer Bennett
Jaci Burton
PC Cast
Deborah Chester
HelenKay Dimon
Leigh Duncan
Stephanie Feagan
Lori Foster
Donna Grant
Wendy Higgins
Alexandra Ivy
Molly Jarrett
Beverly Jenkins
Julie Kagawa
Alison Kent
Kate Kessler
Merline Lovelace
Janice Lynn
Priscilla Oliveras
Michelle M. Pillow
Christopher Rice
Mandy M. Roth

Carrie Ann Ryan
Nalini Singh
Roxanne St. Claire
Susan Stoker
Teri Wilson

BOOK RESOURCES
BOOKS MENTIONED

Digital list: https://books2read.com/rl/AllWriteAlready

1984 by George Orwell
A Theory of Human Motivation by Abraham Maslow
Adventures of Sherlock Holmes by Arthur Conan Doyle
Alice in Zombieland by Gena Showalter
Alice's Adventures in Wonderland by Lewis Carroll
An Extraordinary Union by Alyssa Cole
Any Duchess Will Do by Tessa Dare
The Artist's Way by Julia Cameron
At the Heart of Christmas by Jill Monroe
Barefoot Bay by Roxanne St. Claire
Beautiful Bastard by Christina Lauren
The Best Worst Man by Mia Sosa
Bird by Bird by Anne Lamott
The Bluest Eye by Toni Morrison
The Captain's Baby Bargain by Merline Lovelace
Can't Let Go by Gena Showalter
Catch a Mate by Gena Showalter
Dark Swan by Gena Showalter
The Darkest Assassin by Gena Showalter
The Darkest King by Gena Showalter
The Darkest Night by Gena Showalter
The Darkest Seduction by Gena Showalter
The Darkest Whisper by Gena Showalter
Dating the Undead by Gena Showalter and Jill Monroe
Deathmaker by Lindsay A. Buroker
The Devil Wears Prada by Lauren Weisberger
Divine by Mistake by P.C. Cast
The Dogfather series Sit...Stay...Beg by Roxanne St. Claire

Down the Rabbit Hole by Gena Showalter
Fifty Shades of Grey by EL James
Firstlife by Gena Showalter
Forget Tomorrow by Pintip Dunn
Frames of Mind: The Theory of Multiple Intelligences by Howard Gardner
Fun & Games by Jill Monroe
Game of Thrones–A Song of Ice and Fire by George R. R. Martin
The Gift of the Magi by O. Henry
The Girl With the Dragon Tattoo by Stieg Larsson
The Glass Queen by Gena Showalter
The Godfather by Mario Puzo
Harry Potter and the Sorcerer's Stone by J.K. Rowling
Silence of the Lambs by Thomas Harris
Sworn Enemies (originally published as Hitting the Mark) by Jill Monroe
House of Night series by PC and Kristin Cast
How to Get Happily Published by Judith Appelbaum
How to Polish Your Manuscript in 10 Days by Anne Victory
Immortals After Dark by Kresley Cole
Intimate Behavior: A Zoologist's Classic Study of Human Intimacy by Desmond Morris
It by Stephen King
Kat in Zombieland by Gena Showalter
Lord of Rage by Jill Monroe
Lord of the Abyss by Nalini Singh
The Master by Kresley Cole
Mastering the Art of French Cooking by Julia Child
The Merchant of Venice by William Shakespeare
Merriam-Webster Dictionary
Moon Chosen by PC Cast
My So-Called Bollywood Life by Nisha Sharma
Naked Thrill by Jill Monroe
Never Naughty Enough by Jill Monroe

New Tax Guide for Writers, Artists, Performers, and Other Creative People by Peter Jason Riley

Nine Rules to Break When Romancing a Rake by Sarah MacLean

The Nymph King by Gena Showalter

Oh My Goth by Gena Showalter

The Playbook series – Intercepted, Fumbled, Blitzed – by Alexa Martin

Playing With Fire by Gena Showalter

Poison Princess by Kresley Cole

The Power of Myth by Joseph Campbell with Bill Moyers

Pride, Prejudice and Zombies by Jane Austen and Seth Grahame-Smith

Sworn by Instinct (originally published as Primal Instincts) by Jill Monroe

Prince of Stone by Gena Showalter

The Princess Bride by William Goldman

Romancing the Beat by Gwen Hayes

The Romanov Prophesy by Steve Berry

Romeo and Juliet by William Shakespeare

Sworn to Duty (originally published as SEALed and Delivered) by Jill Monroe

Sworn by a Kiss (originally published as SEALed With a Kiss by Jill Monroe

Sworn to Protect (originally published as Share the Darkness) by Jill Monroe

Story by Robert McKee

The Story Grid by Shawn Coyne

Tall, Dark and Filthy Rich by Jill Monroe

Temptation in Shadows by Gena Showalter

Twilight by Stephenie Meyer

The Vampire's Mail Order Bride by Kristen Painter

The Wonderful World of Oz by L. Frank Baum and illustrated by W. W. Denslow

The Writer's Market Edited by Robert Lee Brewer

TELEVISION SHOWS AND MOVIES MENTIONED

Breaking Bad (2008) TV series created by Vince Gilligan

Dirty Dancing (1987) Movie directed by Emile Ardolino

The Good Place (2016) TV series created by Michael Schur

Law and Order (1990) TV series created by Dick Wolf

LOST (2004) TV series created by J.J. Abrams, Jeffrey Lieber, Damon Lindelof

A Quiet Place (2018) Movie directed by John Krasinski

Seed of Chucky (2004) Movie directed by Don Mancini

The Shape of Water (2017) Movie directed by Guillermo del Toro

Sixth Sense (1999) Movie directed by M. Night Shyamalan

Star Wars: Episode IV - A New Hope (1977) Movie directed by George Lucas

Supernatural (2005) TV series created by Eric Kripke

The Usual Suspects (1995) Movie directed by Bryan Singer and written by Christopher McQuarrie

Wedding Crashers (2005) Movie directed by David Dobkin

The Wizard of Oz (1939) directed by Victor Fleming based on the book *The Wonderful Wizard of Oz* by L. Frank Baum

The Wrong Bed: Naked Pursuit (2017) Movie directed by Monika Mitchell; written by Angela Russel and Roma Roth based on a book by Jill Monroe

You've Got Mail (1998) Movie directed by Nora Ephron

FINAL RESOURCES

Want to self-publish? There are many great podcasts including:

- *The Creative Penn* by Joanna Penn.

- *The Spa Girls* hosted by Cheryl Phipps, Shar Barratt, Trudi Jaye and Wendy Vella.

- Mark Dawson's *The Self-Publishing Show.*

Mignon Fogerty aka Grammar Girl – Quick and Dirty Tips

Scrivner – https://www.literatureandlatte.com/scrivener/overview

Grammarly – https://www.grammarly.com

ProWiritngAid – https://prowritingaid.com/Premium

National Novel Writing Month (NaNoWriMo) – https://nanowrimo.org

ABOUT GENA SHOWALTER

Gena Showalter is the *New York Times* and *USA TODAY* bestselling author of paranormal and contemporary romance novels, as well as young adult, fantasy and non-fiction. She has been mentioned on Orange is the New Black and chosen as *Cosmopolitan's* Red Hot Read. When she isn't hard at work on her next novel, she's playing with her menagerie of rescue animals—adopt don't shop!—telling her husband and kids about every cute thing done by the rescue animals, or binging favorite TV shows.

f facebook.com/GenaShowalterAuthor

𝕏 twitter.com/genashowalter

O instagram.com/genashowalter

BB bookbub.com/authors/gena-showalter

ABOUT JILL MONROE

Jill Monroe is the international best selling author of over fifteen novels and novellas. Her books are available across the globe and *The Wrong Bed: Naked Pursuit* has been adapted for the small screen for Lifetime Movie Network.

When not writing, Jill makes her home in Oklahoma with her husband, enjoys daily walks with her dog Zoey, texting with her two daughters who are away at college and collecting fabric for items she'll sew poorly.

facebook.com/JillMonroeAuthorPage

twitter.com/JillMonroe

instagram.com/jillmonroebooks

bookbub.com/profile/jill-monroe

ALSO BY GENA SHOWALTER

Gods of War:

Shadow and Ice

Frost and Flame

Lords of the Underworld:

The Darkest Night

The Darkest Kiss

The Darkest Pleasure

The Darkest Whisper

The Darkest Passion

The Darkest Lie

The Darkest Secret

The Darkest Surrender

The Darkest Seduction

The Darkest Craving

The Darkest Touch

The Darkest Torment

The Darkest Warrior

The Darkest King

Forest of Good and Evil:

The Evil Queen

The Glass Queen

Tales of an Extraordinary Girl:

Playing with Fire

Twice as Hot

Angels of the Dark:

Wicked Nights

Beauty Awakened

Burning Dawn

The White Rabbit Chronicles:

Alice in Zombieland

Through the Zombie Glass

Queen of Zombie Hearts

A Mad Zombie Party

Kat in Zombieland

Everlife:

Firstlife

Lifeblood

Everlife

Alien Huntress:

Awaken Me Darkly

Enslave Me Sweetly

Savor Me Slowly

Tempt Me Eternally

Seduce the Darkness

Ecstasy in Darkness

Dark Taste of Rapture

Otherworld Assassins:

Last Kiss a Goodnight

Black and Blue

Dark Swan

Imperia:

Prince of Prince

Prince of Forever

ALSO BY JILL MONROE

At the Heart of Christmas

Fun & Games

Naked Pursuit

Naked Thrill

Lord of Rage

Tall, Dark and Filthy Rich

Never Naughty Enough

Novellas

Treasure in the Sand

Wet & Wild

Dating the Undead

Coming Soon - **Sworn** Series:

Sworn to Duty - (formerly SEALed and Delivered)

Sworn By a Kiss - (formerly SEALed With a Kiss)

Sworn to Protect - (formerly Share the Darkness)

Sworn Enemies - (formerly Hitting The Mark)

Sworn by Instinct - (formerly Primal Instinct)

Sworn by Heart - (formerly Date on the Run)